# MUSIC LAW

## FOR THE GENERAL PRACTITIONER

# THOMAS R. LEAVENS

**AMERICAN BAR ASSOCIATION**
Solo, Small Firm and
General Practice Division

Forum on the
Entertainment & Sports
Industries

17 16 15 14    5 4 3

Library of Congress Cataloging-in-Publication Data

Leavens, Thomas R.
  Music law for the general practitioner / Thomas R. Leavens, Solo, General Practice and Small Firm Division, American Bar Association.
    pages cm
  ISBN 978-1-62722-153-5
  1. Music trade--Law and legislation--United States. 2. Musicians' contracts--United States. I. Liberman, Heather Ryan. II. American Bar Association. General Practice, Solo & Small Firm Division. III. Title.
  KF4291.L43 2013
  343.7307'878--dc23

                                                              2013021038

# Dedication

This book is dedicated to Justin, Mary, Emily, and Molly, with the hope they will better understand what their father does with music when he is not listening to it, reading about it, or playing it.

# Thanks

I first want to thank Heather Liberman for her dedication and excellent work in helping research and edit this book and in authoring two of its chapters. Her fingerprints are embedded throughout. Thanks also to my law partners Peter J. Strand, Jerry W. Glover, and David M. Adler for their support of my efforts to write this book and for their insights along the way. Thank you Todd Carey, Jerry Catalano, Ron Kaplan, Andrew Gelman, and Michele Lowrance for your time unselfishly given and your valuable comments and insights, and thank you David Apatoff for permission to quote your article. Thank you Vincent Roberts for your very helpful graphic design work with the publishing illustrations. Above all, thank you to my music clients, who through the years have taught me so much about not only the business of music, but also the rewards of finding passion in your work. And finally, thanks to Sarah for her always steadfast understanding and support while this project drew my time and attention.

# Contents

Dedication     iii

Thanks     v

About the Authors     xv

Preface     xix

CHAPTER ONE
**What Is Music?**     **1**

    What is Digital Music?     3

CHAPTER TWO
**How Value in Musical Properties Is Created**     **7**

    Copyrights     8

      Copyright Basics     8

      Work for Hire     12

      Assignments     13

      Scope of Copyright Claim     13

      Collaboration     15

      Fair Use     16

      Parody     18

      Copyright Myths     19

    Trademarks     21

      Acquisition of Trademark Rights     21

      Performing Group Names     23

      Trademark Fair Use     26

      Titles     26

      Online Presence     27

    Right of Publicity     28

    Data     32

Interviews                                          34
Contractual Rights                                  35
   Exclusivity                       35
   Right of First Negotiation/Refusal 36
   Key Man                            37
   Credit                             37
   Most Favored Nations               38
   Nondisclosure                      39
Moral Rights                                        40

CHAPTER THREE
**Music Publishing**                               **41**
Performance Rights Organizations                    42
Mechanical Licenses                                 46
Synchronization Rights                              49
Dramatic Rights                                     50
Publisher Agreements                                52
   Single Song Agreements            53
   Exclusive Songwriter Agreements   62
   Copublishing Agreements           64
   Administration Agreements         69

CHAPTER FOUR
**How Bands Are Organized and Financed, and
Planning for the Eventual Breakup**                **73**
Treatment of Assets                                 74
Other Band Agreement Provisions                     78
Leaving Members and Recording Agreements            80
Financing                                           81
   Group Member Capitalization       81
   Outside Financing                 82
Settlements                                         86

CHAPTER FIVE
## How Record Companies and Producers Work    87

Nature of the Relationship    88
Parties    91
Scope    91
Term    92
Production and Release Commitment    94
Obligation to Promote    95
Recording Budgets and Advances    95
Royalties    96
   Royalty Basis    97
   Royalty Rates    97
   Licensing Income    98
   Container Charges    99
   Format, Territory, and Channel of Trade Adjustments    100
   Free Goods    101
   Digital Royalties    101
   Royalty Calculation Example    102
Accountings and Audits    103
Approvals    104
Controlled Compositions    105
Merchandising    107
Videos    109
360 Deals    111
Alternative Recording Agreements    115
Producer Agreements    117
Production Company Agreements    120
   Development Agreement    121
   Established Production Company    124

CHAPTER SIX
## Personal Representatives    125

Agents    126
Personal Managers    130
Business Managers    137

CHAPTER SEVEN
## Personal Appearances                                    139
Busking                                                    139
House Concerts                                             140
Public Venues                                              141
  Compensation                                            142
  Hospitality and Benefits                                143
  Billing                                                 144
  Merchandising                                           144
  Cancellations                                           145
  Technical Riders                                        146
  Exclusivity                                             146
Proceeds of Personal Performances                         147
Ticketing                                                 147

CHAPTER EIGHT
## Distribution                                            151
Distribution of Physical Products                         151
  Distribution Functions                                  153
  Distribution Process                                    153
  Scope of Distribution Agreement                         154
  Warranties and Representations                          156
  Advances                                                156
DIY Distribution                                          157
Digital Distribution                                      158
Digital Distribution Revenue                              159
  Webcasting                                              160
  Music Services                                          162
  Permanent Downloads                                     165
  Ringtones and Ringbacks                                 166
  Satellite Radio and Cable Music Services                167

CHAPTER NINE

**Tax Considerations for the Musician**                                    **169**

By Heather Ryan Liberman

A Musician's Gross Income                                                    171
Ordinary Income vs. Capital Gains                                           171
Capital Gains: Musical Compositions                                         172
Ordinary Income: Compensation for Services Rendered vs.
    Royalties                                                               173
Unqualified Deferred Compensation: Advances                                174
Emerging Income Streams: Crowd-Funded Income                               176
Taxation of the Musician's Income                                           177
Deductions                                                                  177
Hobby-Loss                                                                  178
Ordinary and Necessary Business Expenditures                               179
Passive Loss Deductions                                                     182
Charitable Deductions                                                       182
Abandoned Property                                                          183
Crowd-Funding Considerations                                               184
Tax Credits                                                                 185
Tax Exemptions                                                              186
Audit                                                                       186
Choice of Entity                                                            187
Sole Proprietorship                                                         189
Partnerships                                                                190
Corporations                                                                192
Personal Holding Companies                                                  193
Limited Liability Companies                                                 193
Conclusion                                                                  194

CHAPTER TEN

**The Musician's Estate**                                                   **195**

By Heather Ryan Liberman

What Comprises a Musician's Estate?                                         197
Inventory                                                                   198
Valuation of Assets                                                         199

Generating Income for the Estate                                     201
   Fiduciary Duties                                                  201
   Copyright                                                         204
   Trademark                                                         209
   Right of Publicity                                                210
   Digital Assets                                                    213
   Updating Payors: SAG, AFTRA, ASCAP, BMI, etc.                     214
   Tribute Bands                                                     215
Conclusion                                                           216

CHAPTER ELEVEN

**Music and the General Business Client**                           **217**
   Advertising and Music Branding                                    217
   Sponsorships and Endorsements                                     220
      What the Artist Will Be Required To Do                         220
      Artist's Identity and Trademark Rights                         221
      Creation of Special Material                                   222
      Scope of Exclusivity                                           222
      Morals Clause                                                  223
      Non-disparagement                                              223
   Music at the Work Site                                            224
      Performance of Music in Customer Environment                   224
      Other Workplace Use of Music                                   226
   Jukeboxes                                                         229

CHAPTER TWELVE

**Representing the Musician**                                        **231**
   Beauty Contest                                                    232
   Payment of Fees                                                   233
   Dealing with Representatives                                      234
   Dealing with Groups                                               236
   Shopping Groups                                                   237
   Alternative Fee Arrangements                                      238
   Practical Issues                                                  240

APPENDIX A
## Recommended Further Reading 243

APPENDIX B
## List of Dispute Resolution Service Organizations 245
Arts Mediation Group 245
California Lawyers for the Arts 245
JAMS Headquarters 245
JAMS International Headquarters 246
Lawyers for the Creative Arts 246
National Assn. of Record Industry Professionals (NARIP) 246
World Intellectual Property Organization (WIPO) Arbitration
and Mediation Center 246

Index 247

# About the Authors

**Thomas R. Leavens** is a partner in Leavens, Strand, Glover & Adler, LLC. Tom's career as an attorney has involved transactions, counseling, and litigation in all areas of performing, visual, and literary expression, new media, intellectual property, and technology.

Prior to forming Leavens, Strand, Glover & Adler, LLC, Tom was General Counsel for LRSmedia, LLC, a media production and brand development company, whose initial project was the PBS television series LEGENDS OF JAZZ with Ramsey Lewis. His responsibilities there included general business management, development of business models, artist and other talent agreements, publishing and record company clearance, distribution agreements, business development, union agreements, and intellectual property protection. Prior to joining LRS, Tom was General Counsel for MusicNow LLC, a pioneer digital music company that commercially launched a subscription music service, webcasting, and the sale of music downloads in 2002.

Tom has also served as General Counsel and Senior Executive Vice President of Platinum Entertainment, Inc., a public company which grew from its formation in 1992 to become at one point the largest US-based independent record company. While there he also served as executive producer of various recording and television projects, and compiled and produced 16 House of Blues Essential Blues recordings released by the company under its joint venture with HOB Entertainment. Prior to Platinum Tom was a partner with the law firm McBride, Baker & Coles in Chicago, where he chaired the firm's intellectual property department.

Tom was the first recipient of the Thomas R. Leavens Award, presented by Lawyers For The Creative Arts, for contributions to law and the arts in Chicago, was the recipient of the David C. Hilliard Award, presented by the Chicago Bar Association for Outstanding Committee Service to the Legal Profession and Community, and has served as an elected member of the

Board of Managers of the Chicago Bar Association, the Board of Directors of the Digital Media Association, and the National Recording Preservation Board of the Library of Congress. Tom is also an Adjunct Professor at Northwestern University School of Law and at the S.J. Quinney College of Law at the University of Utah, an Associate with The Henry Lydiate Partnership in London, the premiere arts consultancy in the UK, a voting member of the National Academy of Recording Arts and Sciences, and a member of the Authors Guild. Tom has also served as an expert witness in litigation concerning issues pertaining to the music industry. Tom has also received the highest AV Peer Review Rating from the Martindale-Hubbell Law Directory, is included in The Best Lawyers in America, and is ranked in Band 1 in Media & Entertainment: Transactional by Chambers and Partners. He is a graduate of the University of Michigan (A.B.) and Wayne State University Law School (J.D.) and is admitted in Illinois, Utah, and Michigan.

**Heather R. Liberman** is an associate at Leavens, Strand, Glover & Adler, LLC. Heather has represented transactional and litigation clients in the areas of copyright, trademark and entertainment law. Heather also worked as a licensing agent responsible for the clearance of over 100 musical compositions and sound recordings for a major audio release. Heather is the Vice-Chair of the Chicago Bar Association Media and Entertainment Committee and is an associate board member of Links Hall, a performance arts organization. Heather is a volunteer attorney for Lawyers for the Creative Arts (LCA), a not-for-profit organization providing free legal services to members of the various arts communities in Chicago.

While attending law school at Loyola University Chicago School of Law, Heather was selected to participate in the Chicago Intellectual Property Colloquium Fellowship, was the vice president of the Arts and Law Society and also conducted research for a professor writing an art law casebook. Heather was a member of the International Law Review and was named an International Law Fellow for her work teaching via postal mail international relations to Congolese refugees living in Uganda. Heather has also clerked for a Cook County Judge in the Law Division as well as via the Internet for a trademark law firm located in Beijing, China.

Prior to attending law school, Heather worked for a not-for-profit arts organization in Washington, DC and interned for a U.S. Senator.

Heather received her Bachelor of Fine Arts in dance from the Tisch School of the Arts at New York University and a Bachelor of Arts in politics. Heather is a classically trained ballet and modern concert dancer and has danced with multiple modern dance companies in New York City.

# Preface

Music law is the collection of laws and business customs that affect those who make, market, and use music in all its forms. Music law involves several key substantive areas of law—copyrights, trademarks, identity rights, First Amendment rights, contractual rights that shape competition (noncompetes, exclusivity, rights of first refusal, etc.), and data protections. It is also the body of law that is drawn into play by the transactions that take place between those who market or otherwise use music. Music law also involves technology, customs and practices, and the values our culture has given to music, which sculpt the landscape for the users of music. The intersections of these topics are the subject areas for this book.

The traditional players in the music industry are well known: songwriters, singers, instrumentalists, record companies, music publishing companies, record stores, radio and television broadcasters, and venue owners. While these players remain key in the industry, technological advances in the digital distribution of music and recordings have brought important new players into the mix, such as computer manufacturers and telephone companies, and have created new political constituencies of individuals concerned about their rights to use digital music. Such advances have also drawn masses of ordinary businesses into music-related issues. For example, many businesses have discovered that music is critical to branding or otherwise bringing attention to their products or services because music helps convene an audience that can be receptive to a commercial appeal.

All businesses have found that the emergence of inexpensive duplication technology, the portability and ubiquity of mobile music devices, and the ease of transmitting digital music files have brought music into the workplace in unexpected but pervasive ways. Music law is not just a specialized area of practice devoted to creative individuals, if it ever was. It affects an expanding range of commercial activities that most general practitioners are likely to encounter with their clients.

The goal of *Music Law for the General Practitioner* is found in its title. This is a guide for the general practitioner to learn about the legal and business issues that he or she is likely to encounter when representing a musical talent, producer, or consumer. I have not prepared this book for the expert, although I hope experts find value in these pages. My intent is for it to be a point of entry, with guidance on where additional information may be found for deeper analysis. I have tried to provide background, context, insights, and strategies as a means of introduction. The content of this book is not meant to be the final word on any of its topics, nor is it meant to replace any of the excellent in-depth publications available for the expert.

# Chapter One
# **What Is Music?**

Before we launch our exploration of how the law intersects with music creation, performance, distribution, and sale, we should first understand what music is.

Music is the most abstract of creative works. You can't see or touch it—it exists solely as a sound wave that unless recorded, dissipates within moments. Despite this abstraction (or perhaps because of it), music enjoys an elevated role in our development as human beings. Many researchers and writers believe that music played an adaptive/evolutionary role in the development of speech, other cognitive functions, mate selection, and our social development. Neuroscientists have traced the activities in our brains as music is heard to demonstrate the multiple areas involved in listening and reacting to music, physically and emotionally, and are using music to treat certain brain malfunctions.[1] It is not just something with a good beat that you can dance to (although that is believed to be important itself).

What music actually consists of is not something we tend to think too much about. Daniel J. Levitin, in his fascinating book *This Is Your Brain*

---

1. *See generally* Daniel J. Levitin, This Is Your Brain On Music (Plume 2006) [hereinafter Levitin, Brain on Music]; Daniel J. Levitin, The World In Six Songs (Viking 2008); Oliver Sacks, Musicophilia: Tales of Music and the Brain (Vintage 2008); Ronald Kotulak, *Rhythm, Melody, Life*, Chi. Trib., Sept. 21, 2003.

*on Music*, identifies the following as the fundamental elements that comprise musical expression:

(1) Pitch, or the tone of the sound and its relative position in the musical scale;
(2) Rhythm, or the duration of notes and the units into which they are formed;
(3) Tempo, or the overall speed or pace of a musical piece;
(4) Contour, or the overall shape of a melody;
(5) Timbre, or tonal color of an instrument;
(6) Loudness, or the energy created by an instrument; and
(7) Reverberation, or the sense of distance or spaciousness of a sound. [2]

To that list I would add velocity, or the speed by which any of the foregoing elements are accelerating or decelerating. None of these items in and of themselves are legally protectable—they are the basic building blocks of musical expression and no single person can claim rights to control them. The ability to protect them emerges with the way these elements are combined to form higher order musical features, such as melody and harmony.[3] As we shall see, some of these higher order features are protectable and others are not.

The combinations of these elements to create music are limited by what we consider pleasing in Western culture. These physical limits are a consideration whenever a claim is being weighed that a certain piece of music wrongfully copies other music. The following quotation from 1930 reflects the limitations generally expressed in Western music:

The average composer who indulges in songs has a limited number of tones at his disposal. The combinations and permutations of the thirteen tones give the amazing total of 6,227,020,800 combinations, of which only a small fraction may be used ordinarily. Popular songs, in particular, lie within a very small radius. In a confined space,

---

2. Levitin, Brain on Music, *supra* note 1, at 15–16.
3. *Id.* at 17–18.

similarity of tone construction is inevitable. Practically every original idea the composer can think of has appeared somewhere before; it is a matter of probabilities, and every day the number of new possibilities grows less.

Since it is generally agreed that the original fund of melodic ideas has been exhausted, serious composers, and others, have turned to the other important elements of music—harmony and rhythm. In the use and treatment of these there is a certain originality to be attained; but even that is necessarily limited by obvious physical limitations. Of the three essential elements—rhythm, harmony, and melody—the first two are usually emphasized, whereas the third is taken as a matter of course; and when it is impossible to invent new melodic ideas, the composer may display his skill in the means he uses to develop what theme he has.[4]

## What is Digital Music?

When dealing with music today in a commercial way, it is not enough to understand the artistic components that comprise musical expression. Since digital technology generally governs how music is created, recorded, distributed, and sold, the general practitioner must also have at least a basic understanding of some of the components of digital music formats and files.

Technology has always been put to the demands of the creative impulse. Like photography, sound recordings are an art form that would not exist without supporting technology. And this technology has always had an effect on musical expression. For instance, the three-minute song reflects the upper limit of the recording capabilities of early wax acoustic recording technology. Early acoustic recording technology also favored certain sounds over others and, for example, elevated the clarinet to a featured role in klezmer

---

4. A. Shafter, Musical Copyright (2d ed. 1930), *reprinted in* A. Latman & R. Gorman, Copyright for the Eighties 328 (1981).

orchestras.[5] Electrical recording technology permitted more intimate forms of singing to be captured, which helped make Bing Crosby a star.[6] LPs, and then CDs, begat longer performances, and boom boxes played a key role in the development of hip-hop culture.[7] Electronic instruments and sound processors such as synthesizers, Linn drum machines, MIDIs,[8] and Auto-Tune have created new sounds and compositional possibilities, making new forms of expression possible, such as "mashups."[9]

When digital music is referenced, it is often referred to in a shorthand way as an "MP3." The term MP3 refers to a format for compressing and then decompressing a digital file representing a sound recording. There are many formats used for the distribution and sale of digital music, but MP3 is the most popular. The MP3 compression format was developed by the Moving Pictures Experts Group in 1988 as part of that group's effort to develop a format for compressing television video and soundtracks generally. The part of the format that described sound compression was Layer 3, which became known as MP3. The specifications for the MP3 standard were developed under the auspices of the International Organization for Standardization (IOS), unlike the proprietary compression formats such as ALAC or WMA developed by Apple and Microsoft, respectively.

When sound is recorded digitally, the analog sound wave is sampled 44,100 times per second. The sound is recorded for the left channel and for the right channel (stereo), and each sample is stored as sixteen bits for frequency (pitch) and amplitude (loudness). As a result, one second of digitally recorded music is made up of 1,411,220 bits. This is what is generally known as a WAV or AIFF file—the raw data from which the recording can

---

5.  Mark Katz, Capturing Sound: How Technology Has Changed Music 39 (University of California Press 2004).

6.  Gary Giddins, Bing Crosby: A Pocketful of Dreams—The Early Years 1903–1940, at 117–18 (Little, Brown 2001).

7.  Lyle Owerko, The Boombox Project: The Machines, the Music, and the Urban Underground (Abrams Image 2010); The History of the Boombox, National Public Radio, Apr. 22, 2009, http://www.youtube.com/watch?v=e84hf5aUmNA.

8.  MIDI is an acronym for Musical Instrumental Digital Interface. See MIDI Manufacturers Association, www.midi.org (last visited Jan. 20, 2013).

9.  Lae, Elina, Mashups—A Protected Form of Appropriation Art or a Blatant Copyright Infringement? (December 2011). Available at SSRN: http://ssrn.com/abstract+2003854 or http://DX.DOI.ORG/10.2139/SSRN.2003854.

then be processed. An MP3-formatted version of the raw data file is created by sampling the bits in the file at certain rates. The higher the "bit rate," the more information contained in the MP3 file and, thus, the greater fidelity to the original file. The "art" of the compression format is in how the format decides which bits to include and which to leave out. The format uses psychoacoustics (how people perceive sounds) to discard quieter or non-perceptible sounds and arrive at a playback that is acceptable to the listener. The advantage is a smaller file size. Early compressed digital files were reduced to 128,000 bits per second (128 Kbps), but higher bit rates reproducing recordings with greater fidelity are more common today as file size storage and electronic transmission capabilities increase. There are also other file formats in use today, such as FLAC and ATRAC, which do not lose data and thus can more accurately reproduce the sound of the original file.

As digital files overtake physical products as the means by which music is delivered to and consumed by people, the formats in which such digital products are offered and the interoperability of the devices with which such digital products may be used becomes more important to understand. This is due to the fact that file or format distinctions may implicate different rights for the owners of the recordings and compositions that are featured in such files.

## Chapter Two

# How Value in Musical Properties Is Created

It is no secret that the music industry has been troubled in the last decade. Revenue from the sale of prerecorded music has declined almost 40 percent[1] as new methods of digital distribution have not produced sufficient income to overcome the loss of revenue caused by the decline in the sale of physical media, such as compact discs. The U.S. Department of Labor also reports that there are 41 percent fewer paid musicians in the United States since 1999.[2] In addition, new business models for the distribution, sale, and consumption of music have stressed traditional music business models and legacy contractual relationships and terms in ways that remain to be fully sorted.

But value certainly remains in music properties and transactions. This chapter will touch on the topic of value in a transaction, including:

---

1. Robert Andrews, *Music Industry Can See the Light After "Least Negative" Sales Since 2004*, PAIDCONTENT (Mar. 26, 2012) http://paidcontent.org/2012/03/26/419 -music-industry-can-see-the-light-after-least-negative-sales-since-2004/.

2. Paul Resnikoff, *Recording Sales Declines & Musician Employment, 1999– 2011 . . .*, DIGITAL MUSIC NEWS (Aug. 25, 2012) http://www.digitalmusicnews.com/ permalink/2012/120824recording.

copyrights, trademarks, rights of identity, website addresses, social media platforms, data, and contractual competitive rights. These rights and properties form the basis for the transactions that will be discussed throughout this book.

# Copyrights

## Copyright Basics

Copyright is the most important source of value in a musical property. Copyright protects creative expression, which includes music, lyrics, and sound recordings. Copyright also protects the photographs, text, drawings, and other works of visual art that are used in the packaging, advertising, and promotion of musical properties. It is important to understand that each recording of a musical composition is protected by a claim to copyright that is separate from the copyright to the musical composition performed in the recording and to every other recording of that composition. For example, there is only one copyright claim to the composition "Yesterday," but there are separate copyright claims to each of the hundreds of recordings of that composition.

The United States Copyright Act[3] has exclusive jurisdiction for the rights in creative expression that are included in the Act. The exclusive rights of a copyright owner of a musical composition or sound recording are set forth in § 106 of the Copyright Act, which are as follows:

(1)  to reproduce the copyrighted work in copies or phonorecords;

(2)  to prepare derivative works based upon the copyrighted work;

(3)  to distribute copies or phonorecords of the copyright work to the public by sale or other transfer of ownership, or by rental, lease, or lending;

(4)  in the case of literary, musical, dramatic, and choreographic works, pantomimes, and motion picture and other audiovisual works, to perform the copyrighted work publicly;

(5)  in the case of literary, musical, dramatic, and choreographic works, pantomimes, and pictorial, graphic, or sculptural works, including the

---

3.  United States Copyright Act, 17 U.S.C. §§ 101-1332 (2011).

individual images of a motion picture or other audiovisual work, to display the copyrighted work publicly; and

(6) in the case of sound recordings, to perform the copyrighted work publicly by means of a digital audio transmission.

In addition, the anti-bootlegging provisions of the Uruguay Round Agreements Act of 1994,[4] which are found at § 1101(a) of the Copyright Act, bar the unconsented recording, transmission, sale, or rental of copies of live musical performances. We will revisit these rights throughout this book as we discuss the various ways these rights are implicated and exercised.

Federal copyright protection in a musical composition or sound recording arises immediately and automatically upon the creation of that work.[5] A work is "created" when it is fixed in a copy or phonorecord for the first time.[6] A work is "fixed" in a tangible medium of expression when its embodiment in a copy or phonorecord, by or under the authority of the author, is sufficiently permanent or stable to permit it to be perceived, reproduced or otherwise communicated for a period of more than transitory duration.[7] This means that an artist or an author has federal copyright protection in any musical or lyrical work that is original to the author immediately after the work is fixed in some way, such as by writing it down or capturing it by some method of recording. The same principle holds true for sound recordings.

Registration with the United States Copyright Office of any claim to a copyright in a composition or sound recording is not a condition to copyright protection.[8] Registration of one's claim to copyright with the Copyright Office is just that—it is not an application to obtain a copyright. It is the registration of the copyright that you already have. This is important to understand because from a transactional point of view, the person creating the work starts by holding everything and can only give away rights in subsequent transactions. However, registration of one's copyright claim is a

---

4. Uruguay Round Agreements Act, Pub. L. No. 103-465, Sec. 512, 108 Stat. 4809 (1994).

5. 17 U.S.C. § 302(a) (2011).

6. 17 U.S.C. § 101 (2011).

7. *Id.*

8. 17 U.S.C. § 408(a) (2011).

prerequisite to the commencement of any claim in federal court for infringement.[9] Also, registration permits the awarding of important remedies to a copyright owner not available for claims against an infringer who commenced before the registration became effective.[10] These remedies are the right to an award of one's attorney fees incurred in pursuing the claim[11] and the right to elect to receive damages in an amount defined by the Copyright Act in lieu of proving actual damages. The latter remedy—statutory damages—is beneficial as actual damages may be very difficult to establish or of a lesser amount than the statutory range. Consequently, registration of one's claim to copyright is always recommended.[12]

Registration of one's copyright claim is a relatively straightforward process and has been made easier through the online process found at the Copyright Office website: www.copyright.gov. The process has been developed with the goal of encouraging copyright claimants to register their works with minimum obstacles or need for specialized advice. Registration requires a relatively modest registration fee of $35 for applications made through the Copyright Office's online system. While registration can be conducted via the traditional method of submitting completed paper forms through the mail (which requires an application fee of $65), online registration is highly encouraged to avoid lengthy delays that have recently been caused by the security requirements of processing governmental filings. Registration also requires submission of deposit copies of the work for which registration is sought.

When a musical property is published, it should bear a proper copyright notice. This notice is not dependent on whether the work is registered because, since March 1, 1989, failure to include the notice does not invalidate the copyright claim. However, failure to include the notice allows a defendant to interpose a defense that his or her infringement was innocent in mitigation of damages.[13]

---

9.  17 U.S.C. § 411 (2011).
10.  17 U.S.C. § 412 (2011).
11.  17 U.S.C. § 505 (2011).
12.  17 U.S.C. § 504(c) (2011).
13.  17 U.S.C. § 405(b) (2011).

The notice of copyright for musical properties takes one of two forms. For lyrics or music appearing in print form, or for any artistic or text work used in connection with the packaging, advertising, or promotion of a work or performer, the notice is comprised of either the word "Copyright" or the copyright symbol ©, the name of the copyright owner, and the year the work was first published. An example of the notice on printed lyrics first published in 2013 would be: © Thomas R. Leavens 2013. Publication is like a birth year—it does not change unless the work with which it appears changes, in which case the changed work get its own new birth year.

For sound recordings, the notice is composed of either the word "Copyright" or the copyright symbol ℗, the name of the copyright owner, and the year the sound recording was first published. An example of the notice on a compact disc of a sound recording first published in 2013 would be: ℗ Thomas R. Leavens 2013. When you look at a commercially released compact disc, you will see both of these notices. The notice with the © is for the artwork and text of the packaging, and perhaps a separate © for the lyrics if they are printed in the packaging. The ℗ will be for the sound recording embodied in the compact disc.

The term of copyright protection for works created after January 1, 1978, is the life of the author, plus seventy years.[14] In the case of a joint work that was prepared other than as a work for hire, the period is the life of the last survivor, plus seventy years.[15]

Sound recordings have some special rules that apply only to them. Federal copyright protection was only extended to sound recordings in the United States starting in 1972. As a result, recordings created prior to that time are currently protected by state law, which varies from jurisdiction to jurisdiction.[16] This situation will continue until February 15, 2067, when pre-1972 sound recordings enter the public domain.[17]

---

14. 17 U.S.C. § 302(a) (2011).

15. 17 U.S.C. § 302(b) (2011).

16. *See, e.g.*, Capitol Records Inc. v. Naxos of Am., Inc., 372 F.3d 471 (2d Cir. 2004); Briggs v. State, 638 S.E.2d 292 (Ga. Sup. Ct. 2006); People v. Williams, 920 N.E.2d 446 (Ill. 2009); Capitol Records Inc. v. Naxos of Am., Inc., 830 N.E.2d 250 (N.Y. Ct. App. 2005).

17. 17 U.S.C. § 301(c) (2011).

## Work for Hire

While ordinarily the creator of a musical work will be the copyright owner, there are circumstances under which someone other than the creator will own the copyright. Those circumstances occur when a work is created in what is called a "work for hire" situation, which can occur under two scenarios. First, musical works created within the scope of a person's employment are works for hire,[18] and the copyright to those works belongs to the employer. For example, if you are regularly employed in the marketing department of a company and it is your job to write music and lyrics for advertisements for your company, then the copyright to those music and lyrics will belong to your employer. Whether one is an "employee" will depend principally on the general common law test of agency and control.[19] A person may be an employee even if his payment is in the form of an advance on royalties.[20]

The second work-for-hire scenario involves independent contractors who are commissioned to create a musical work. The copyright to the commissioned work will belong to the party commissioning the work, rather than the creator, if (1) the parties so agree in writing signed by the creator and (2) the work that is created falls within one of the following categories of works:

> A work specially ordered or commissioned for use as a contribution to a collective work, as a part of a motion picture or other audiovisual work, as a translation, as a supplementary work, as a compilation, as an instructional text, as a test, as answer material for a test, or as an atlas, if the parties expressly agree in a written instrument signed by them that the work shall be considered a work made for hire. For the purpose of the foregoing sentence, a "supplementary work" is a work prepared for publication as a secondary adjunct to a work by another author for the purpose of introducing, concluding, illustrating, explaining, revising, commenting upon, or assisting in the use of the other work, such as forewords, afterwords, pictorial illustrations,

---

18. 17 U.S.C. §§ 101(b), 201 (2011).
19. Community For Creative Non-Violence v. Reid, 490 U.S. 730 (1989).
20. Fred Fisher Music Co. v. Leo Feist, Inc., 55 F. Supp. 359 (S.D.N.Y. 1944).

maps, charts, tables, editorial notes, musical arrangements, answer material for tests, bibliographies, appendixes, and indexes, and an "instructional text" is a literary, pictorial, or graphic work prepared for publication and with the purpose of use in systematic instructional activities.[21]

In the absence of such a signed written agreement, or with respect to works that do not fall within the specifically identified categories of works, the copyright will remain with the creator.[22] The term of copyright protection for a work made for hire is the shorter of ninety-five years from publication or 120 years from creation.[23]

## Assignments

As with other forms of property, ownership of a copyright may be assigned from one party to another. However, to be effective, a copyright assignment must be in writing and signed by the copyright owner. Undocumented assignments are not effective. For example, endorsed checks written in payment for the purchase of a copyright interest are invalid as written assignments of the copyright that is the subject of the transaction.[24] Also, mere reference to the assignment of compositions in an otherwise valid recording agreement is not sufficient to pass title to compositions that might be recorded under the recording agreement.[25]

## Scope of Copyright Claim

Copyright ownership attaches to what is *original* with an author.[26] It is irrelevant whether an author's contribution to a composition or recording is new, novel, or unique.[27] The test is only whether the contribution originated

---

21. 17 U.S.C. § 101 (2011).

22. Note, however, that under some circumstances a court may find that while ownership of a copyright has not passed as a work for hire, the employer may nevertheless have acquired rights by means of a nonexclusive implied license. *See, e.g.,* Kolton v. Universal Studios, Inc., 73 U.S.P.Q.2d 1603 (C.D. Cal. 2004).

23. 17 U.S.C. § 302(c) (2011).

24. Papa's-June Music, Inc. v. McLean, 921 F. Supp. 1154 (S.D.N.Y. 1996).

25. Pamfiloff v. Giant Records, Inc., 794 F. Supp. 933 (N.D. Cal. 1992).

26. 17 U.S.C. § 102(a) (2011).

27. Vargas v. Pfizer, Inc., 418 F. Supp. 2d 369 (S.D.N.Y. 2005).

with the author. If the author's effort to create a work is independent, the work will be accorded copyright protection no matter how similar it may be to a prior work. As stated by one court many years ago, "[I]f by some magic a man who had never known it were to compose anew Keats's 'Ode on a Grecian Urn,' he would be an 'author,' and, if he copyrighted it, others might not copy that poem, though they might of course copy Keats."[28] Also, copyright protection only extends to the particular *expression* fixed in a work, which is original with the author. Copyright does not protect any idea, concept, plan, or discovery that might be revealed in the expression.[29] Further, an author who has rearranged or adapted a particular composition or created a compilation of separate works, such as a song folio or revue, gains copyright protection only in the original material, such as the selection and sequence of compositions, contributed by the author to the rearrangement, adaptation, or compilation.[30]

As a result of this originality test, more than one author can compose a song about a certain event or idea,[31] use a common word or phrase[32] or rhyme scheme,[33] or take a melody or verse from the public domain and express it in his own original fashion.[34] However, to gain protection in an arrangement of a work already in the public domain, the author's contribution must be more than a trivial addition or variation.[35] Originality is generally viewed as a low bar, and to give you an example of how low that bar might go, copyright protection has been extended to a single note "melody,"[36] to stage makeup,[37] to certain distinctive vocal effects (although

---

28. Sheldon v. Metro Goldwyn Pictures Corp., 81 F.2d 49, 54 (2d Cir. 1936).

29. 17 U.S.C. § 102(b) (2011).

30. 17 U.S.C. § 103(b) (2011).

31. Stratchborneo v. Arc Music Corp., 357 F. Supp. 1393 (S.D.N.Y. 1973).

32. Currin v. Arista Records, Inc., 724 F. Supp. 2d 286 (D. Conn. 2010).

33. Peters v. West, 692 F.3d 629 (7th Cir. 2012); Lil' Joe Wein Music, Inc. v. Jackson, 245 Fed. Appx. 873 (11th Cir. 2007).

34. Scott v. Paramount Pictures Corp., 449 F. Supp. 518 (D.D.C. 1978), *aff'd*, 607 F.2d 494 (D.C. Cir. 1979); Withol v. Wells, 231 F.2d 550 (7th Cir. 1956); Plymouth Music Co. v. Magnus Organ Corp., 456 F. Supp. 676 (S.D.N.Y. 1978); Newcomb v. Young, 43 F. Supp. 744 (S.D.N.Y. 1960); Whitney v. Ross Jungnickel, Inc., 43 F. Supp. 744 (S.D.N.Y. 1960).

35. Smith v. George Muelebach Brewing Co., 140 F. Supp. 729 (W.D. Mo. 1956).

36. Levine v. McDonald's Corp., 735 F. Supp. 92 (S.D.N.Y. 1990).

37. Carrell v. Shubert Org., Inc., 104 F. Supp. 2d 236 (S.D.N.Y. 2000).

in the context of the appropriation of other performance features),[38] and to the use of the word "dog" as musical punctuation and rhythmic panting.[39] Copyright protection, however, does not extend to the conventions and tools of printed musical expression, such as scales, keys,[40] chords, notations, markings, and symbols, nor does it extend to chord progressions or standard "licks" in and of themselves. If the latter were the case, hundreds of performers and composers would be paying royalties to early blues performers or to Chuck Berry, or both. Where unprotectable ideas leave off and original expression begins is not always a bright line.

With respect to sound recordings, the scope of copyright protection is limited to the actual sounds fixed in the recording. Therefore, so-called soundalike recordings, if independently fixed, do not infringe the copyright in prior recordings no matter how closely the prior recordings are imitated or simulated.[41]

## Collaboration

The creation of music and recordings of music is often a collaborative process. Whether co-authors will separately own or control their respective contributions to a song or recording or whether they will co-own the song or recording as a single unitary work is a question of intent. If their intent is that their contributions be merged, or they have worked in furtherance of a preconcerted common design, the composition or recording will be considered a joint work that they own as co-owners.[42] This intent must be present at the time the work is co-authored or at the time the author makes his contribution, not later.[43] Lyricists and composers involved with musical-dramatic productions for the stage often expressly agree that their respective contributions to a musical stage play will not merge until the

---

38. Tin Pan Apple v. Miller Brewing Co., 1994 WL62360 (S.D.N.Y. 1994).

39. Bridgeport Music, Inc. v. UMG Recording, Inc., 585 F.3d 267 (6th Cir. 2009).

40. Velez v. Sony Discos, 2007 WL 120686 (S.D.N.Y. 2007).

41. 17 U.S.C. § 114(b) (2011); Griffin v. J-Records, 398 F. Supp. 2d 1137, 1142 n. 14 (E.D. Wash. 2005).

42. 17 U.S.C. §§ 101, 201(a) (2011).

43. Janky v. Lake County Convention & Visitors Bureau, 576 F.3d 356 (7th Cir. 2009); see also Shapiro, Bernstein & Co. v. Jerry Vogel Music Co., 161 F.2d 406 (2d Cir. 1946); H. Rep. No. 1476, 94th Cong., 2d Sess. 120 (1976).

play has been performed for a certain minimum number of performances, thereby permitting each contributor to use his material in another situation if the play is not produced or is produced unsuccessfully.

## Fair Use

The exclusive rights that the Copyright Act grants to the owner of a copyright are not absolute. Instead, the rights of the copyright holder are always balanced against the rights of other parties, particularly the First Amendment rights of someone using a work protected by copyright without the owner's consent. The doctrine that provides this balance is called the fair use doctrine, which is a court-created, equitable defense to a claim of copyright infringement that permits unconsented uses of a copyrighted work on certain public policy grounds. Fair use, as codified in the Copyright Act, permits unconsented uses "for purposes such as criticism, comment, news reporting, teaching, . . . scholarship, or research."[44]

The following four factors set forth in § 107 must be analyzed determine if a use is fair and thus not an infringement:

(1) the purpose and character of the use, including whether such use is of a commercial nature or is for nonprofit educational purposes;
(2) the nature of the copyrighted work;
(3) the amount and substantiality of the portion used in relation to the copyrighted work as a whole; and
(4) the effect of the use upon the potential market for or value of the copyrighted work.[45]

It is important to understand that fair use is a defense. Whether one's fair use defense is valid is not conclusively known unless and until there is a judicial determination—it is not fair use unless and until the judge says it is fair use. As a result, reliance upon fair use to justify an unconsented use comes with the risk of uncertainty.

---

44. 17 U.S.C. § 107 (2011).
45. *Id.*

Also, the fair use defense must be assessed on a case-by-case basis. There are no absolute rules that either permit or bar the defense in all cases. The most useful general rule could be characterized as the Fair Use Golden Rule—only take what you would be comfortable others taking from you, and only use what you need to use and no more. That is not the expression of any legal doctrine, but it is generally a good initial measure to assess in association with the factors set out in the Copyright Act.

The following are examples of cases involving music in which the fair use defense was successfully interposed:

(1) *Lennon v. Premise Media Corp. L.P.*[46] (fifteen-second use of song "Imagine" held fair principally on the basis that such use was critical of song's message and did not usurp market for licensing the song for non-transformative uses).

(2) *Bill Graham Archives LLC v. Dorling Kindersley Ltd.*[47] (use of photographs of posters and tickets in book held fair principally on the basis that such use was transformative of the original work and not financially harmful).

(3) *Italian Book Corp. v. American Broadcasting Cos.*[48] (television broadcast of film and sound recording of parade band performing plaintiff's composition held fair on the basis of no harm to plaintiff).

(4) *Karll v. Curtis Publishing Co.*[49] (publication of plaintiff's composition held fair on the basis of implied consent).

(5) *Keep Thomson Governor Committee v. Citizens for Gallen Committee*[50] (use of song identified with one candidate in political campaign by his opponent in the opponent's responding commercials held fair).

---

46. Lennon v. Premise Media Corp. L.P., 556 F. Supp. 2d 310 (S.D.N.Y. 2008).

47. Bill Graham Archives LLC v. Dorling Kindersley Ltd., 386 F. Supp. 2d 324 (S.D.N.Y. 2005).

48. Italian Book Corp. v. American Broadcasting Cos., 458 F. Supp. 65 (S.D.N.Y. 1978).

49. Karll v. Curtis Pub'g Co., 39 F. Supp. 836 (E.D. Wis. 1941).

50. Keep Thomson Governor Comm. v. Citizens for Gallen Comm., 457 F. Supp. 957 (D.N.H. 1978).

(6) *Shapiro, Bernstein & Co. v. P.F. Collier & Son Co.*[51] (reprinting of lyrics from play in fictional serial in which characters in serial hear performances of the play while listening to radio broadcast).

(7) *Broadway Music Corp. v. F-R Pub'g Corp.*[52] (publication of portions of song in article about death of actress with whom song was associated).

The fair use defense has often been cited by politicians who have used musical compositions in political campaigns without consent, but the defense in such cases has generally been found to be unavailing.[53]

## Parody

Parody is a form of fair use. The success of a parody depends upon its perceived relation to a familiar object, person, or work, so parodists are permitted a somewhat greater freedom to borrow in order to "recall or conjure up" the original work as needed to link conceptually the parodist's work to the work being copied. However, to be defensible as a parody, the work being copied must be the work being parodied. For example, a parody defense interposed in a case involving use of a musical composition in a political ad was unsuccessful, as the "parody" took as its subject the user's opponent, rather than the song or those associated with the song.[54] The same result occurred when a salacious reworking of a popular song from the 1940s was included in a musical stage play and unsuccessfully defended as comment on the original composition.[55]

In the case of *Campbell v. Acuff-Rose Music, Inc.,*[56] the Supreme Court stated that, to the extent a parody does not take as the object of its criticism the work being copied, it diminishes the fairness of the borrowing but held that "parody, like other use, has to work its way through the relevant [fair use] factors, and to be judged case-by-case, in light of the end of copyright law."[57] The Court ruled that "It was error for the Court of

---

51. Shapiro, Bernstein & Co. v. P.F. Collier & Son Co., 26 U.S.P.Q. 40 (S.D.N.Y. 1934).
52. Broadway Music Corp. v. F-R Pub'g Corp., 31 F. Supp. 817 (S.D.N.Y. 1940).
53. *See, e.g.,* Browne v. McCain, 612 F. Supp. 2d 1125 (C.D. Cal. 2009).
54. Henley v. DeVore, 733 F. Supp. 2d 1144 (C.D. Cal. 2010).
55. MCA Music v. Earl Wilson, 425 F. Supp. 443 (S.D.N.Y. 1976).
56. Campbell v. Acuff-Rose Music, Inc., 510 U.S. 569 (1994).
57. *Id.* at 581.

Appeals to conclude that the commercial nature of 2 Live Crew's parody of 'Oh, Pretty Woman' rendered it presumptively unfair."[58] The following are other examples of cases involving music in which the parody defense was successfully interposed:

(1) *Elsmere Music, Inc. v. National Broadcasting Co.*[59] (use of "I Love New York" advertising jingle in NBC *Saturday Night Live* sketch as "I Love Sodom").

(2) *Berlin v. E.C. Publications, Inc.*[60] (publication of satirical lyrics that copied the meter of plaintiff's songs with directions to the reader to mentally supply the melodies).

(3) *Brownmark Films, LLC v. Comedy Partners*[61] (parody of popular music video in episode of television series "South Park").

## Copyright Myths

The rules of copyright law are often the subject of myth—there are some ideas that seem hard to put to rest, notwithstanding the efforts of many to dispel the errors in the myths. Here are some often-heard misconceptions:

(a) "It is okay to use someone's music if you do not use more than thirty seconds of it or make at least [fill a number in the blank] changes in the melody or words." The only rule of thumb with respect to the use of musical compositions is that there is no rule of thumb. This myth seems to arise as a result of the use of thirty-second preview samples at online stores that permit a prospective purchaser to confirm whether the track they are about to buy is in fact the one they want, and not something by another artist or a rerecorded or live version. These thirty-second sample rights accompany the right to sell the recording being offered and do not exist independently as a general right to use thirty

---

58. *Id.* at 594.

59. Elsmere Music, Inc. v. National Broadcasting Co., 482 F. Supp. 741 (S.D.N.Y. 1980), *aff'd*, 623 F.2d 252 (2d Cir. 1980).

60. Berlin v. E.C. Publications, Inc., 329 F.2d 541 (2d Cir. 1964), *cert. denied*, 379 U.S. 822 (1964).

61. Brownmark Films, LLC v. Comedy Partners, 682 F.3d 687 (7th Cir. 2012).

seconds (or some lesser period) of a composition. And there is no minimum number of changes that one can make to a melody or words to construct a shield against liability against a claim of copyright infringement. The legal test for liability is substantial similarity, which may not necessarily be escaped through the device of a minimum number of note or word changes. Each use of a composition or a recording has to be considered on a case-by-case basis, and while some use of even greater duration may be permitted without consent, even shorter uses may require permission.

(b) "To save yourself the cost of registering your work with the United States Copyright Office, just send a copy of your work to yourself by certified or registered mail and do not open the package." This myth has persisted for decades despite equally persistent efforts to debunk it. There is no value, from a copyright perspective, in such a process as it is easily corruptible (just mail yourself an empty, unsealed envelope and seal within it whatever you want at a later date). Standing to enforce a copyright in litigation requires a registration. Further, just from a practical point of view, the difference in price is immaterial given the relatively low cost of undertaking an application with the Copyright Office. While it may seem odd that some people still have this belief, the myth of the registered letter is like a vampire that will not die.

(c) "The work I want to use does not have a copyright notice on it, and I could not find it registered in the Copyright Office, so it must be in the public domain." This myth falls in the "it depends" category. It may be true that a work published without a copyright notice prior to January 1, 1978, or published between 1978 and March 1, 1989, without a notice and not registered within five years thereafter, is in the public domain. However, works published after March 1, 1989, do not require a copyright notice or a registration in order to remain protectable—it's just that a registration needs to be undertaken before a lawsuit is commenced. The upshot is that whether a work is in the public domain is a complex question that cannot be answered on the basis of these two simple factors.

(d) "It is okay to use another person's work because I am not charging people for what I am producing, I have given the original creator credit, and the original creator will benefit from the promotion I am giving to their work." Whether one charges for a work that incorporates the work of others is not relevant to whether an infringement has occurred—it is only a factor in assessing how damages will be determined. Further, while giving credit is a recommended practice, it is not a shield to liability. An unconsented use remains actionable, whether the borrowing is acknowledged or not. Finally, the owner of a copyright interest in a work is the sole person entitled to determine whether a proposed use of that work will provide a promotional incentive strong enough to forego more customary methods of compensation. No matter how strongly the second person may believe his or her use of a work will help create value in the work being used, the copyright owner has the right to be wrong about that.

# Trademarks

## Acquisition of Trademark Rights

Trademarks are usually thought of as words or logos that are used to identify the products or services of a person or company. However, trademarks go beyond simple words and logos—trademarks can comprise anything that has source identifying significance, including such things such as color, sound, and scents.[62] Trademarks represent the goodwill of their owners and, in the music industry, make possible the merchandising, packaging, licensing, and sponsorship opportunities that are so important to musical performing groups. Trademarks are to be distinguished from trade names, which are simply the names of the business entities that use the trademark or services marks.

Trademark rights are acquired in one of two ways in the United States. The first is simply by adoption and use of a mark with a product or service. The trademark owner's rights will be measured by the following factors: (1) strength of the mark in relation to the goods or services with which it is

---

62. For an interesting case concerning a claim to protect a performer's "costume," see *Naked Cowboy v. CBS*, 844 F. Supp. 2d 510 (S.D.N.Y. 2012).

used, (2) the territory in which the mark is used, (3) the channels of trade in which the trademarked goods or services are marketed, and (4) the success the trademark owner has in creating an association in the public mind between the mark and the owner's goods or services. The owner's rights will begin as of the date the mark is first used with the product or service. Federal registration of the owner's mark under the Lanham Act[63] after the mark has been used in commerce will give nationwide rights to the mark, along with certain remedies for the owner in the event of an infringement.

The second way trademark rights are obtained in the United States is by an application to register a proposed mark under the intent-to-use provisions of the Lanham Act.[64] An intent-to-use application, or ITU, permits the filing of an application to register a mark prior to the actual adoption of a mark based on the applicant's bona fide intention to adopt the mark with the goods or services identified in the application. Under an ITU, rights in a proposed mark can be obtained as of the filing date of the application for registration, as long as the applicant eventually files evidence within the time limits proscribed by the Lanham Act that he or she has commenced use of the mark in commerce in association with the goods or services identified in the application. This process protects the efforts of a trademark owner during the interim period between conceptualization of the mark and the actual use of the mark in commerce, which is the prerequisite event for a regular application.

Registration of one's trademark or service mark creates a legal presumption of one's ownership of the mark and one's exclusive right to use the mark nationwide on or in connection with the goods or services listed in the registration. A registration may also be recorded with the U.S. Customs and Border Protection Service to prevent importation of infringing goods and may be used as a basis for obtaining registrations in foreign countries. The registration symbol ® may only be used in connection with a mark that has been registered. It is highly recommended to use the registration symbol because failure to give such notice of registration means no profits and no damages may be recovered in a suit under the Lanham Act unless

---

63.  15 U.S.C. §§ 1051–1141n (2012).
64.  15 U.S.C. § 1051(b) (2012).

the defendant had actual notice of the registration.[65] Absent a registration, one may use "TM" or "SM" next to a mark to designate a claim of ownership, but such use does not confer legal rights comparable to those arising from a registration.

## Performing Group Names

Trademark rights are important for music companies such as record or music publishing companies, production companies, event promoters, and merchandising companies. However, the most interesting trademark issues generally arise in connection with the names of musical performing groups.[66]

The first trademark issue an emerging group faces is what the group is going to call itself. This is not an easy problem to solve, given the number of performing groups in the United States and the longevity of the careers of some groups. Additionally, the national online platforms available for groups to promote themselves, such as Facebook and Myspace, mean that concurrent users of the same name cannot carve out separate geographic regions for themselves as they may have done in the past. It was reported in 2010 that 2.5 million hip hop and 1.8 million rock acts registered accounts on Myspace alone,[67] and of course that list is not static. The satirical publication, *The Onion,* made the observation in 2007 that there were only seven good band names left.[68] The best group names convey a sense of the values associated with the creative output of the group, such as Metallica, Funkadelic, Insane Clown Posse, or the Clash. But the availability of such names has grown increasingly scarce, leading to the emergence of many names consisting of absurd non sequiturs, approaching narrative sentences, or reflecting a very low level of aspiration. One of the benefits of the appearance of online social media platforms as a promotional tool

---

65. 15 U.S.C. § 1111 (2012).

66. While we generally think of musical performing groups as the owners of the names of the groups, the names may be actually owned by others, such as the record company for which the group records. For a case where the party enforcing rights in the name and "persona" of the musical group The Supremes was the record company, see, e.g., Motown Record Corp. v. Hormel & Co., 657 F. Supp. 1236 (C.D. Cal. 1987).

67. *Investing in Music,* INTERNATIONAL FEDERATION OF THE PHONOGRAPHIC INDUSTRY (2010), http://www.ifpi.org/content/library/investing_in_music_2010.pdf.

68. *Report: Only 7 Band Names Remaining,* THE ONION (May 17, 2007) http://www.theonion.com/articles/report-only-7-band-names-remaining,5697/.

for musical performers is the greater ability to search the availability of proposed names as more names already being used are detectable through conventional online search methods.

The test for infringement under trademark law is whether use of a mark for a particular good or service is likely to cause confusion as to source, sponsorship, or approval of such goods or services with a prior user of a mark.[69] A group that presents itself with the same name as a different prior group would certainly cause people to believe that the new group is either the original group or a group that had the approval of the original group.

Beyond use of identical names, the question of whether one name for a musical performing group is likely to be confused with the name of another musical performing group must be determined on a case-by-case basis, generally taking into account the following factors: (1) similarity of the marks, (2) strength of plaintiff's mark, (3) sophistication of consumers when making a purchase, (4) intent of defendant in adopting the mark, (5) evidence of actual confusion (or lack thereof), (6) similarity of marketing and advertising channels, (7) extent to which the targets of the parties' sales efforts are the same, (8) product similarity, and (9) other factors suggesting that consumers might expect the prior owner to be involved with the defendant's product, service, or market.[70] With respect to music groups, the most important factors are the strength of the original user's mark and the similarity or dissimilarity of the marks in their entireties as to appearance, sound, connotation, and commercial impression.[71]

---

69. 15 U.S.C. §§ 1114, 1125 (2012).

70. Interpace Corp. v. Lapp, Inc., 721 F.2d 460 (3d Cir. 1983).

71. Notwithstanding the rights trademark law provides to a mark's owner, the commercial music market seems to tolerate similar names for performers that might be more problematic in other commercial situations. For example, two groups with the name Nirvana agreed to coexist, and the group fun. was able to distinguish itself from another Fun group by lower-casing the first letter and adding a period. Some other groups adopt certain modifications to their names, depending on the territory in which they are appearing or releasing recording. For example, the English Beat in the United States is The Beat in the rest of the world, and the Spinners in the United States were the Detroit Spinners in the United Kingdom. The passage of time also sometimes permits tolerance of names that would otherwise be confusingly similar. For example, the eighties country music supergroup featuring Johnny Cash, Willie Nelson, Waylon Jennings, and Kris Kristofferson called The Highwaymen was able to reach an arrangement with the sixties folk group The Highwaymen to coexist.

Whatever the name a group might select, it should be guided by at least two goals. First, the name should be selected with the goal of having offensive rights as opposed to defensive rights. The goal should not be to see what the group might be able to get away with, which is the defensive approach. The goal should be to select a name distinctive enough that it will enable the group to keep other groups from adopting names that are close in meaning—the group will have offensive rights against others. The second goal is to make sure that the name is available as a URL for the group's website and on social media platforms that will support the group's marketing efforts.[72]

Assuming the name a group selected does not run afoul of the rights of a prior user, conveys the values the group wants associated with its music, and is available for the online marketing platforms that will be critical for its marketing efforts, the next step is to seek protection of the name selected. This is often a moment of truth for many groups. If the group wisely elects to seek a federal registration of its name (perhaps under the intent-to-use provisions of the Lanham Act if use in interstate commerce has not yet occurred), the application requires the identification of the owner of the mark. Is the owner the group as an entity, and if so, what is the form of that entity? Or, is the owner of the name one of the group members (or less than all in some configuration)? Or is the owner the manager of the group?[73] Or the company producing and releasing the group's performances?[74] Each of these options is a viable election—the application requires that the issue be resolved before it is filed.

Issues relating to a group name do not end with adoption. Given how fragile and fluid the makeup of many musical groups can turn out to be, the ownership and use of a group's name as members come and go has caused

---

72. Two resources for checking the availability of a proposed name across multiple platforms, or monitoring how one's selected name might be in use by others, are www.knowem.com and www.namechk.com.

73. Rick v. Buchansky, 609 F. Supp. 1522 (S.D.N.Y. 1985) (manager found to be the owner of group name Vito and the Salutations).

74. Bell v. Streetwise Records, Inc., 640 F. Supp. 575 (D. Mass. 1986) (record company's claim of group name ownership rejected).

many interesting dustups in the past.[75] How to deal with these issues is considered in Chapter Four.

## Trademark Fair Use

Like copyright ownership, trademark rights do not convey an absolute ability to prevent others from using a mark. Under the doctrine of nominative fair use, performers' names can be used without liability to editorially refer to the performers themselves. For example, a newspaper used the name of the group New Kids On The Block (NKOTB) without the group's consent in a promotion asking young readers to vote for their favorite member of the group by means of a telephone number that produced revenue for the newspaper. The court hearing NKOTB's claim held that the newspaper's use met the following three requirements for a nominative fair use defense: "First, the product or service in question must be one not readily identifiable without use of the trademark; second, only so much of the mark or marks may be used as is reasonably necessary to identify the product or service; and third, the user must do nothing that would, in conjunction with the mark, suggest sponsorship or endorsement by the trademark owner."[76]

## Titles

While trademark protection extends to products and services, it does not apply to titles. From the perspective of the U.S. Patent and Trademark Office, titles are descriptive of an individual item and thus may not be registered.[77] However, while song or record titles will not be protected under trademark

---

75. *See, e.g.*, Crystal Entertainment & Filmworks, Inc. v. Jurado, 643 F.3d 1313 (11th Cir. 2011) (Expose); Marshak v. Treadwell, 240 F.3d 184 (3d Cir. 2001) (The Platters); Kassbaum v. Steppenwolf Productions, Inc., 236 F.3d 487 (9th Cir. 2000) (Steppenwolf); Robi v. Reed, 173 F.3d 736 (9th Cir. 1999) (The Platters); Marshak v. Schaffner, 2012 WL 1658393 (S.D.N.Y. 2012) (The Marvelettes); Densmore v. Manzarek, 2008 WL 2209993 (Cal. App. 2d Dist. 2008) (DOORS); Grondin v. Rossington, 690 F. Supp. 200 (S.D.N.Y. 1988) (Lynyrd Skynyrd); Kingsmen v. K-Tel Int'l Ltd., 557 F. Supp. 178 (S.D.N.Y. 1983) (The Kingsmen); HEC Enterprises, Ltd. v. Deep Purple, Inc., 213 U.S.P.Q. 991 (C.D. Cal. 1980) (Deep Purple); Griffin v. Gates, 205 U.S.P.Q. 1150 (N.D. Ill. 1979) (Bread); Giammarese v. Delfino, 197 U.S.P.Q. 162 (N.D. Ill. 1977) (Buckinghams); Noone v. Banner Talent Assocs., Inc., 398 F. Supp. 260 (S.D.N.Y. 1975) (Herman's Hermits); Rare Earth, Inc. v. Hoorelbeke, 401 F. Supp. 26 (S.D.N.Y. 1975) (Rare Earth); Tate v. Jackson, Case No. 12-2-21829-3 (King Co. Sup. Ct.) (Queensryche).

76. New Kids on the Block v. News America Pub'g, 971 F.2d 302 (9th Cir. 1992).

77. Herbko Int'l, Inc. v. Kappa Books, Inc., 308 F.3d 1156 (Fed. Cir. 2002).

principles, they may be protected under theories of unfair competition if they have achieved secondary meaning, which means that the public principally associates the title with a particular work.[78] Courts have noted, however, that a musical composition could not serve as a trademark for itself.[79]

## Online Presence

Accompanying the need to develop and protect trademarks and service marks for a performer or company is the need to build a strong online presence with associated domain names and social media addresses. By itself, a domain name, or uniform resource locator (URL), only offers its owner control of activity implemented by means of the URL. Variations on an established URL may be obtained—perhaps with a different extension (.net instead of .com, for example)—without any formal review or examination process to determine whether the second URL infringes the rights of an existing URL owner. If a trademark owner finds that a URL has been obtained that features the owner's mark, or is a name that is confusingly similar to the owner's mark, and the trademark owner is also able to establish that the registrant has no legitimate interest in the domain name and that the name has been obtained and used in bad faith, in addition to possible litigation the owner can initiate an arbitration proceeding to recover the offending URL under the Uniform Domain-Name Dispute Resolution Policy of ICANN.[80] Mere similarity of URLs will not be enough to obtain relief, which is why savvy website owners obtain multiple versions of their URLs as a defensive move against cybersquatters. While it is not practical to obtain all variations of a particular URL, the cost of maintaining at least a portfolio of the more common extensions, together with some

---

78. Robert Stigwood Group Ltd v. Sperber, 457 F.2d 50, 56 (2d Cir. 1972); Jubilee Industries, Inc. v. Roulette Records, Inc., 153 U.S.P.Q. 431 (N.Y. Sup. Ct. 1967); Glory Records, Inc. v. RCA, 213 N.Y.2d 875 (1961) *see also* Life Music, Inc. v. Wonderland Music Co., 241 F. Supp. 653 (S.D.N.Y. 1965) (protection of word "supercalafrajalisticexpialidocious" against use in dissimilar song denied).

79. EMI Catalogue Partnership v. Hill, Holliday, Connors, Cosmopulos Inc., 228 F.3d 56 (2d Cir. 2000); *see also* Mattel, Inc. v. MCA Records, Inc., 296 F.3d 894 (9th Cir 2002), *cert. denied,* 537 U.S. 1171 (2003) (use of "Barbie" doll character name in title and lyrics of composition and recording protected fair use).

80. Internet Corporation for Assigned Names and Numbers, http://www.icann.org/en/help/dndr/udrp (last visited Jan. 20, 2013).

other predictable variations,[81] is insignificant in comparison to the cost of pursuing an infringer.

With respect to infringing addresses and sites on social media services such as Twitter, Facebook, or Tumblr, a recommended first step is to provide notice of the infringement as a violation of the terms of use of the service through the service's complaint procedure. It has been my experience that the services are cooperative in disabling sites and addresses that make unauthorized use of prior owners' names and marks, which provides effective relief with minimal expense.

## Right of Publicity

The right of publicity is the right of an individual to control the commercial exploitation of his identity. This right is the foundation for many of the same sources of revenue for a performer as provided by trademarks, including: merchandising, touring, licensing, fan clubs, sponsorships, and packaging.

The right of publicity originally developed out of the common law protection of the right of privacy but assumed its own standing as a right protected under both common law and by state statutes. The right protects any element of an individual's identity—likeness, name, biography, voice—from unconsented commercial exploitation. This right was famously recognized by the U.S. Supreme Court in the case of *Zacchini v. Scripps-Howard Broadcasting Co.*[82] In *Zacchini*, the plaintiff was "The Human Cannonball," whose entire performance of being propelled through the air as he was shot from a cannon was filmed and broadcast by a television station. The Court recognized the commercial value of Mr. Zacchini's performance had been wrongfully appropriated and protected his commercial stake in his act over the First Amendment claims of the broadcasters.

Since the right of publicity is governed by state law, there are variations in its scope and application. In some states (such as New York), where the

---

81. It is not uncommon to defensively obtain URLs for websites that might otherwise be used for critical purposes, such as www.XXXXXSucks.com or www.XXXXXBlows.com. Of course, this could go on forever as well.

82. Zacchini v. Scripps-Howard Broadcasting Co., 435 U.S. 562 (1977).

right is interpreted as a personal right, the right of publicity terminates upon the death of the individual.[83] In other states (such as California), the right is interpreted as a property right and is descendible.[84] In states where the right is protected by statute, the period of time the right may be protected after death is as long as 100 years.[85] Since the matter protectable by the right of publicity is distinguishable from the scope of matter protectable by the Copyright Act, state statutory protection of the right of publicity is not preempted by the Copyright Act.[86] A claim for violation of one's right of publicity may be easier to establish than a trademark claim because proving a likelihood of confusion is not required. Instead, one only need establish that an element of one's identity has been used without consent and that such use was for a commercial purpose.

One of the most important right of publicity cases in the music area involved the performer Bette Midler. On her debut album, Ms. Midler delivered a distinctively seductive performance of what had theretofore been a much-covered up-tempo song called "Do You Want to Dance." Ms. Midler's version was popular, and she was later approached by the Ford Motor Company to obtain her consent to use her recording in a television commercial for one of its cars. When Ms. Midler declined, Ford instead arranged for the production of a recording of the same song by one of Ms. Midler's former backup singers that mimicked Ms. Midler's performance and used that recording in its commercial. Ms. Midler was successfully able to claim that her voice was an element of her identity and that, as such, her identity had been wrongfully appropriated by Ford in its sound-alike recording.[87]

Following Ms. Midler's success, Tom Waits sued Frito Lay in 1992 under similar circumstances. After Waits had declined to authorize the use of his performance for the soundtrack of a Doritos commercial, Frito Lay used a known impersonator to record a song that was not identical to one Waits

---

83. N.Y. CLS Civ. R § 51 (2000); Milton H. Greene Archives, Inc. v. Marilyn Monroe LLC, 692 F.3d 983 (9th Cir. 2012).

84. Cal. Civ. Code § 3344.1 (West 1997).

85. Right of Publicity Act, Ind. Code §§ 32-36-1-1-20.

86. Toney v. L'Oreal USA, Inc., 406 F.3d 905 (7th Cir. 2005).

87. Midler v. Ford Motor Co., 849 F.2d 460 (9th Cir. 1988).

had earlier released, but the vocals captured Waits's distinctive stylings. Waits was not only able to successfully assert that his identity had been misappropriated, but also that use of an impersonator under such circumstances created a likelihood of confusion as to Waits's sponsorship, approval, or endorsement of the Frito Lay product in violation of Section 43(a) of the Lanham Act.[88]

While performers with distinctive vocal characteristics have been successful in establishing that such vocal characteristics are a feature of their identity, performers have had less success establishing that a particular recording or song has become so identified with an artist that a secondary meaning has developed granting that artist trademark or identity rights.[89] For example Nancy Sinatra, whose biggest hit record was "These Boots Are Made for Walking," was unsuccessful in asserting a claim against the use of that song in a commercial extolling "wide boots" tires.[90] In like manner, the performing group The Romantics, whose major hit was "What I Like About You," were unsuccessful in asserting a claim against the developer of the electronic game "Guitar Hero" when it included a version of that song in the game as performed by other people.[91] However, a different result was achieved in a case involving the identity of performer Guy Lombardo, where a recording was one piece of several elements associated with Mr. Lombardo that were imitated in an advertisement.[92]

Identity rights, as with the case of trademarks and copyrights, are not absolute rights and must be balanced against the First Amendment rights of those who use a performer's identity noncommercially. For example, a song written by Bob Dylan about Rubin "Hurricane" Carter included the name of a witness involved with the actual trial. The witness sued Dylan, his publisher, and his record company on a variety of grounds, including

---

88.  Waits v. Frito-Lay, Inc., 978 F. 2d 1093 (9th Cir. 1992), *cert. denied*, 506 U.S. 1080 (1993); *see also* Prima v. Darden Restaurants, Inc., 78 F. Supp. 2d 337 (D. N.J. 2000) (right of publicity of performer Louis Prima violated by use of soundalike recording in background of television commercial).

89.  *See, e.g.*, Oliveira a/k/a Gilberto v. Frito-Lay, Inc., 251 F.3d 56 (2d Cir. 2001).

90.  Sinatra v. Goodyear Tire & Rubber Co., 435 F.2d 711 (9th Cir. 1970), *cert. denied*, 402 U.S. 906 (1971).

91.  Romantics v. Activision Pub., Inc., 574 F. Supp. 2d 758 (E.D. Mich. 2008).

92.  Lombardo v. Doyle, Dane & Berbach, 396 N.Y.S.2d 661 (1977).

misappropriation of her identity. While the song and the recording of the song are certainly commercial undertakings, the song did not promote a product or a service, which is a key element of the right of identity claim.[93] On the other hand, a musical featuring performers imitating the Beatles performing Beatles songs was found to appropriate the group's persona. The court found in favor of the Beatles, notwithstanding the argument that the musical work was an expressive commentary on the culture and politics of the 1960s that was entitled to First Amendment protection. The court used the fair use factors under the Copyright Act to find that the taking of the Beatles' identity overwhelmed the other elements of the musical work, as the performers imitating the Beatles were on stage for 95 percent of the presentation.[94]

Further, the First Amendment may be inapplicable if the use of a performer's identity is wholly unrelated to the material with which it is used. In this situation, the use could be said to be for the purpose of attracting commercial attention to the material. For example, the name of the civil rights icon Rosa Parks was used as the title of a song by the group Outkast. Parks sued for violation of her right of publicity and was able to reverse a summary judgment entered against her on the grounds that a genuine issue of material fact existed as to whether the title of the song was or was not "wholly unrelated" to the content of the song.[95]

As a result of the various claims brought against advertisers based on performers' identity rights, the use of licensed preexisting music for commercials has become more prominent than the use of newly recorded material. Licensed music brings certainty. This circumstance has also created new opportunities for artists to use commercials as a promotional vehicle, creating more competition for participation in commercials and, in many cases, reducing the amount advertisers have to pay for such recordings as a result of the perception that exposure from being included in a commercial creates

---

93. Valentine v. C.B.S., Inc., 698 F.2d 430 (11th Cir. 1983).

94. Apple Corps Ltd. v. Leber et al., 229 U.S.P.Q. 1015 (1986). For a discussion concerning identity rights and "tribute" bands, see Brent Giles Davis, *Identity Theft: Tribute Bands, Grand Rights, and Dramatico-Musical Performances*, 24 CARDOZO ARTS & ENT. L.J. 845 (2006).

95. Parks v. LaFace Records, 329 F.3d 437 (6th Cir. 2003), *cert. denied*, 540 U.S. 1074 (2003).

value. For some performers, commercials are viewed as a desirable platform, particularly as the playlists of commercial radio stations have become more restrictive and difficult to break through.

# Data

Access to market and customer data improves commercial decision making in the music business.[96] Online transactions and other data collection tools enable artists to directly connect with their fans in ways never before possible. In the past, the artist-fan relationship was mediated by record companies and retailers. While information might have been available about how many records featuring a particular artist had been sold, and perhaps generally where in the United States and through what general channel of retailer, no one knew who bought those records so that they could be contacted and persuaded to buy the next one. An artist's fan club was perhaps the only form of direct relationship that existed, and that vehicle, even when available to an artist, was cumbersome and inexpert.

In addition to having a direct link to those likely to support the artist with their purchasing decisions, knowing where an artist's fans are located helps to more precisely route personal appearances and support appeals to promoters making booking decisions. Data also helps measure the effectiveness of promotional efforts and can provide validation to actual and potential sponsors of the ability of the artist to draw an audience and influence buying behavior. Analysis of other data metrics also helps an artist identify trends in their own performances and measure that performance relative to other artists.

Data is also critical with respect to digital marketing and distribution and the tracking of music usage.[97] Before releasing recordings, performers should insure that correct metadata concerning each of their recordings is properly embedded as part of the mastering process. This metadata should

---

96. *See, e.g.*, Derrick Harris, *Data Isn't Just the New Oil, It's the New Money. Ask Zoe Keating*, GIGAOM (Nov. 20, 2012), http://gigaom.com/data/data-isnt-just-the-new-oil-its-the-new-money-ask-zoe-keating.

97. *See generally* Ed Christman, *Database Dilemma*, BILLBOARD, June 2, 2012 at 8.

include each master's International Standard Record Code (ISRC),[98] which is a unique number assigned to each recording for identification and reporting purposes. The ISRC will assist the detection of usage of the recording and make possible the tracking of proper payments for the use of the recording to the correct recipient.

Online sites that offer music, such as music services or online retailers, obtain album cover artwork, reviews, titles, composers, and other metadata concerning the music they feature so that the music, and information about the music, can be properly presented to their customers. These music sites obtain such metadata from suppliers that create, compile, and sell metadata. These metadata suppliers include www.gracenote.com, www.artistdata.com, and www.allmusic.com. It is important for performers to ensure that such metadata suppliers have correct data concerning the performers and their work within their files so that the performers and their work are correctly presented by the music sites using those metadata suppliers.

Data may be collected by the artist or company itself, by platforms used by the artist or company, or by third parties such as Next Big Sound that, in turn, format and market access to the data. An artist's efforts to collect data that personally identifies an individual fan or consumer will be governed generally by state and federal law.[99] In addition, efforts by an artist to collect data by mining social media platforms will generally require disclosure of the artist's privacy policy concerning how such collected information may be used and may be subject to additional specific restrictions of the social media platform as well.[100]

Ownership of data associated with an artist is not always within the artist's reach. For example, many artist recording agreements provide that the record company will administer the artist's website during the term of the recording agreement. Under such circumstances, data collected by the

---

98. ISRCs may be obtained online through the Recording Industry Association of America at this website. International Standard Recording Code, http://www.usisrc.org (last visited Jan. 20, 2013).

99. *See, e.g.*, Children's Online Privacy Protection Rule, 16 C.F.R. pt. 312 (2003); Privacy of Consumer Financial Information, 16 C.F.R. pt. 313 (2003); Standards For Safeguarding Customer Information, 16 C.F.R. pt. 314 (2003); Cal. Civ. Code §§ 1798.29, 1798.82.

100. *See, e.g.*, Facebook, *Statement of Rights and Responsibilities*, Section 9 (Apr. 15, 2009), http://www.facebook.com/note.php?note_id=183538190300.

record company and associated with the artist will not be available to the artist. In like manner, ticket sellers collect information concerning ticket purchaser, which information is not generally shared with the artist. If an artist engages the services of a third-party payment provider, such as PayPal, to facilitate the sale of their products from the artist's website, or third- party product development or fulfillment providers such as Café Press, certain information concerning purchasers of artist-related merchandise may also not be shared.

When representing an artist, it is important to anticipate how data concerning that artist and the artist's work will be collected. Determine how the artist will be able to control and use that data, and keep in mind that transactions and professional relationships run their course and are superseded by new transactions and relationships. In the event the performing group itself collects personally identifying information about their fans, the privacy policy under which such information is collected should anticipate all intended uses and how the group members have determined the data will be shared if the group disbands.

## Interviews

Musicians view interviews as both the desired result of promotional efforts and a nuisance. Whatever may be the view at the moment the interview occurs, the principal issue for the musician being interviewed is, "Who owns the results of the interview?" The answer to that question is not clear. An interview is by definition collaborative, which may lead to a conclusion that the interviewer and interview subject are joint owners of the interview, or owners of their respective contributions. Alternatively, each party could claim sole ownership of the entire questions and answers. The issue is further complicated if the interview is recorded by a third party, who may have their own independent rights in the recordings they are producing.[101]

---

101. Mark Fowler, *Who "Owns" an Interview?*, RIGHTS OF WRITERS (Jan. 7, 2011), http://www.rightsofwriters.com/2011/01/who-owns-interview.html.

The best way to address the issue of ownership is to agree in writing prior to the event. Although this practice may not be appropriate with respect to quick promotional telephone interviews in anticipation of an appearance, or interviews conducted to develop material for inclusion in a larger work such as a book, it does apply to extensive interviews to be published as stand-alone works. In the written agreement, attention should be given to how recordings of the interview may be used, if at all, and how ownership of such recordings will be held.[102]

# Contractual Rights

For purposes of this chapter, the term "contractual rights" are certain provisions that sculpt the market in some manner and help create competitive advantages. Such provisions often found in entertainment contracts, particularly agreements related to music, include: exclusivity, right of first negotiation and refusal, key man, credit, most favored nations, and nondisclosure.

## Exclusivity

Grants of rights, whether for copyrights, trademarks, identity rights, or personal services, fall into one of two categories. The rights are either exclusive or they are nonexclusive. If rights are exclusive, that means they are exclusive even as to the grantor, absent a specific reservation of that right. This may seem obvious, but it is an important consideration in any transaction involving a musical property or talent. The broader the scope of exclusivity as to territory, product or service, channel of trade, or duration that is defined in an agreement, the more valuable the right. Exclusivity is particularly applicable to performers. Recording agreements define the scope of exclusivity of rights the record company has in the results of the performances of the talent, the songwriter agreements and his or her output, or

---

102. Lennon, et al, v. Pulsebeat News, 143 U.S.P.Q. 309 (N.Y.Sup. 1964) (records of taped interview enjoined from distribution).

the personal appearances within a certain period of time within a certain geographic range.

In some instances, rights are not available on an exclusive basis. For example, licenses that permit the manufacture and sale of phonorecords of sound recordings, or mechanical licenses, are nonexclusive because music publishers want to have as many performers recording their songs as possible. However, the exclusivity of a mechanical license may be unimportant, as the artist and quality of the specific performance in the recording, which would be exclusive, may create the real market value. Some transactions can be structured so that rights are exclusive for a period of time but become nonexclusive thereafter.

## Right of First Negotiation/Refusal

Parties to a music-related transaction often do not know the true value of a property or a talent at the time the agreement is entered. Therefore, the parties may want to leave themselves with some flexibility to adapt their agreement terms as the project unfolds and they can measure the project's success. However, to negotiate all the details and "what-ifs" involving all the possible contingencies of what that success might be, and how the terms of the agreement would be affected and addressed, can derail or smother the progress of a successful negotiation.[103] A right of first negotiation is one method of preventing a battle about hypotheticals from overcoming negotiations. A right of first negotiation means the artist or property owner will engage with the producer or distributor first before soliciting interest from any other party. The right gives the producer or distributor the first chance to assess the opportunity available from the artist or property owner and reach terms to continue the relationship. The right also prevents a competitor from initiating negotiations directly with the artist or property owner prior to the expiration of the initial agreement unbeknownst to the producer or distributor.

---

103. In such circumstances, the talent or property side of the transaction (the seller) may opt to have a shorter agreement to avoid being bound to terms that might become unfavorable in light of an achieved success. However, the production or distribution side of the transaction (the buyer) may want the ability to continue the relationship in some manner if the success occurs.

A right of first negotiation is often paired with a right of first refusal, or ability to meet an offer made by another party subsequent to the first negotiation period if that first negotiation period ends without reaching an agreement. Under such circumstance, the producer or distributor in effect gets a second shot at continuing the relationship, which can be a powerful combination.

## Key Man

A key man provision in an agreement generally means that in the event a particular person is no longer affiliated with a company, or is otherwise not available to manage the relationship of the talent with an organization, then the talent has the right to terminate the agreement. This may be significant in a management or agency agreement, where the personal relationship of the talent with an individual may be the principal reason the talent is signed to the organization. I also had the experience of representing a musical performer who insisted on what I came to call a "reverse" key man provision in his agreement with a recording company. In the event a certain named individual ever became associated with the record company, the artist would have the right to terminate the agreement. The label was small enough that it felt my client's *bête noir* would never be affiliated with it so it conceded the point.

## Credit

Credit for a performer, producer, songwriter, or company is a key component of the consideration they will receive in a transaction. What credit is given, and how and where that credit is accorded in a project and the packaging and advertising for products embodying the project, is usually heavily negotiated. Credit influences industry and public perceptions of an artist or company, enables participation in further and better projects, and can drive financial compensation arrangements. However, credit obligations will only be enforced by means of contractual provisions, whether through direct agreements between talent or licensors and producers or indirectly through the provisions of certain union or guild agreements covering talent to which a producer becomes a signatory.

There is no general statutory right to receive a credit for one's contribution to a work. Efforts to bring a cause of action under the federal trademark laws against a work that fails to accord credit on the grounds that such work is mislabeled have failed. In the case of *Dastar v. Twentieth Century Fox Film Corp.*,[104] the Supreme Court held that § 43(a) of the Lanham Act[105] did not address the misappropriation of authorship, which in that case involved a "reverse passing off" claim concerning repackaged public domain content that did not accord credit to those originally involved with the content. The Court ruled that the word "origin" in § 43(a) did not include the intellectual contribution made to a good or service, only the producer of the product or service. Since that decision, courts have invalidated claims concerning misattribution of credits brought under the Lanham Act and have pointed out that one desiring credit has the right to obtain such credit by contract or union collective bargaining agreements.[106] Further, failure to properly accord credit is not a violation under the Copyright Act.[107]

The takeaway from this circumstance is that the credit provisions of an agreement—whether for an artist or a production company licensing rights to its works—and the remedies available to the artist or production company if credit is not properly accorded are to be given very careful attention in any transaction, as valuable consideration may be lost if not found within the terms of the agreement.

## Most Favored Nations

A most favored nations clause essentially says that in the event one party to an agreement enters a second transaction involving the property that is the subject of the initial agreement with a third party under terms or conditions that are more favorable than the terms and conditions in the initial agreement, then the more favorable terms and conditions of the

---

104. Dastar v. Twentieth Century Fox Film Corp., 539 U.S. 23 (2003).
105. 15 U.S.C. § 1125(a) (2012).
106. *See, e.g.*, Dutch Jackson IATG, LLC v. Basketball Mktg. Co., 846 F. Supp. 2d 1044 (E.D. Mo. 2012); Williams v. UMG Recordings, Inc., 281 F. Supp. 2d 1177 (C.D. Cal. 2003); *see also* King v. Ames, 179 F.3d 370 (5th Cir. 1999) (claim that individual falsely accorded himself credit on packaging of CDs to be producer of live recordings rejected).
107. UMG Recordings, Inc. v. Disco Azteca Distribs., 446 F. Supp. 2d 1164, 1178 (E.D. Cal. 2006).

second agreement will be deemed incorporated into the initial agreement and applicable. Most favored nations provisions appear in a number of circumstances. For example, when a sound recording is being licensed for use in an audiovisual work, the financial terms for use of the recording and the underlying composition performed in the recording are often negotiated on a most favored nations basis—the master rights holder and the composition publisher receive the same payment. Also, when multiple works are being assembled for a compiled work, the terms applicable to each of the individual works are often offered on a most favored nations basis. All terms are equal, with no individual owner receiving more favorable terms than any other. Credit provisions are also often established on a most favored nations basis, with each credit recipient receiving credit in the same manner as everyone else.

A most favored nations approach to a negotiation can expedite a transaction because the party receiving the benefit of the most favored nations treatment knows that he or she will not receive less than any other party and that he or she will be the beneficiary of any improved terms that might be obtained by a stronger party.

## Nondisclosure

Nondisclosure provisions prevent the recipient of certain information, such as a contractual party, from disclosing that information to others. In music transactions, nondisclosure of the terms of an agreement, particularly the financial terms, protects the business model of a producer and prevents terms from being known to other artists that could be used to the detriment of the producer in other negotiations. Nondisclosure of material transactional terms may also be beneficial to artists, who may wish to shield such sensitive information from public scrutiny and any possible resulting negative reactions. Maintaining privacy of terms is also wise when the musician may not want to inform other possible transactional partners of the terms under which they are prepared to work.

# Moral Rights

Artist moral rights do not refer to questions of ethics but to the rights of an artist (among others) to control works they create to prevent their revision or distortion (integrity), to determine how their works may be presented, and to receive proper credit for their contribution to a work (attribution). In the United States, the moral rights of visual artists are addressed in the Copyright Act as the result of the Visual Artists Rights Act of 1990.[108] Although the moral rights of a composer are not recognized in the United States,[109] moral rights may extend to the visual artists who create album cover artwork unless such rights have been waived by the visual artist.[110]

---

108. 17 U.S.C. § 106A (2011).
109. *See, e.g.*, Shostakovich v. 20th Century-Fox, 80 N.Y.S.2d 575, *aff'd*, 87 N.Y.S.2d 430 (1949).
110. 17 U.S.C. § 106A (2011).

# Chapter Three
# Music Publishing

Music publishing is the engine that drives the music industry. There is not a transaction involving music that does not implicate publishing in some manner. While some of the practices of the industry are arcane, or may seem so, the industry also relies upon sophisticated systems to track music uses, collect payments, and disburse proceeds throughout the world. The music publishing industry can be characterized as centralized in the context of the large international companies affiliated with the few major international record companies. However, the industry beyond the few majors is quite Balkanized, with low organizational and financial barriers to successful launch and operation. Since the business of music publishing today is principally the administration of the rights that are derived from the copyright interest in a composition, without the need to physically distribute products, there are many tens of thousands of music publishing companies operating within a wide range of size. And it all starts with a song.

As explained in the section about copyright, copyright rights in a musical composition arise automatically upon the fixation of that composition in some tangible form—the song is written down in some form of transcription or is recorded. Music publishing involves dealing with the question of who owns the composition's copyright at that moment of fixation and the terms under which the various rights in that composition are exploited.[1]

Most musical compositions will begin their lives owned by the composer. It is possible, however, for someone other than the composer to own the copyright when created. For example, if music is being composed by an employee within the scope of his or her employment, such as for a commercial jingle production company, the composition will belong to the employer as a work made for hire. Another common circumstance involving a composition being deemed a work made for hire would include a composer hired to create music for an audiovisual work, such as a film or television program. Remember, to constitute a work made for hire, there must be a written agreement that defines the work as one made for hire.

To illustrate and explain how music publishing works, we will organize this chapter around the fictitious circumstances of a new songwriter who is not working in a work for hire relationship and has composed a group of songs he now wants to exploit. What should the composer do? Assuming the songwriter is not already affiliated with a music company (which we will discuss later), the songwriter should first become affiliated with one of the performance rights organizations.

## Performance Rights Organizations

Copyright owners were first granted the exclusive right to publicly perform their musical compositions for profit in 1897. The American Society of Composers, Authors and Publishers (ASCAP) was formed in 1914 to enforce this right for composers, and the Society of European Stage Authors & Composers (SESAC) and Broadcast Music, Inc. (BMI) were formed in 1930 and 1939, respectively, for the same purpose.[2] Since 1941, ASCAP

---

1. *See generally* Darren M. Richard, *Music Licensing 101*, 29 ENT. & SPORTS LAW, No. 4, 2012 at 12.

2. The early history of ASCAP, and the circumstances of the formation of BMI as an alternative to ASCAP, are recounted in the following titles: JOHN RYAN, THE PRODUCTION OF CULTURE IN THE MUSIC INDUSTRY: THE ASCAP-BMI CONTROVERSY (University Press of America 1985), and RUSSELL SANJEK & DAVID SANJEK, AMERICAN POPULAR MUSIC BUSINESS IN THE 20TH CENTURY (Oxford 1991).

and BMI have operated under consent decrees resulting from antitrust actions brought by the government which, *inter alia*, limit their authority to the nonexclusive licensing of nondramatic performances and establish procedures for setting license rates and conditions.[3] These three organizations now license for composers, on a nonexclusive basis, the nondramatic performance rights in almost all domestic compositions to entities publicly performing music, such as commercial radio and television stations, restaurants, clubs, online music services, and other such establishments. Most arrangements are through blanket licenses of each organization's entire repertoire.[4] While the blanket licensing practices of ASCAP and BMI have been challenged on antitrust and copyright misuse grounds in several private actions, they have been upheld as to broadcast television networks,[5] local television broadcasters,[6] and as applied to small establishments offering music, such as bars, nightclubs, and restaurants.[7] The blanket licensing practices of a single publisher of religious music granting performance and reprint rights to Catholic parishes has also been upheld.[8] As of the writing

---

3. United States v. Broadcast Music, Inc., 1996-1 Trade Cas. ¶ 71,378 (S.D.N.Y. 1994); United States v. BMI, 1966 Trade Cas. ¶71,941 (S.D.N.Y. 1966); United States v. ASCAP, 1950-1951 Trade Cas. ¶ 62,595 (S.D.N.Y. 1950); United States v. ASCAP, 1940-1943 Trade Cas. ¶ 56,104 (S.D.N.Y. 1941); United States v. BMI, 1940-1943 Trade Cas. ¶ 56,096 (E.D. Wis. 1941).

4. However, DMX, a background and foreground music service provider, was recently able to successfully establish a rate for its service through ASCAP that allowed it to offset the costs of direct licenses with ASCAP members. *See* Broadcast Music, Inc. v. DMX Inc., 683 F.3d 32 (2d Cir. 2012). Also in 2011, one of the largest music publishers, EMI Music Publishing, withdrew the right to license digital services from ASCAP in favor of direct licenses. *See* Ed Christman, *EMI Music Publishing Taking Over Licensing Digital Rights From ASCAP*, Hollywood Reporter, May 4, 2011, http://www.hollywoodreporter.com/news/emi-music-publishing-taking-licensing-184688. This move has been followed by Sony/ATV, which acquired EMI Music Publishing in 2012. *See* Martin Bandier, *Cutting But Not Running*, Billboard, Oct. 20, 2012, 8. The subsequent direct negotiation by Sony/ATV of digital performance rights with Pandora resulted in a 25 percent increase in the license rate paid to Sony/ATV. *Sony/ATV Ups Fee With Direct Pandora Pact*, Billboard, Feb. 2, 2013, 10.

5. Broadcast Music, Inc. v. Columbia Broad. Sys., Inc., 441 U.S. 1 (1979), *aff'd on remand*, 620 F.2d 930 (2d Cir. 1980), *cert. denied*, 450 U.S. 970 (1981); Columbia Broad. Sys., Inc. v. American Soc'y of Composers, Authors & Publishers, 400 F. Supp. 737 (S.D.N.Y. 1975), *rev'd*, 562 F.2d 130 (2d Cir. 1977), *rev'd sub nom.*

6. Buffalo Broad v. American Soc'y of Composers, Authors & Publishers, 744 F.2d 917 (2d Cir. 1984), *cert. denied*, 469 U.S. 1211 (1985).

7. Broadcast Music, Inc. v. Moor-Law, Inc., 527 F. Supp. 758 (D. Del. 1981), *aff'd*, 691 F.2d 490 (3d Cir. 1982).

8. F.E.L. Publ'ns, Ltd. v. Catholic Bishop of Chicago, 214 U.S.P.Q. 409 (7th Cir. 1982).

of this chapter, private antitrust actions are pending against SESAC by com-mercial television and radio broadcast stations.[9]

Until 1948, ASCAP also licensed to theater operators and exhibitors the right to publicly perform music in motion pictures. That practice was ended by court order in the case of *Alden-Rochelle, Inc. v. ASCAP.*[10] The right to perform music in motion pictures by way of theatrical exhibition is now acquired directly by motion picture producers. The performance rights to the same music when the motion picture is transmitted by other means, such as by broadcast or satellite, are still controlled by the perfor-mance rights organizations.

Registering with one of the performance rights organizations, or PROs, is relatively easy. One may apply to ASCAP (www.ascap.com) and BMI (www.bmi.com) online, as either a songwriter, a publisher, or both. Affilia-tion with SESAC requires submission of one's work and an invitation from SESAC to become a member. Since our fictitious songwriter is not already affiliated with an existing music publishing company, he or she may wish to affiliate as both a songwriter and as a publisher by way of establishing his or her own self-owned publishing company.

The financial considerations impacting our fictitious songwriter's selection of which PRO to join are beyond the scope of this book but are comprehen-sively reviewed in the book *Music, Money, and Success* by Jeffrey Brabec and Todd Brabec,[11] wherein ASCAP, BMI, and SESAC are profiled in detail. The authors write:

> The primary areas that need to be considered include the length of a writer's or publisher's contract and the procedures to terminate that contract if one wants to leave; fairness and equality of treatment in the distribution of royalties; recognition of the value of all of a writer's and publisher's copyrights whether they be new or old works; procedures whereby each organization changes its payment rules; relationships

---

9. Meredith Corp. v. SESAC, LLC, 2011 WL 856266 (S.D.N.Y. 2011); Radio Music License Comm., Inc. v. SESAC, LLC, et al., Civil Action No. 12 5807 (E.D. Pa. 2012).

10. Alden-Rochelle, Inc. v. ASCAP, 80 F. Supp. 888 (S.D.N.Y. 1948).

11. Jeffrey Brabec & Todd Brabec, Music, Money, and Success 309–357 (Schirmer Trade Books 2011).

with foreign performing right organizations; maximum and accurate collection of foreign income; and the actual dollar payments each organization is making for specific types of uses in specific media.[12]

Sometimes the selection of a PRO is made on other grounds. Some people select on the basis of affinity with the historical background of the organization. ASCAP began its life in New York and has a legacy strong in the Tin Pan Alley and show tune tradition that existed there. BMI gathered its initial repertoire among certain genres of music that had been overlooked by ASCAP, such as country, jazz, and R&B. This factor is of much less importance today, as both organizations are now strong in each genre, but some songwriters may feel a stronger connection with one over the other because of the songwriters and catalogs they and their songs may be joining.

Another factor may be how the songwriter feels about the ownership of the PRO. ASCAP is an unincorporated membership association. BMI is owned by members of the radio and television broadcasting industries. SESAC is privately owned by an investor group.

Another factor may be the methodology and technology by which a PRO detects and collects performances. Each of the PROs—ASCAP, BMI, and SESAC—uses digital technology to detect and track performances. This enables each PRO to obtain more comprehensive and accurate data concerning such performances and more correctly allocate their license proceeds among their members. BMI and ASCAP use digital fingerprinting technologies called Blue Arrow and Mediaguide, respectively, that can identify music and compare it to an existing file for recognition. SESAC uses digital watermarking technology called Digisound that embeds a recognizable signal in a recording.[13]

Finally, another way to help the selection process is to compare actual results between the organizations. The only "apples-to-apples" comparison that would yield helpful results is the respective payouts for a song

---

12. *Id.* at 315.

13. *Frequently Asked Questions*, PRODUCTION MUSIC ASSOCIATION (July 8, 2010), http://pmamusic.com/pma/?page_id=45.

co-written by, for example, an ASCAP member and a BMI member. Unfortunately, that information is not generally available or, if so, is anecdotal.

Once the songwriter has selected which PRO to affiliate with, the next most significant issue is the name of his or her proposed publishing company. ASCAP and BMI will ask the songwriter for three name choices of his or her proposed publishing company, in order of preference. Creative name selections are encouraged, as there are tens of thousands of music publishing companies and each organization will check for confusingly similar names not only within their own membership, but also within the membership of one another and their respective foreign affiliates. Once affiliation is completed, the songwriter will submit his or her compositions to the PRO he or she has joined so that any performances of such songs that are logged by the PRO can be tied to the composer.

The form of business entity that the songwriter takes for his or her publishing company—sole proprietorship, corporation, or limited liability company—will of course depend upon the individual circumstances of the songwriter. However, affiliation with a PRO is suggested as a first step, as clearance of the proposed name of the publishing company through the PRO will be the most important consideration in name selection.

There are many alternative next steps our fictitious songwriter might take after the organization of his or her own publishing company. For our purposes, let us assume the songwriter initially elects to operate on his or her own as a self-publisher. The principal business of the company will be to administer the granting of rights in the compositions controlled by the company, the most important of which are mechanical rights and synchronization rights.

## Mechanical Licenses

Observation tells us that, as people, we tend to integrate change through the use of analogy. For example, the first automobiles looked like wagons, many of man's first efforts to fly mimicked the flapping of birds' wings, and the first on-screen digital music players looked like CD players. That is the only way one can explain why, after over one hundred years, the music industry still uses the term "mechanical" to describe a circumstance that has long lost any association with a mechanical process.

Piano rolls were an early form of musical exploitation. The mechanical process involved scrolling paper in which holes had been punched through a specially equipped piano, which caused the piano to perform a composition. The Copyright Act of 1909 recognized that the scrolling of punched-paper constituted a reproduction of the composition that was within the scope of the exclusive rights of the composition's copyright. The license to produce such piano rolls was called a mechanical license, as the composition was considered to be mechanically reproduced by the piano rolls. This same terminology was later applied to sound recordings on wax cylinders and then to recordings on flat discs or records. As discs became magnetic tapes, and then discs again in the form of compact discs, the terminology remained. Today, the term "mechanical license" refers to the permission given to fix a recording of a musical composition in any form, whether physical, such as a compact disc (which the Copyright Office calls "phonorecords"), or digital, such as a download transmission (what the Copyright Office calls a "digital phonorecord delivery"), or the copy of a recording fixed on a server to facilitate the digital stream of the recording.

Since the Copyright Act of 1909, mechanical licenses have been the subject of a compulsory license recognized under copyright law that essentially permits anyone to market (for private use) a recording of a musical composition that has already been released in recorded form. The caveat is that the second user of the composition must comply with the statutory requirements of the compulsory license.[14] There are a number of requirements for qualifying for the compulsory license, but the most significant requirement is that the second user of the composition must pay the statutory license rate that has been set by the Copyright Office for such use.[15]

---

14. 17 U.S.C. § 115 (2011).

15. The compulsory license permits the performer to make an arrangement of the composition "to the extent necessary to conform it to the style or manner of interpretation of the performance involved, but the arrangement shall not change the basis melody or fundamental character of the work . . . ," 17 U.S.C. § 115 (2011). For a discussion concerning some of the implications of this "arrangement privilege" for the music business, see Spender C. Martinez, *The Phonorecord Compulsory License Statute and the Unresolved "Arrangement Privilege,"* Ent. L. & Fin., Feb. 2009.

The statutory royalty rates set for mechanical licenses under the compulsory licensing provisions of the Copyright Act of 1909 and the current copyright law eventually became the prevailing standard in most privately negotiated mechanical license agreements. This is because both publishers and users of music knew that if they did not come to terms, the user could elect to pay the statutory rate to the publisher for a recording of the publisher's song once a recording of that song had been released domestically. These rates were 2 cents per recording, per copy, for many years, and were initially raised by the Copyright Act of 1976. They have been adjusted periodically since. The rates for physical phonorecords, on a per-unit basis, are currently set as either 9.1 cents or 1.75 cents per minute of playing time or fraction thereof, whichever amount is larger.[16] In reality, very few marketers of recordings avail themselves of the compulsory licensing provision of the Copyright Act because of the notice and accounting provisions that must be observed to ensure the license's effectiveness, but the rate set by the Copyright Office continues to be the benchmark for private licenses.

There are essentially two methods of issuing or obtaining a mechanical license for a musical composition in the United States. The first is a direct license from the publisher of the composition, which for purposes of this chapter is our hypothetical beginning songwriter/self-publisher. If the songwriter is approached to have his or her songs recorded by others and released in an audio-only format, the mechanical license is the agreement that would be issued by the songwriter to the proposed user. The terms of the license agreement would address the rate, the format in which the recordings are to be released, the territory in which the recordings would be distributed, the frequency of accountings, and other provisions.

A far more frequent method of issuing and obtaining mechanical licenses in the United States is through an organization called the Harry Fox Agency. The Harry Fox Agency was formed in 1927 by the Music Publishers Association as a central clearing house for the issuance of mechanical licenses on behalf of its members. Today, the Harry Fox Agency issues licenses for the production and distribution of digital downloads, CDs, tapes, and other audio-only configurations for the great majority of music publishers

---

16. Royalty Rates for Making and Distributing Phonorecords, 37 C.F.R. 385.3(a) (2011).

in the United States, monitors the payments of fees due under such agreements, and acts as a source of information about music licensing on behalf of the music publishing industry. Our hypothetical beginning songwriter might consider affiliating with the Harry Fox Agency as a self-publisher to handle mechanical licensing for a number of reasons. The Harry Fox Agency is generally the first place the music industry checks for licensing information about a composition, contact information for the writer and publisher is made easily available, the Harry Fox Agency has a convenient online system for the issuance of licenses under publisher-favorable terms without the writer/publisher involvement, and the Harry Fox Agency has the collective power to enforce payment of license fees that can be more effective than the individual action of a single writer/publisher. Affiliation as a writer/publisher requires that at least one composition controlled by the publisher has been recorded and commercially released by a third party. The current commission charged by the Harry Fox Agency for its services is 8.5 percent of collected license proceeds.

## Synchronization Rights

The so-called synchronization right is the right of musical composition owners to control the right to have their compositions reproduced in timed sequence in an audiovisual work. The synchronization right is implicated whenever the recorded performance of a musical composition is used in a motion picture, television program, music video, commercial, or other form of audiovisual work. Even if the audiovisual work itself is in the public domain, one who commercially reproduces the public domain work can be subject to an obligation to license the music incorporated in the work.[17]

The synchronization right is derived from the owner's exclusive right of reproduction.[18] The synchronization right first appeared when sound became a feature of motion pictures, which involved the reproduction of a recording of the composition on a separate track appearing on the film

---

17. Maljack Prods., Inc. v. Good Times Home Video Corp., 81 F.3d 881 (9th Cir. 1996).
18. 17 U.S.C. § 106(1) (2011).

stock of the sequential images comprising the motion picture. The reproduction of a composition's recording may be sequenced differently today,
but the right remains.

Unlike a mechanical license, there is no compulsory license or statutory
rate for a synchronization license for a musical composition that might
provide a backup alternative to a user of a composition in the event negotiations are unsuccessful. Instead, the terms for each synchronization license
are individually negotiated. Compensation for a synchronization license can
range from no charge (if the owner of the composition believes there is promotional benefit from a proposed use) to seven figures, depending on the
status of the composition, the type of use being made (commercial, opening
credits for movie, background for scene in television program, etc.), territory, length of use, and format. If a preexisting sound recording is licensed
for synchronization use in an audiovisual work, it is not uncommon for the
fee paid for use of the master recording and the underlying composition to
be determined on a most favored nations basis, meaning each rights holder
receives the same compensation for the use of their respective property—the
master and the composition. While the consideration under some synchronization licenses may be determined on a royalty basis, which would take
into account contingent sales volume or other factors, many synchronization licenses today are issued on a flat fee basis. This enables the producer of
the audiovisual work the flexibility to exploit the work across all platforms
without having to obtain additional rights or anticipate new royalty models.

## Dramatic Rights

Whenever a musical composition is incorporated into a theatrical work, such
as a musical play or revue, the rights that must be obtained are referred
to as either dramatic rights or grand rights. The two terms are often used
interchangeably, but generally dramatic rights refer to the right to incor-
porate a composition in a staged work and grand rights refer to the right
to use a portion of a staged work in a second staged work, or to reproduce
the staged work in a different medium. In any event, like synchronization
licenses, there are no compulsory licenses or statutory rates applicable to

dramatic or grand rights licenses. Each such license is negotiated individually, and the rights holder, the publisher, is free to withhold consent to the
use of the composition without fear of a statutory license as a backup alternative for the producer.

One significant issue that arises in connection with dramatic and grand
rights licenses is determining when the nondramatic performance rights
for compositions licensed by ASCAP, BMI, and SESAC end and the need
to obtain a separate dramatic rights license from the publisher for a work
begins. A series of cases involving the work *Jesus Christ Superstar* several
years ago provides some guidance in helping draw that line.

When *Jesus Christ Superstar* was first released, it existed only as a double-
disc vinyl LP. While the songs from the work were sequenced to provide a
narrative and the performers of the songs on the album assumed certain
character voices, the work did not exist as a dramatic presentation. When the
album became successful, certain producers conceived the idea of presenting
choral performances of the songs from the album in the same sequence as
they appeared on the album. For the right to present the performances, the
producers relied upon the nondramatic performance licenses from ASCAP
and BMI already in place with the performance venues. This practice was
successfully challenged in several lawsuits, the opinions to which set out
some of the features of a stage presentation that distinguish a nondramatic
performance —a singer or group performing a series of songs—from a dramatic performance.[19] A key element is whether the performance features
a narrative—meaning, does it tell a story? Are there characters, is there
character costuming, is there scenery tied to a story being told?[20] To the
extent such elements exist, the presentation takes the form of a dramatic
work, for which the nondramatic rights controlled by ASCAP, BMI, and
SESAC do not suffice.

---

19.  Robert Stigwood Group Limited v. Sperber, 457 F.2d 50 (2d Cir. 1972); Rice v. Ameri-
can Program Bureau, 446 F.2d 685 (2d Cir. 1971); John R. Allison, *Protection of Performance
Rights to "Jesus Christ Superstar": The Dramatic-Nondramatic Dilemma*, 4 PERFORMING
ARTIST REVIEW 13 (1973).

20.  *See* Gershwin v. The Whole Thing Co., 208 U.S.P.Q. 557 (C.D. Cal. 1980); April Prods.
v. Strand Enters., 221 F.2d 292 (2d Cir. 1955).

The phenomenon of so-called tribute bands raises issues in a number of areas, including whether the staging of a tribute performance incorporating the "characters," iconography, and other elements of a performing group implicates any dramatic rights in the compositions being performed.[21] The issue has generally been more theoretical than real. While some artists have sought to bar the performance of tribute bands (e.g., the Beatles, Blues Brothers, Bon Jovi), such actions generally have been grounded on trademark or right of publicity rights rather than music copyright rights.

In the case of a composer or lyricist preparing work for a musical stage play, the composer, lyricist, and playwright generally receive an equal portion of the advance and royalty pool made available for the play's creators. There are a number of ways in which such pools may be determined,[22] but the contributions of each generally are considered of equal value in the allocation. With respect to preexisting compositions that are incorporated in a musical stage play, the compensation will depend on how the song is used in the play, the capacity of the theater in which the work is presented, ticket prices, number of performances per week, and whether the production is commercial or not-for-profit. Payment may take the form of a set per-performance fee, a percentage of the gross box office receipts, or a combination of the two.

## Publisher Agreements

While our hypothetical songwriter/self-publisher may elect to continue as an independent, self-administrating entity through all levels of success, success alternatively may bring the need to affiliate with another publishing company in one form or another. These various arrangements can be generally categorized as a single song agreement, an exclusive songwriter agreement, a copublishing agreement, or an administration agreement. The features of each of these arrangements are described below.

---

21. Brent Giles Davis, *Identity Theft: Tribute Bands, Grand Rights, and Dramatico-Musical Performances*, 24 Cardozo Arts & Ent. L. Rev. 845 (2006).

22. *See generally* Donald C. Farber, Producing Theater ch. 4 (3d ed. Limelight Editions 2006).

## Single Song Agreements

The structure of a single song publishing agreement is essentially this: the songwriter assigns full ownership of the song—the copyright—to the publisher in return for the services of the publisher to promote the song, administer rights in the song when used by others, collect proceeds from uses of the song, and account for those proceeds to the songwriter. Although referred to as a single song agreement, the agreement could apply to a group of songs assigned to the publisher in a single document and transaction, each of which would be treated in the same manner as described below.

The compensation payable to the songwriter will generally fall into two categories: compensation for uses of the song that are made by the publisher and compensation for uses of the song that are made by others under license from the publisher. Today, almost all publishing income under song publishing agreements falls in the second category, as very few music publishing companies actually exploit rights in compositions themselves. Nevertheless, music publishing agreements almost universally contain provisions describing the royalties due to the songwriter from the sale of print or piano roll copies of the composition. Why do agreements include provisions for such marginal forms of music use? First, remember that the music publishing industry is generally very tradition-bound, and changes in the form agreements used by publishers have been slow to occur. Second, music publishing companies are frequently bought and sold. In the lifetime of the copyright in a composition, it may be owned by a music publishing company that actually exploits that composition in print or as a piano roll, in which case the royalty to be paid has been determined. Rates for sheet music and piano rolls are generally stated in a certain number of cents per copy sold, which generally ranges from 8 to 12 cents.

Tradition has determined that when a songwriter assigns rights in a composition to a publishing company, most of the compensation received by a music publishing company from the licensing of rights in that composition is divided equally between the publishing company and the songwriter (or songwriters as a group). The 50 percent songwriter portion is paid to the songwriter as a royalty. This arrangement applies to mechanical licenses, synchronization licenses, print licenses, and other, more specialized categories of licenses for such products as apparel, greeting cards, or the use of a song's title, characters, or narrative as the basis for adapted works in other media, such as audiovisual works or books. The 50 percent portion of the proceeds retained by the publisher is generally referred to as the "publisher's share," and the other 50 percent portion that is paid by the publisher to the writer is generally referred to as the "writer's share." If there is more than one writer, the writers share the writer's share and the publisher's share remains at 50 percent. While this math is about as simple as one might encounter, it nevertheless leads to confusion. This generally occurs when negotiation depends upon how the respective shares of the writer and the publisher might be allocated.

One source of income from music publishing that is treated differently when a publisher is not a self-publishing extension of the songwriter but is an independent, separately owned entity is performance income. The performance rights organizations—ASCAP, BMI, and SESAC—have elected to directly pay music publishers and songwriters their respective shares of performance income. The payment by the PROs of the writer's share and the publisher's share is in the same allocation as the payments made by music publishers of other proceeds. Each receives 50 percent of performance income directly from the respective performance right organizations. Because the songwriter is already receiving his or her portion of performance income directly from the PROs, the publishing company does not account to the songwriter for any of that income, which is generally recognized in the single song agreement.

The following are some additional issues that are typically included in a single song agreement.

### Initial Payment

Generally, a songwriter receives a payment from the publisher when the publisher obtains ownership of the song or songs from the writer. This payment can be categorized either as an advance paid by the publisher against royalties to be paid under the publishing agreement or the purchase price of the copyright being assigned. The latter would not necessarily be recoupable from future royalties. The difference is clearly material. If the payment is characterized as an advance, then the songwriter has in effect received the benefit of a guaranteed payment for the future use of his or her song, but will not receive any further payments until that advance is recouped from actual credits to the songwriter's account. In effect, while the publishing company is taking the risk whether future proceeds will be enough to earn back the advance, the publishing company is paying for the composition with the songwriter's money (or, to be fair, with the songwriter's potential money). If the initial payment is characterized as a purchase price in exchange for the assignment of the copyright interests in the songs, then the publishing company will obtain the songs subject to an obligation to pay royalties to the songwriter from the first proceeds received by the publisher.

Whether an initial payment is characterized as an advance or as a purchase price may turn on the status of the compositions being acquired. The payment for the acquisition of an established composition, with a history of revenue over a period of time (or a clear projection based on success achieved at that time), is more likely to be treated as a purchase price, particularly if the seller is not the songwriter. Payment for the acquisition of an unproven composition directly from the songwriter is more likely to be treated as an advance.

## Approvals

Songwriters, particularly emerging songwriters, generally are not granted the right to approve how their compositions are used by the publisher. However, there is one area that songwriters should seek approval of, and that is for the issuance of synchronization licenses. Using a composition in connection with a visual image contextualizes the composition—it creates an association that is very powerful and which might change the way audiences relate to the composition. Use of a tender ballad to ironically underscore a violent scene, for example, could materially impair performance of that ballad in the future if it conjures up the violent association to audience members. Writers may also not want their compositions used in connection with certain audiovisual works generally, such as movies of a certain genre, commercials generally, or commercials specifically in support of such things as politics, religion, alcohol, tobacco, firearms, personal care products, or certain foods. Because of this sensitivity, many music publishing companies will seek input from writers before authorizing a license.

However, songwriters are always on firmer ground if their songwriter agreement specifically requires approval for such licenses.

Another area of possible approval for the songwriter is to authorize the first artist to record of one of the writer's compositions. An initial recording of a composition often defines the composition, although there are many examples of subsequent recordings of compositions creating new or more popular perceptions or values.[23] Writers often write with specific performers in mind and wish to see the initial commercial release of a recording of that composition feature that performer, or at least a performer of enough perceived stature to boost the likely success of the composition.

Finally, another general topic area in which writer approval is considered has to do with the integrity of the song itself and how the song might be adapted. For example, at what point is the song considered "complete"? May the publisher add new words or new musical material, or authorize the inclusion of the song in a medley or as a portion of a different song? Will the writer be able to approve translations of the song, or parody versions? Unless addressed, general rights language in a single song agreement might permit adaptations along these lines (although the right of a publisher to do something does not always mean that right is exercised without seeking consultation and approval from the writer).

### Obligation to Promote

The exclusive nature of the relationship between the composer and the publisher creates an implied general obligation to use commercially reasonable efforts to promote the composition.[24] It is also possible to contractually require the publisher to use its "best" efforts, but since it is not clear what that standard actually implicates, any specific efforts meant to be undertaken should be described in the agreement. The relationship between the composer and the publisher, in and of itself, is generally not considered one of a fiduciary that creates any special form of trust or obligation.[25]

---

23. For a comprehensive collection of information about the initial recordings of well-known songs, see Dick Rosemont, The Originals Project, http://www.originalsproject.us (May 10, 2013).

24. Wood v. Lucy, Lady Duff-Gordon, 118 N.E. 214 (N.Y. 1917).

25. Mellencamp v. Riva Music, Ltd., 698 F. Supp. 1154, 1159 (S.D.N.Y. 1988).

Indeed, the holder of exclusive rights in a property has the right to reject opportunities as long as the intent is not to harm the royalty participant.[26] However, a breach of the implied obligation to exploit a composer's work with no motive other than to harm the composer would constitute a tort.[27]

## Demo Costs

A key method of promoting compositions is to create demonstration recordings, or demos, that can be circulated to record companies, producers, managers, and artists. Demos can bring a song alive and present arrangement details that might otherwise be lost to the person to whom the song is being presented. Demos may be produced independently by the songwriter or under the auspices, and at the expense, of the publishing company. Demo costs may be recoupable either in full or up to 50 percent and may be recouped from either the songwriter's share of income or from first receipts generally. The publishing agreement could provide limits on the amount a publisher might spend on each demo and should address how the songwriter might be reimbursed for costs incurred in producing demos on his or her own. The agreement should also address ownership of the demos and acknowledge that they will not be commercially released.

## Warranties and Indemnifications

Similar to all agreements granting rights in copyrighted works, music publishers will want to receive warranties from the songwriter that the works being conveyed are innocent and freely obtainable by the music publisher. These are some typical warranties:

- The song is original with the songwriter, and the songwriter is the sole writer/composer (or all cowriters are identified)
- The song has not already been published
- There are no prior agreements pertaining to the song
- The song does not infringe the rights of any third party

---

26. Third Story Music, Inc. v. Waits, 41 Cal. App. 4th 798 (Ct. App. 1996).
27. Mellencamp v. Riva Music, Ltd., 698 F. Supp. 1154, 1159 (S.D.N.Y. 1988).

- No claims have ever been asserted against the song, and the writer knows of no unasserted claims
- The songwriter is free to enter the transaction with the music publisher
- There are no existing agreements that would impair the ability of the publisher to fully exploit the song and all rights in and to the song

Coupled with the warranties and representations will be the songwriter's indemnification of the music publisher, which is subject to the same considerations as indemnification provisions generally. Two additional key points should be addressed. First, because of the continued obligation of the publisher to pay royalties to the songwriter, the single song agreement will often permit the music publisher to withhold payments that might otherwise be due to the songwriter in the event a claim is made against the publisher which implicates the indemnification terms. The terms under which such funds can be held, including when the withholding may be triggered and how long thereafter the funds may be held, should be negotiated. Second, the agreement may state that the indemnification may be asserted against any funds otherwise due under the music publishing agreement, or "any other agreement between Music Publisher and Writer." The language in quotations permits cross-collateralization between agreements, the implications of which needs to be fully considered.

### Accountings and Audits

Accountings under music publishing agreements are generally provided quarterly, generally within forty-five to ninety days following the end of each calendar quarter. It is not uncommon for music publishing agreements to feature a contractual limitation on the period of time the recipient may challenge the accuracy of the statement, after which the recipient will be barred from pursuing any claim for unpaid royalties. Such provisions are enforceable,[28] so the period of time—generally between two and three years after submission of the statement—should be carefully considered. As with any circumstance involving periodic contingent payments, the royalty

---

28. Clinton v. Universal Music Group, 2011 WL 3501818 (C.D. Cal. 2011); Allman v. UMG Recordings, 530 F. Supp. 2d 602 (S.D.N.Y. 2008).

recipient should have the right to audit the publishing company in order to know if a claim for unpaid funds exists.

The terms considered in an audit clause in a publishing agreement include: when and where the audit may take place, how long it may take place, the frequency of audits, what materials may be reviewed, any cost shifting in the event a discrepancy is discovered, confidentiality of disclosures, and whether any audit report will be shared. How the audit provisions tie to the contractual limitations on when claims for unpaid royalties may be initiated should be carefully reviewed.

The relationship between a songwriter and music publisher will generally not rise to one of fiduciary, so the writer's right to receive accountings and royalties will not create a special publisher obligation. Efforts have been made to impose a higher obligation to pay royalties on the part of the publisher by contractual language that defines license proceeds as funds held in trust by the publisher on behalf of the songwriter,[29] but acceptance of such language by a publisher is rare, if nonexistent. While failure to pay royalties will result in a claim for the unpaid amount, such failure will generally not give rise to an action for recession of the publishing agreement and reassignment of the copyright to the author unless the failure to pay was nearly total.[30] Agreements can provide, however, that in the event a commercial recording of a composition is not secured by the publisher within a certain period or royalties are not paid, all rights shall be reassigned to the composer.[31]

## Credit and Identity

The music publisher will generally want to have the right to use the name, likeness, and other elements of the songwriter's identity in connection with

---

29. *See, e.g.*, THE SONGWRITERS GUILD OF AMERICA, THE SONGWRITERS GUILD OF AMERICA POPULAR SONGWRITERS CONTRACT ¶ 4(l) (1978), *at* http://www.songwritersguild.com/sandboxsga2010/contract.pdf (hereafter SONGWRITERS CONTRACT).

30. *See, e.g.*, Nolan v. Williamson Music, Inc., 300 F. Supp. 1311 (S.D.N.Y. 1969); *see also* Peterson v. Highland Music, Inc., 140 F.3d 1313 (9th Cir.), *cert. denied*, 525 U.S. 983 (1998) (rescission granted for failure to pay sound recording royalties).

31. *See, e.g.*, THE SONGWRITERS GUILD OF AMERICA, THE SONGWRITERS GUILD OF AMERICA POPULAR SONGWRITERS CONTRACT, ¶¶ 6(a), 8 and 12, (1978) http://www.songwritersguild.com/sandboxsga2010/contract.pdf [hereinafter SONGWRITERS CONTRACT].

the exploitation of the compositions. This is particularly true with respect to popular singer/songwriters. How this right extends to the publisher's licensees must be addressed, particularly with respect to the licensing of nontraditional uses of compositions, such as on apparel or posters, where use of the writer's identity might add value. The writer might also have particular interests in how his or her identity is credited. If the songwriter wants his or her name presented in a particular fashion, or if cowriters have agreed on the order in which their names should appear in connection with their compositions, then the music publisher should be instructed on these decisions.

### International

A songwriter is presented with several choices in how to deal with exploitation of his or her compositions outside of the United States. For example, many large music publishing companies have an international presence, so their agreements would generally extend to all territories (although more limited rights could be granted, if the publisher were to agree). Even if the publishing company is not a multi-national entity, it may nevertheless have established relationships with local sub-publishers throughout the world, effectively creating a network administered by the domestic publisher. Finally, the songwriter has the option of entering agreements directly with publishers on a territory-by-territory basis outside of the United States.

Each option has advantages and disadvantages. A territory-by-territory approach has the advantage of a potentially larger aggregate advance than one may receive from a single publisher. Having separate agreements also prevents cross-collateralization between the activities of the separate territories and reduces the risk of loss or withheld payments if a particular publisher experiences financial difficulty or has a dispute with the writer. On the other hand, entering and administering multiple publisher relationships in foreign territories requires greater dedicated resources, and unless a foreign entity has a presence in the United States making it subject to the jurisdiction of the courts in the United States, dispute resolution and enforcement may be difficult, expensive, or impossible.

Whichever option a songwriter selects, there are several key issues that should be addressed in the publishing agreement. First, if the music publishing agreement permits the music publisher to enter agreements with sub-publishers in territories other than the United States, the payments made to the songwriter for such foreign territories should be calculated by the music publisher on the basis of the payments made "from the source." Being paid "from the source" means that the songwriter's royalties are calculated on the basis of reported revenue from uses of the songwriter's compositions within the territory in which the revenue was earned—the source of the revenue. This language is necessary to prevent an unfortunately common situation where sales are earned in one territory, then reported to a publisher in another territory (which takes its cut), then reported to a publisher in another territory (which takes its cut), then reported to the entity reporting to the songwriter, by which time the royalty amount has been significantly diminished. Such sequential arrangements are usually with related companies, which results in an overall benefit to the publisher at the artificially inflated expense of the author.

Sub-publishers generally charge a fee of between 10 percent to 25 percent of collected funds for their services in their designated territory. This fee may increase with respect to revenue derived from local recordings of the composition the sub-publisher may arrange. Requiring the domestic publisher to calculate the songwriter's portion of payments from the sub-publisher "from the source" means that the songwriter will receive his or her payment based on what the sub-publisher collects, less the sub-publisher's direct fee, not on any lesser amount that might result if such sub-publisher payments were to be channeled through a series of intermediate parties (perhaps affiliated with the U.S. publisher), each of which extracts its own fee and thereby creates a greatly diminished sum delivered to the domestic publisher from which it then might calculate the songwriter's portion.

Performance income generated in a foreign territory is treated the same way as in the United States: the amounts due to the songwriter and the publisher are allocated by the performing rights organization. The songwriter portion is remitted by the foreign performing rights organization directly to its U.S. counterpart and then paid to the songwriter. The publisher portion can either be remitted to the local representative of the U.S.-based publishing company or paid to the U.S. counterpart performing rights organization, which will then pay the publisher. Whether one elects to have performance income paid to a local sub-publisher or processed through interorganiza-tional means may turn on whichever method results in quicker payment.

Another international consideration for publishers and songwriters is to ensure that any translations or other adaptations of compositions will be undertaken only with the consent of the songwriter. Consent protects the integrity of the composition, ensures that there is not a dilution of interest in the composition by those who may claim rights for the translation, and ensures that any new title to the translation is properly tied to the original composition for purposes of logging performances that result in revenue.

The songwriter will also want to ensure that approval must be obtained for any synchronization licenses or grant of rights for any grand or dra-matic uses. Since the distribution of works using such rights (movies, plays, television shows) often extends across multiple countries, a publisher/song-writer will want to license such uses directly to protect the integrity of the composition and avoid paying sub-publisher fees for revenue generated by such works beyond the territory controlled by the sub-publisher. The publisher/songwriter will also be in the best position to understand how a use licensed in a foreign territory might impact the broader market for the composition or other anticipated or developing projects.

## Exclusive Songwriter Agreements

The most common form of agreement between a music publishing com-pany and a songwriter is the exclusive songwriter agreement. In essence, the exclusive songwriter agreement provides that all compositions created by the songwriter during the term of the songwriter agreement will be assigned to the publishing company. The agreement may also address compositions already in existence at the time the agreement is entered by assigning such compositions to the publishing company in the same way that a single song agreement might operate. The key difference with an exclusive songwriter agreement from a single song agreement is that the publishing company knows it will receive the full creative output of the writer for the term of the agreement.

Exclusive songwriter agreements are generally structured with an ini-tial defined term, which can be renewed at the option of the publisher for a certain number of renewal periods of like duration. If the songwriter agreement is with a recording artist signed to a record company that is affiliated with the music publishing company, the term of the music publishing agreement, and perhaps other terms, might be aligned with the term of the recording agreement.

The exclusive songwriter agreement will generally describe the delivery requirements of the songwriter during each contract period, which is usually stated in terms of a minimum number of acceptable compositions. This number will be described with respect to songs written 100 percent by the songwriter, so if the songwriter delivers cowritten material, such material would satisfy the delivery obligation only to the extent of the songwriter's proportionate share of such collaborations. To be acceptable, the material must also be deemed reasonably satisfactory to the publisher.[32] In the event the required number of acceptable compositions is not delivered during the defined contractual period, the songwriter agreement generally will permit the publisher to extend the term of the agreement until such minimum number of compositions are delivered. If the songwriter is also a recording artist, the minimum composition delivery commitment might further require that recordings by the songwriter of a certain number of compositions be delivered during a contractual period be commercially released by the songwriter or his or her record company.

The royalty compensation payable to a songwriter under an exclusive songwriter agreement will be the same as described for the single song agreement. The key additional compensation issue is advances. The exclusive nature of the songwriter agreement requires some form of guaranteed payment to the songwriter in consideration for the exclusive commitment the songwriter has given to the publisher. The advance may take the form of an initial portion upon signing and additional portions as the songwriter's delivery requirement is satisfied. Some exclusive songwriter agreements schedule regular periodic payments on a monthly or even bimonthly basis, akin to a paycheck. Merit advances for the commercial release of a recording,

---

32. For a discussion concerning the acceptability of compositions delivered by a songwriter under an exclusive songwriter agreement, see RICHARD SCHULENBERG, LEGAL ASPECTS OF THE MUSIC INDUSTRY 277–80 (Billboard Books 2005).

the achievement of a certain level of success of such recording (sales or chart position), or the receipt of certain awards might also be negotiated.

Additional terms of the exclusive songwriter agreement might address the fact that the agreement involves compositions not in being at the time the contract is entered. Managing the creative process between the publishing company and the songwriter for the creation of songs might involve a key person from the songwriter's perspective, the loss of whose relationship might cause the songwriter to want to avoid contract extensions. Also, because the scope of an exclusive songwriter agreement embraces all compositions created by the songwriter during the term of the agreement, irrespective of the commercial prospects of such songs, the songwriter might wish to have rights in compositions that remain unrecorded after a period of time revert to him or her. If such a reversion right were to be agreed to by the publisher, it would generally be subject to the reimbursement of any advances associated with such compositions.

The issues discussed earlier with respect to the single songwriter agreement concerning approvals, warranties and indemnifications, accounting, sub-publishing, and credit will also be present in the exclusive songwriter agreement.

## Copublishing Agreements

Copublishing agreements generally arise under two circumstances. First, whenever two or more writers collaborate in the creation of a composition, a copublishing agreement will need to be put in place to address their respective interests in the composition (unless they are both published by the same publishing company). The second copublishing circumstance occurs when a publishing company with greater administrative resources than another obtains a co-ownership interest in the composition through an assignment of a partial interest from the original publisher. Why would either party enter such an agreement? From the perspective of the original publisher, such an agreement might involve a substantial advance payment from the second copublisher to the original publisher, or periodic guarantees, or both, that might not be available under an administration agreement. From the perspective of the acquiring publisher, such an agreement might be the best compromise the publisher can achieve with an original publisher unwilling to give up all of its interests in the compositions.

Decision making concerning the use of a composition between co-owners begins with one of the principles of copyright law, which is that a co-owner of a copyright is permitted, absent a contractual obligation not to do so, to authorize nonexclusive uses of the rights in the co-owned copyright without the consent of the other co-owners. All the authorizing party must do is account to the other co-owners for their share of the proceeds from such nonexclusive uses. Many valuable rights in a composition, such as mechanical, synchronization, and dramatic rights licenses, can be issued on a nonexclusive basis. Therefore, it is important for co-owners to have an understanding between themselves concerning which rights, if any, an individual co-owner could exercise with a third party on a nonexclusive basis. The issue does not arise with respect to the granting of exclusive rights, since such grants require the consent of all owners in order to be effective.

In the case of copublishing agreements between collaborators, the respective interests of the publishing companies generally reflect the allocation of interests agreed to by the collaborators. This may be fifty-fifty, or it may be some other allocation. Whatever the proportion, it applies to the full ownership of the song—both publisher and songwriter. The key issue to be determined in such an agreement (apart from the respective shares of the publishing proceeds each collaborator will receive) is administrative control—which one of the co-owners will have the responsibility of issuing licenses and collecting proceeds. Each of the publishing companies could receive proceeds directly from their respective performance rights organizations, such as ASCAP or BMI, and could also receive their respective shares of mechanical license proceeds issued by the Harry Fox Agency. However, the process by which other rights and licenses are administered should be resolved in the copublishing agreement.

In the event one of the co-owners does perform administrative functions, it normally would be entitled to receive an administration fee, perhaps 10 percent, in consideration for the services. Like a shareholder agreement in a closely held corporation, or an operating agreement in a limited liability company, a copublishing agreement could also address issues relating to the transfer of the interests in a composition held by either of the companies.

Assuming the parties to a copublishing agreement between co-composers reach terms concerning control and administration, it is important to understand structurally how the proceeds from the exploitation of the copublished compositions will flow. Conceptually, each publishing company will have some form of agreement with the co-composer of the composition from whom the publishing company derives its rights. In reality, there may not be a distinction between the songwriter and his or her sole proprietorship publisher, but in concept each publishing company is bound to an obligation to account to the songwriter from whom it derives its rights for the proceeds. Publisher A accounts to its songwriter and Publisher B accounts to its songwriter. The structure of this arrangement can be illustrated like this:

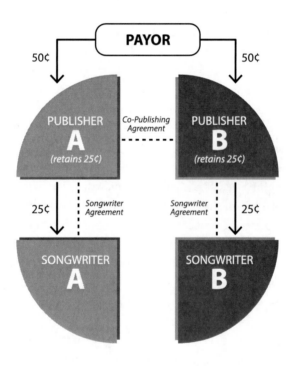

If one of the copublishers exclusively administers the composition for a fee (let us use a 10 percent administration fee as an example), the structure would be along these lines:

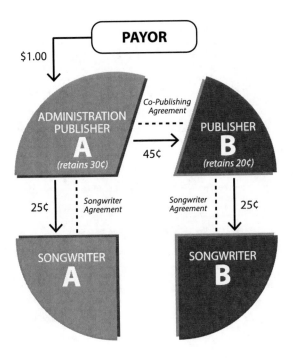

When the co-owner of a composition is not a collaborator, but a purchaser instead, the issues discussed above still pertain. However, unlike the copublishing arrangement between co-composers, which deals with 100 percent of the interests in the composition, the copublishing arrangement involving a purchaser is with respect to the publisher's interest in the composition only. Also, in most such circumstances, the purchaser will require that it exclusively administer all rights in the co-owned compositions and be compensated with the payment of an administration fee (generally 10 percent) in addition to the co-ownership share of the composition that it holds. Co-ownership allocations of the publisher's interests under these circumstances are generally fifty-fifty. This is the structure of the arrangement, assuming a 10 percent administration fee:

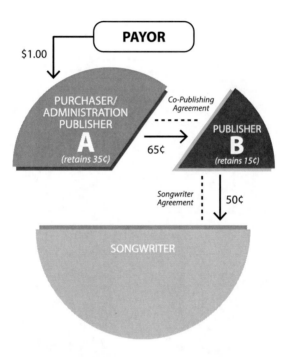

Note in this case that the publisher with the direct relationship with the composer remains obligated to account and pay to the composer, while the administrating copublisher is only required to account to and pay the other copublisher. The parties can agree to direct the administrating copublisher to pay the other copublisher and the composer for their respective portions of the proceeds derived from the song, which would look like this:

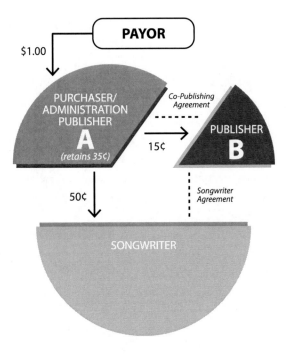

A copublishing agreement will also contain customary warranty and indemnification provisions from each party to the other and accounting and auditing provisions for the party providing administrative services. The agreement should also address decision making with respect to the selection of sub-publishers and the terms under which they may be engaged, whether adaptations of a composition may be made, and how litigation to enforce rights in the composition against infringers will be handled.

## Administration Agreements

Administration agreements for music publishers are as they sound. The publishing administration company agrees, for a specific period of time, to provide to the publisher administration services such as the issuance of licenses, the collection of license proceeds, and the accounting of the resulting activity. Companies such as BMG Rights Management (the acquirer of Bug Music) and Kobalt Music provide such services generally to artist-owned publishing entities that do not require the promotional and placement services that a regular publishing company might undertake. The most likely candidate for an administration agreement is a singer/songwriter who performs and records their own material and, through the release and promotion of his or her recordings through a record company, is creating recognition, market demand, and revenue for their compositions. A catalog of well-known songs, or "standards," featured on recurrent recordings or often rerecorded without the need for promotional effort would also be a good candidate for an administration agreement. Even a music publishing company with a small administrative staff might avail itself of the services of an administrator, particularly with respect to the collection of publishing income generated in foreign territories where the publishing company may not have a presence.

Under the terms of an administration agreement, the administration company does not take ownership or co-ownership of the compositions. The company is simply engaged for a defined period of time to act on behalf of the publisher in providing the defined services. A typical fee arrangement may be 15 percent of the proceeds collected by the administrator. This is the structure of such an arrangement, assuming a 15 percent administration fee:

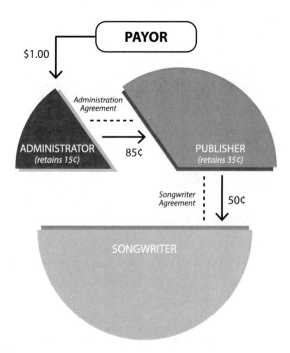

Some administration agreements further provide that, in the event the administrator is able to achieve a recording of one of the songs in the publisher's catalog, the fee arrangement for the proceeds of that recording might be higher. A typical period of time for the administration agreement to be in place is between three and five years. An important feature for any administration agreement is the scope of authority the administrator has to issue licenses for the use of the songs subject to the agreement. At a minimum, a publisher will want to approve any synchronization licenses, for the same reasons stated earlier with respect to songwriter and sub-publishing agreements.

## Chapter Four
# How Bands Are Organized and Financed, and Planning for the Eventual Breakup

Assembling a band may be fun, but maintaining a musical performing group over a period of time is tough business. First, there are the pressures that doom any kind of business collaboration—different visions for the direction of the company, disputes concerning control or compensation, unequal contributions of commitment, effort, financing, or other resources, or incompatible temperaments. When one adds differing levels of musical ability, different views on creative direction, the sacrifices necessary to succeed against extraordinary odds, the short windows of commercial opportunity that can open and close without regard to the personal feelings of the individuals involved, the corrupting influence of outsiders to the group, and the demands imposed on those who do succeed, it is little wonder that the makeup of musical groups is fluid.

Most musicians recognize these circumstances. Further, many musicians are required, as a condition of surviving as a performer, to play in more than one performing group, the members of which may change for reasons that may involve no more than availability. This is neither good nor bad, just the reality of the industry. For this reason, most musical groups are organized informally. The exact form of organization under such circumstances may not be declared. A group may be the enterprise of a single individual, who owns the identity associated with the group either as a sole proprietor or through an organized business entity. This person may be one of the performers in the group or may be a manager or agent. The group could also be simply an assembly of backup performers, engaged by the lead performer on a fee basis to rehearse, perform, and record with the lead performer. The group could also be an undeclared partnership, with revenue, expenses, and properties shared between the group members but without a more formal documentation of the arrangement.

At a certain point, a group may cohere and reach an understanding that a more formal form of business entity is desirable to establish grounds for moving ahead with shared commitment. Recommendations for the selection of one form of entity over another are beyond the scope of this book, given the great range of individual considerations that impact the selection of a form of organization and the differences between the laws of the various states concerning business entities. Whichever form of business entity is selected, the band member owners will need an organizational document—a partnership agreement, a shareholder agreement, or an operating agreement. These documents will assist the band with issues surrounding the business of the band and are the subject of this chapter.

## Treatment of Assets

The first key issue is the scope of the rights that will be handled by the entity. Is the entity intended to be the owner of the sound recordings produced by the group, or the publisher of the musical compositions written by the members? Will the entity be the owner of the identity of the group for purposes of establishing trademark rights or authorizing the use of such trademark rights? How will personal appearance revenue be handled? And very importantly, what is the scope of the exclusive rights that the entity has in the entertainment careers of the individual owners? Is the entity the means by which all activities are facilitated and the payee of all earnings from such activities? May any of the members of the group make personal appearances apart from the group, or otherwise contract for his or her talent services in any way?[1] Or are there certain areas that are left within the control of the individual members, who may personally retain any compensation resulting from such activities? For example, may individual members perform, write, or record with other performers and retain whatever earnings that might result, or engage in other expressive activities unrelated to music, such as book publishing or acting, and retain compensation for that?

These questions are critical for several reasons. First, reaching an agreement on terms helps establish shared expectations among band members that can reduce disagreements in the future. But even more important is the fact that written agreements are necessary if the entity is to be the owner of certain works for which copyright, trademark, and identity rights may exist. Those written agreements may include employment agreements, work for hire arrangements, or assignments. If such agreements are not in place, the entity may not have the ownership interest the band-member owners may believe and rely upon. Further, if the group is going to expend resources for purposes of preparing to present personal appearances, and commit to such personal appearances, the group members should be committed to performing at such personal appearances by means of an employment agreement. Finally, defining the scope of rights held by the entity, and specifically carving out certain areas that are retained by the individual owners, will assist those owners in securing individual arrangements for the retained rights and properties.

The likelihood of a band breakup needs to be taken into account when deciding which rights and properties are to be lodged with the entity. In that respect, the agreement acts as a form of prenuptial agreement. For example, if the entity is intended to hold all rights in the group name and identity, then the rights of the then-current members of the band to use the name and identity of the band following a breakup should be addressed. If a band member is expelled, may the remaining members continue using the name? If so, how many original members of the group need to remain

---

1. For a description of the fallout affecting personal appearances caused by a leaving member, see Billy Shields, *Pretty Ricky Leaving Member Spurs Litigation*, ENT. L. & FIN., Feb. 2008.

before the name has to be abandoned? Is there any key member who must be an active member of the group in order for the group to use the name? May leaving or expelled members of the group regroup at some point and begin using the name again? Or is the name simply something that belongs to the entity and, consequently, whoever ends up owning the entity?[2] If any registrations of a trademark or service mark have been undertaken, who will be the successor to the ownership of the registrations? What about URLs and social media site addresses—in whose name will such properties be acquired, and is there any understanding about the ownership and maintenance of such properties in the event of a dissolution?

Whether the band's entity is the owner of music publishing rights to compositions composed by group members must be carefully considered in light of the potential period such rights may be of value. The length of time a composition will be protected by copyright—the lifetime of the composer, plus seventy years—far surpasses the period any of the band members may be collaborating and/or personally operating their entity. Some groups approach this issue by having each member retain their interests in compositions with their own individual publishing companies. These individual publishing companies may then enter copublishing agreements for collaborative songs. Other groups grant their jointly-owned entity the publishing right in songs written by individual members in an effort to recognize the value non-composing members may add to a song by helping arrange compositions, contributing key instrumental flourishes, or performing the compositions in personal appearances. The individual member-composers would retain 100 percent of the songwriter's share of the compositions, and all the group members would share the publisher's share of the compositions in accordance with their interest in the overall entity. If the group agrees to share publishing interests in some manner with non-composing

---

2. Through the passage of time, some groups eventually end up with no original members, or no members who performed in the recordings that are famously associated with the group. Efforts have been undertaken on the state level to protect consumer interests by prohibiting misrepresentations concerning the authenticity of live performers appearing under the names of famous group recording artists. *See, e.g.,* New Jersey Truth In Music Act, N.J. STAT. ANN. § 2A:32B–2; False, Deceptive, or Misleading Advertisement of Live Musical Performances, FLA. STAT. § 817.4115 (2007); Unfair Trade Practices, S.C. CODE ANN. § 39-5-38 (2012); Singer Mgmt. Consultants, Inc. v. Milgram, 650 F.3d 223 (3d Cir. 2011).

group members, there is a third option, which is to lodge the compositions in a separate company owned by the group and dedicated solely to publishing, with the songwriter retaining his or her full songwriter share. In that manner, the interests of the group members in the compositions are undisturbed regardless of the makeup of the band entity generally, which may be owned by different people over time for reasons which should not affect the ownership or treatment of publishing revenue as originally established.

Recordings produced by the group, using group resources, are generally owned by the group's business entity. Post-breakup, if the business entity retains any interests in recordings, there may be issues concerning how such recordings may be used. For example, the group may have produced a number of demonstration recordings that were not meant for commercial release. May such recordings be released by whoever eventually succeeds to the interests of the business entity? If they may be released, who will be the credited artist for such recordings? A former group member may not want to be individually identified as the credited artist, particularly if they go on to success in another arrangement. In like manner, certain group members may object to the use of recordings in which they perform in connection with advertising for certain products, services, or causes, or for premiums. There may also be obligations to accord credit for producing or otherwise contributing to the production of such recordings. What will be the status of artwork (drawings, graphics, and photographs) for the packaging of sound recordings that may have been released by the band, which is subject to its own claims of copyright?[3] Who will be the custodian of original multitrack tapes or files of recordings? Finally, may the group's recordings be remixed or otherwise changed in any way without the participation of each group member in the decision-making process for such changes?

Other asset categories that should be addressed include both tangible and intangible properties. For example, will the ownership of instruments be vested in the group's jointly owned company, or will the instruments be individually owned? Does it make any difference if company resources are used to acquire or maintain the instruments? What about other equipment,

---

3. Zamoyski v. Fifty-Six Hope Road Music Ltd., Inc., 718 F. Supp. 2d 128 (D. Mass. 2010); Smith v. Trans-Siberian Orchestra, 689 F. Supp. 2d 1310 (M.D. Fla. 2010).

such as sound, lights, vehicles, or other staging equipment—is there any understanding about how such equipment will be distributed in the event of a dissolution? Will any such equipment be part of the capital contribution of a member, and if so, will that member have the right to reclaim such equipment? Also, the business of the band will develop a significant amount of data that can be valuable, such as e-mail lists and Twitter followers. Is the collection of such data by the business done so pursuant to policies that permit the data to be shared among band members in the event of a dissolution?

## Other Band Agreement Provisions

Decision making within the band's entity is similar to the decision-making process in any business entity. The organizational agreement should identify the voting percentages that are required, any category of decisions that might require a greater percentage of votes, or even unanimity, and any possible key person votes that may be required for particular decisions. Voting may be equal or follow the percentage of ownership interests in the entity, which could be equal or disproportionate. The issue of distributions may also be tied to how the voting structure is set up. Compensation may be distributed equally, in amounts equal to disproportionate ownership interests among the members, or in different amounts, depending on the source or type of revenue. Each group will have its own range of competing interests to resolve in a structure that works for them.

A group's organizational agreement should also address issues concerning the makeup of the group. For example, under what circumstances may a member be expelled or added, and what are the consequences of a person quitting the group. Standard shareholder, partnership, and operating agreements generally deal with grounds for expulsion, but membership in a musical group may present more particular grounds in recognition of the special requirements of artistic collaboration. Under such circumstances, the group members could agree to an expulsion without cause with the affirmative vote of a percentage of the ownership. The risk of expulsion under such circumstances would be one each of the members would take, and the gravity of the risk would depend on the percentage vote required to expel a member and the valuation of each member's interest in the event of such expulsion without cause were to occur.

Valuation of a group member's interest in the event of certain transfers is a key provision in partnership, shareholder, and operating agreements. Organizational documents generally bar any voluntary transfer of an owner's interest without giving the organization and/or the other owners a right to purchase the interest. The method of valuing the interest under such circumstances would generally be the price offered by a third party. Valuation in the event of an involuntary transfer, however, may vary, depending on the circumstances of the transfer. For example, valuation in connection with a foreclosure action involving the owner may be different than valuation triggered by a divorce action. Valuation in the event of a member's death, disability, or expulsion without cause may be established closer to actual value, which may be agreed to periodically by the members as either a set amount or a certain multiple of a financial feature of the entity, such as net taxable income or gross revenue. Valuation under such circumstances might also be determined by an appraisal process if the parties cannot come to an agreement at the time. Valuation could be established in the form of either (1) a set amount, which takes into account projected future revenue from the assets held by the entity, reduced to present value, (2) contingent compensation based upon a certain percentage of revenue or earning over a defined period, or (3) a combination of both.

Valuation in the event of an expulsion for cause (which would be defined in the agreement) may be an entirely different matter, which may relate to an accounting calculation such as book value. Whatever may be the method of valuation, or the amount paid to the selling owner, the payout by the purchasing party could also be scheduled to avoid cash flow issues, which payments from the former group member's perspective should be secured with a security interest in the remaining assets.

## Leaving Members and Recording Agreements

Recording agreements generally seek to obtain the exclusive recording services of the members of a group, both as a group and as individual performers apart from the group. Therefore, solo records by individual group members will generally be subject to the claims of the record company. This same circumstance comes into play if a group is signed to a recording agreement at the time one of its members leaves. Group recording agreements frequently contain provisions obligating each individual signatory to remain as a recording artist with the record company even if he or she is no longer a member of the group. The leaving member provisions of a recording agreement will frequently spell out the terms applicable to the leaving member, such as length of agreement, number of recordings to deliver, and royalty rate (which is often less than the rate payable to the group as a whole).[4] To erase any doubt about the enforceability of the leaving member provisions of a group agreement, and to address the particular circumstances that may exist at the time a group member becomes a leaving member, it is not uncommon for the record company to enter a new agreement with the leaving member, should it wish to retain the leaving member as an artist.

There are several implications for both the leaving member and the group. First, the status of the royalty accounts should be clearly delineated for: (1) the group with the leaving member included, (2) the group without the leaving member going forward, and (3) the leaving member individually.[5] The leaving member does not want to have his or her royalty account cross-collateralized with the royalty account for the group's recordings. The leaving member is not in control of any of the costs incurred by or on behalf of the group going forward that might become recoupable under the recording agreement. Therefore, the leaving member will not want royalties otherwise payable to him or her to be applied to the recoupment of the group's unrecouped account, even if such royalties were only applied to costs associated with recordings in which the leaving artist performed. In

---

4. *See, e.g.,* The Gordy Co. v. Mary Jane Girls, Inc., 1989 WL 149290 (S.D.N.Y. 1989).

5. For an example of the consequences of not clarifying how royalties will be handled for leaving group members, see Mitchell v. Faulkner, 2013 WL 150254 (S.D.N.Y. 2013).

like manner, the remaining members of the group will not want any costs associated with the leaving member to be associated with their account (although they would probably not object if the leaving member's royalty earnings helped reduce their own account). Further, the leaving member should arrange for his or her proportionate share of any royalty income from the group's account to be paid directly to him or her rather than to any group entity in which the leaving member may not have any further ownership interest.

# Financing

Financing a group's music business is often a cloudy, ad hoc undertaking, with inexact contributions made to the entity in combinations of cash, properties, and services. It is a beautiful thing if the band members agree that their contributions are satisfactory for the interests they have obtained in their business. Of course, it doesn't always work out that way, and a lot of resources can be expended unraveling who owes what to whom if the business fails. Also, the consequences for each of the band members can be different, depending on the nature of their contribution.

## Group Member Capitalization

If a group is going to be self-financed, it is first important for the members to understand whether their cash contributions are capital contributions in consideration of their ownership interests in the group or are a loan, to be paid back in some manner. Of course, cash can be contributed to the business of the group in both forms, and financial planning may recommend one form over another. The key point is that the group members should note and accept the distinction.

In the event services are provided in consideration of an ownership interest in the business, the value of the interest will be considered income to the service provider as compensation for the services provided. From an accounting perspective, the value of an interest in a recently organized band may be insignificant enough that any reportable income to the service provider could be disregarded. However, gaining an interest in an established group in return for services may produce a different result. With respect to equipment and other physical property, the issue will be the same as with cash—is ownership of the equipment being assigned to the business or is it being offered on loan?

If musical compositions or sound recordings are being contributed to the business, it is important to note that ownership or possession of the material object in which a sound recording may be embodied, such as recording tape or acetates, does not create ownership of the copyright interest in such sound recording,[6] nor does the transfer of any such material object transfer any copyright interest.[7] An assignment of copyright interest in compositions or sound recordings, to be effective, must be in writing and signed by the copyright owner.[8] Further, filing of the assignment in the Copyright Office will be constructive notice of the transfer if the assignment references a registered work. If the work is unregistered, then a filing will not give a priority, as there is no constructive notice. Under those circumstances, the UCC and the particular state law will control.[9] Section 205(d) of the Copyright Act identifies the priority of claims with respect to assignments.[10]

## Outside Financing

Outside financing for a musical performing group is generally difficult to obtain, given the significant risks involved with such business. Nevertheless, financial support may be available to a group in the form of patronage, loans, or investments.

---

6. Forward v. Thorogood, 985 F.2d 604 (1st Cir. 1993).

7. 17 U.S.C. § 202 (2011); Polygram Records, Inc. v. Legacy Entm't Grp., LLC, 205 S.W.3d 439 (Tenn. Ct. App. 2006).

8. 17 U.S.C. § 204 (2011).

9. In re World Auxiliary Power Co., 305 F.3d 1120 (9th Cir. 2002).

10. 17 U.S.C. § 205(d) (2011), "Priority between Conflicting Transfers. — As between two conflicting transfers, the one executed first prevails if it is recorded, in the manner required to give constructive notice under subsection (c), within one month after its execution in the United States or within two months after its execution outside the United States, or at any time before recordation in such manner of the later transfer. Otherwise the later transfer prevails if recorded first in such manner, and if taken in good faith, for valuable consideration or on the basis of a binding promise to pay royalties, and without notice of the earlier transfer."

## Patronage

Patronage is a centuries old form of support for creative endeavors. In its contemporary mode, patronage may simply be a gift in the form of the payment of funds to a group, or providing access to services such as rehearsal or recording facilities. The only legal issue that might arise in connection with such support is whether there is clarity concerning the actual status of the payments or the provision of services. It is not unknown for a group to accept what it understands is gratuitous support, only to encounter a demand for repayment, or a claim of ownership, at a later date. Another form of patronage may be a presale of a product, which generally may be a recording in some form. For example, the performer Sam Phillips offered a series of recordings released over a period of time on a subscription basis from her website.[11]

An entirely new form of patronage made possible by online tools that is particularly well suited to musical artists is the crowd sourcing services provided by websites such as Kickstarter, Indiegogo, Rockethub, Sellaband. com, AKAMusic.com, Artistshare.com, and Pledgemusic.com.[12] In essence, each of these services permits musical performers to post a description of a project (an album, a tour, an equipment purchase) for which they are seeking funding, the amount of funding they are seeking, and the form of consideration that will be provided to those who make pledges. Akin to a pledge drive by a not-for-profit organization (but without the charitable contribution treatment), the form of premium given to contributors will vary by level of contribution. A musical group seeking funding for a recording project may, for example, give each contributor a copy of the album when it is completed, and increase the value of the premium all the way up to a live personal appearance for contributors at the top end. The contributions provided by the supporters are not an investment, as the supporters are not obtaining any ownership interest in the group, the project, or any

---

11. Randy Lewis, "For Musicians, Economy is the Mother of Invention," *Los Angeles Times*, May 9, 2010, *available at* http://www.latimes.com/entertainment/news/la-ca-0509-sam-philips-20100509,0,5342881.story.

12. The federal JOBS Act of 2012 (H.R. 3606) contained a section permitting "crowd-funding" by means of equity or debt offerings of not more than $1 million, but as of the preparation of this chapter, the Securities Exchange Commission had not issued its regulations implementing this new method of financing.

intellectual property resulting from the project, but they will be deemed prepayments and counted as revenue to the individual or group making the offer. The commissions charged by current online financial crowd sourcing services range from 4 percent to 15 percent. Some performing groups with strong existing fan bases have adopted the crowd sourcing financing model for offerings made through their own websites and other platforms.[13]

### Investors

Certain investors are attracted to the idea of investing in performers, or in certain projects associated with a performer. Terms for such arrangements lie within a broad range and within an environment in which information about the music industry as a whole and the experience of individual performers is often imprecise and anecdotal. Consequently, musicians and producers sell into a market where investor perceptions have been forged to reflect the belief that music investments are risky ventures. Music financing also must be judged on the economic merits of a project, since there are no significant tax incentives to cause an investor to invest, regardless of the likely success of the project. Investors also know success in the music industry is dependent upon public taste, which is unpredictable and subject to change without warning or explanation. Also, since the performer controls the circumstances of how his or her project is developed and marketed and the investor does not, the investor views the risks of production and financial return as greater than the performer does. Further, whatever business history there may be for a musical performer or group in a traditional form (balance sheet, income statement, management stability and performance, etc.) that an investor might investigate as part of his due diligence, this information is of lesser utility for an investment in a music project. As a result, an investor will generally end up putting his faith in his or her assessment of the creative and personal skills and reliability of the performer and his or her team to develop and produce the project.

---

13. *See, e.g.,* Paul Resnikoff, *Indie Band Figures Out How to Raise Money Without Using Kickstarter . . .,* DIGITAL MUSIC NEWS (Sept. 14, 2012), http://www.digitalmusicnews.com/permalink/2012/120914kickstarter.

The following are some key points of negotiation of an investor agreement, which are driven in their development by the foregoing dynamics:

- The amount of investment and how and when it will be contributed
- Any preconditions to payments if made in tranches
- Use of proceeds, e.g., to fund a recording or tour, engage in a marketing plan, etc.
- Scope of interest obtained, e.g., co-ownership of property developed with investment or contractual right to receive portion of revenue generated by property. If the latter, the duration of the period payments would be made
- Any requirements for the payment of additional funds
- Accounting and auditing provisions
- Any decision-making involvement regarding career direction or transactions for the talent or the results of the talent's services

### Loans

From an investor perspective, if the investment takes the form of a loan rather than an equity or ownership position, the loan should be secured by a security interest in the copyright and trademark interests in the group or performer. For copyright interests that have been registered, the security interest should be filed in the Copyright Office to be perfected and should reference the copyright registration.[14] If the works are unregistered, then the UCC and the applicable state law where the debtor is located will control.[15] With respect to federally registered trademarks, there is not a requirement that a security interest be filed in the United States Patent and Trademark Office (USPTO) to perfect a security interest.[16] Trademarks are considered general intangibles and are controlled by the UCC and the applicable state law where the debtor is located. Nevertheless, it may be advisable to file a notice of security interest with the USPTO as a matter of general notice.

---

14. 17 U.S.C. § 205(c) (2011).

15. *In re* World Auxiliary Power Co., 305 F. 3d 1120 (9th Cir. 2002).

16. *In re* Roman Cleanser, 225 U.S.P.Q.140, 142 (Bankr. E.D. Mich. 1984), *aff'd*, 802 F.2d 207 (6th Cir. 1986).

## Settlements

In the event a group disbands or one of the members leaves, the best practice is to document the terms under which the group members have settled to reduce the likelihood of future disputes and litigation.[17] In the event the attorney has represented the group, and not the individual members of the group, the attorney may document the settlement terms as collectively directed by the group. However, individual group members may nevertheless perceive the attorney as bound by a requirement to represent their individual interests as continued band members.[18] This would certainly be the case if the attorney were to participate in strategizing with certain group members about how to expel other members. Attorneys are best advised, when confronted with contested claims between band members, to refer individual members to other counsel for representation.

A settlement agreement will take into account the band assets mentioned above: recordings, compositions, equipment, band identity, royalty streams, and data. Additional items of value could include insurance claims or proceeds, existing infringement claims, upcoming performance commitments, inventory of recordings and merchandise, website and social media addresses, unpublished works, and so-called pipeline income, or income that has been earned but is in the hands of third parties as it moves through various accounting relationships. A non-disparagement provision is also a recommended practice, although its observance may not be respected. Further, provision should be made with respect to decision making about future exploitation of works controlled by the group. If any group members will no longer participate in decision making concerning such exploitation, specific credit obligations should be included in the settlement agreement to ensure proper credit is accorded all group members going forward.

---

17. *See generally* R. Robin McDonald, *Sugarland Suit Offers Look at Dynamics of Litigating Intra-Band Disputes*, Ent. L. & Fin., Dec. 2010.

18. *See, e.g.*, Adler v. Manatt, Phelps, Phillips & Kantor, L.A. Supr. Ct. BC O5307 (Apr. 1992) (former member of group Guns N' Roses sued the group's law firm for malpractice in connection with group settlement agreement).

# Chapter Five

# How Record Companies and Producers Work

Recording agreements for artists are generally the first thing people think about when the topic of the music business is discussed. Achieving the status of a recording artist, sometimes on a particularly prestigious record label, has historically been the goal of many musicians and performers. This vision has been shaped by the promises of financial, artistic, and social success associated with being featured on a sound recording. Yet, stories of artistic and financial loss, ruin, and frustration as a result of dealings between record companies and recording artists are almost just as common. There is validity to each of these characterizations.

The functions of a record company generally fall into five areas: (1) discovery (identifying performers, songs, and cultural developments); (2) capital (providing the resources required to engage creative personnel and create sound recordings); (3) production (operating and staffing the recording studios where sound recordings for the company are produced); (4) distribution (providing the means by which recordings can be purchased or otherwise used for value received); and (5) promotion (creating demand for the recordings and the recording artists). While these functions have historically been beyond the resources of most individual musicians, recent technological developments have created tools that make each of these functions more available outside the traditional record company relationship. In fact, with respect to production, few record companies own and operate their own recording studios today. Nevertheless, record companies continue to play a key role in the development and success of musical artists.

Today, recording agreements are not always with the company that ultimately owns and releases the recordings produced under the agreement. It is common for recordings to be produced by independent producers and then delivered to the record companies under the terms of production agreements. We will address the features of each of these arrangements, but initially we will describe the structure and typical terms found in a direct recording agreement between a performing artist and record company.

## Nature of the Relationship

The recording agreement, at its most basic level, will generally be for the services of the musician as a recording artist for the production of sound recordings. The relationship may be exclusive for a defined period or it could be nonexclusive and related to a specific project only. The most important issue is one of copyright. Is the relationship between the musician and the company engaging the musician's services one for hire?

As discussed earlier, the implications of whether or not a contribution to a copyrightable work (in this case a sound recording) is made as a work for hire are very important. If the contributions are deemed to be a work made for hire, the copyright in the sound recording will arise automatically with the record company[1] and will not be subject to any right of later termination by the musician. The term of copyright protection for a work made for hire is the shorter of 95 years from publication or 120 years from creation.[2] However, if the contributions are deemed to have been assigned to the record company, then the musician can reclaim his or her interest in the copyright thirty-five years after the assignment. An almost universal

---

1.  17 U.S.C. § 201(b) (2011).
2.  17 U.S.C. § 302(c) (2011).

provision of recording agreements is a section that describes the contributions of the recording services of the musician subject to the agreement as being works made for hire. Most agreements will also provide some form of savings language to the effect that if the contributions are at any point found to not constitute works made for hire that all interests in the copyright in such contributions are nevertheless assigned to the record company. In addition to the contributions of musicians, courts have said that the contribution of a recording engineer, coproducer, and mixer fall within ambit of sound recording authorship.[3] Even the spontaneous contribution of a guest at a recording session has resulted in a claim of rights.[4] Why is work for hire an issue for sound recordings?

Section 101 of the Copyright Act defines two circumstances under which a work may be deemed to be a work made for hire.[5] First, a work produced within the scope of the employment of the creator will be deemed a work made for hire and owned by the employer. Whether one is an "employee" will depend principally on the general common law test of agency and control.[6] A sound recording produced by an in-house employee of a commercial jingle production company is an example of a sound recording that would fall within the first circumstance of the work for hire definition. A person may be an employee even if his payment is in the form of an advance on royalties.[7]

Next, a work may one made for hire if it is specially ordered or commissioned to be created by a nonemployee pursuant to a written agreement with the creator identifying the work as one made for hire. With respect to the second circumstance, the Copyright Act is very specific about which types

---

3. Diamond v. Gillis, 357 F. Supp. 2d 1003 (E.D. Mich. 2005); JCW Invs. Inc. v. Novelty Inc., 289 F. Supp. 2d 1023, 1032 (N.D. Ill. 2003) ("A record producer may be an author when he or she is 'responsible for setting up the session, capturing and electronically processing the sounds, and compiling and editing them to make a final sound recording,"); *see* Systems XIX, Inc. v. Parker, 30 F. Supp. 2d 1225, 1228 (N.D. Cal. 1998) (quoting H.R. Rep. No. 94-1476, 94th Cong., 2d Sess. 56 (1976)); *see also* the dissent in Brown v. Flowers, 196 Fed. Appx. 178 (4th Cir. 2006), which discusses the creative role of a recording engineer in the production of sound recordings.

4. Ulloa v. Universal Music & Video Distrib., 303 F. Supp. 2d 409 (S.D.N.Y. 2004).

5. 17 U.S.C. § 101 (2011).

6. Community for Creative Non-Violence v. Reid, 490 U.S. 730 (1989).

7. Fred Fisher Music Co. v. Leo Feist, Inc., 55 F. Supp. 359 (S.D.N.Y. 1944).

of works are capable of being deemed works made for hire by independent contractors. Unfortunately for record companies, the list of specifically identified works that may be specially ordered or commissioned as works made for hire that was originally included in the 1976 Copyright Act did not include sound recordings. In 1999, Congress amended the Copyright Act to specifically include sound recordings within the classes of works that could be created within a work for hire arrangement.[8] After a firestorm of dissent from the artistic community, however, this revision was repealed retroactively, without prejudice to either artists or the record companies.[9]

Recordings produced under agreements beginning in 1978 will be subject to the conflicting interpretations of the work for hire provisions contained in those agreements by the record companies and the recording artists who are parties to those agreements. The recording artists will seek termination of the record companies' rights to the recordings on the grounds that such works are not valid works made for hire and the record companies will counter that the sound recordings are valid works made for hire and thus termination does not apply. Given that termination, if valid, occurs thirty-five years following the granting of rights, the first actual terminations will begin to occur in 2013 (although the Copyright Act permits notices of intent to terminate up to ten years prior to actual termination and many notices of termination have already been served).[10] As of this writing, it is not clear how this issue will be resolved. However, one court has held that recordings delivered between 1972, when sound recordings first were protected by copyright in the United States, and 1978, when the Copyright Act of 1976 became effective, were works made for hire.[11]

---

8. Intellectual Property and Communications Omnibus Reform Act of 1999, Pub. L. No. 106-113, app. I, § 1011(d), 113 Stat. 1501, 1501A-554 (1999).

9. Work Made for Hire and Copyright Corrections Act of 2000, Pub. L. No. 106-379, 114 Stat. 1444 (2000).

10. *See generally* Jay Rosenthal, *As 2013 Approaches, Artist Termination Right Faces Record Labels' Work-For-Hire Argument*, ENT. L. & FIN., Mar. 2008.

11. Fifty-Six Hope Road Music Ltd. v. UMG Recordings, Inc., 2010 WL 3564258 (S.D.N.Y. 2010).

## Parties

The signatory on a recording agreement is not always an individual musician. First, the musician may have formed a business entity through which he or she provides their personal entertainment services. This entity is typically referred to as a loan-out company. If the loan-out company signs the recording agreement, the individual musician will sign an accompanying "inducement" letter. The inducement letter essentially states that the individual musician agrees to provide all the services required of the loan-out company under the recording agreement and acknowledges that the musician will look to the loan-out company exclusively for all compensation to be received by the musician for their services under the recording agreement.

When a group is the signatory, they may also have organized a loan-out company for the delivery of their entertainment services, in which case the same inducement letter would come into play for each of the owners of the loan-out company. If the group has not organized a loan-out company, the recording agreement may be another moment of truth in the life of the group—will all the group members be signatories, or only a subset? From the record company point of view, it will want to contractually obligate every contributor to the production of the sound recordings to be produced under the agreement. However, it may make its offer to less than all of the current members of the group for any number of reasons. Whether the group goes ahead under such circumstances may depend on the agreements between the group members existing at that time.

## Scope

Over the decades the scope of rights in recording agreements has changed as new forms of expression, distribution, and markets have developed. Early recording agreements applied only to the recordings produced during a particular recording session, for which an artist may or may not have been promised royalties in addition to whatever set amounts they received at the time. Then agreements became exclusive and engaged artists over a defined period for the purposes of producing recordings for use in the production of phonograph records.[12] At a certain point, as the means for producing sound recordings became more widely distributed, and the use of sound recordings more varied than just for purposes of the production of phonograph records, the scope of recording agreements began to apply to *any* sound recordings produced during the term of the agreement, whether produced by the record company or not, and to any use of such sound recordings. For example, recording agreements began to apply to live recordings produced by others than the record company or recordings produced for inclusion in motion pictures or television programs. In like manner, recording agreements grew to embrace interests other than sound recordings—first music publishing for compositions created by the recording artist, then such things as music videos, merchandising, and fan clubs.

Today, it is not uncommon for a record company, particularly one of the major three companies (Sony Music Entertainment, Universal Music Group, and Warner Music Group), to insist on a broad range of rights in a musical performer's creative output under what have been characterized as "360" deals for the breadth of their application. We will review specific topic areas further in this chapter, but major recording agreements now frequently bring within their scope not only recordings of all types and methods of exploitation, but also merchandising, touring, fan clubs, websites, social media platforms, management, and other aspects of the entertainment career of the artist. Whether this expanded scope of rights makes sense to the artist will depend on the capabilities of the company requesting the rights and the consideration being given in return for the grant.

## Term

Recording agreements generally have an initial period during which a certain minimum number of recordings will be produced and delivered to the record company. While this period is sometimes defined by a certain number

---

12. *See, e.g.*, Polygram Records, Inc. v. Legacy Entm't Grp., LLC, 205 S.W.3d 439 (Tenn. Ct. App. 2006) (recordings produced for syndication as radio programs were distinguished from recording produced for purposes of sale as records).

of months, it will quite often be tied to the delivery and/or release of a certain minimum number of recordings satisfactory to the record company. For example, the initial period might commence at the execution of the agreement and end six to eighteen months following the initial commercial release of the recordings required to be delivered by the artist during the initial period. This method of determining the duration of the agreement has the benefit to the record company of extending its exclusive rights to the artist's work for however long it actually takes the musician to complete his or her creative recording process. The label also has the time to measure the commercial prospects of the artist following the release of the recordings. Of course, the artist may find their interests are best served by a shorter period, particularly if success is not occurring at the rate envisioned by the artist. If the initial album to be delivered under the recording agreement was already independently produced by the artist prior to the agreement, then the risk attendant to the production of new recordings does not exist for either party and the initial period should be correspondingly reduced.

Following the initial period, the recording agreement will generally have a certain number of options for the record company to extend the agreement. The options may vary between three and five, and the duration of these option periods will generally mirror the duration of the initial period. The options might be exclusively exercisable by the record company, but it may be possible to negotiate certain contingencies that must be satisfied in the prior period in order for the exercise to be valid, such as the commercial release of a certain number of recordings, the obtainment of a certain method of distribution, or the achievement of a certain level of sales. In contrast, the record company will want its exclusive rights to extend for a period of time following the delivery of the final recorded works required under the agreement in order to give it sufficient time to market such recordings as the musician's newest release without competition with recordings released by the artist's new label.

# Production and Release Commitment

The delivery requirement of the artist under the recording agreement is generally described in terms of a minimum number of individual masters that are satisfactory to the record company. The required number of masters generally will be enough to comprise an album featuring a certain minimum number of recordings. The record company may want a certain number of additional recordings for such uses as so-called B sides, for inclusion in albums released in foreign territories or through exclusive retailer arrangements in order to distinguish such albums from the regularly available editions, or for seasonal, tribute, or other thematic collections.

The nature of the masters to be delivered is often described in detail, such as whether the recordings are studio recordings rather than live, what their minimum and maximum length may be, that the songs not be previously recorded by the artist, etc. The level of record company satisfaction that must be obtained is sometimes a negotiated point. Must the master be commercially satisfactory to the record company, or must the artist only deliver masters that are technically satisfactory for the production of phonorecords?

Delivery may also be described in actual physical terms, as the record company will want to possess the actual multitrack master tapes, digital files, or other physical media in which the recordings featuring the artist are embodied. This is important not only because the record company will want to ensure safekeeping of such physical media, but also because future playback formats or uses such as multichannel surround-sound formats may require access to such original multitrack media rather than second generation media prepared for reproduction in a specific earlier format.

While the artist is required to deliver a certain number of recordings to the record company, the record company is not required generally to release any particular number of such recordings, or to do so in any particular format or sequence. A release commitment should therefore be negotiated on behalf of the artist. The release commitment should include the dates by which the release would be achieved and the configuration in which the recordings would appear (digital only, compact disc, vinyl, etc.). If negotiated correctly, the failure to affect a release could trigger the right of the artist to terminate the agreement, block the exercise of an option to extend the agreement, or obtain the return of masters delivered under the agreement.

## Obligation to Promote

The relationship between a recording artist and the record company is generally considered a conventional business relationship and does not rise to the status of a fiduciary relationship. Because of the exclusivity of the arrangement, the record company will have a general obligation to use its reasonable commercial efforts to promote the recordings subject to the agreement.[13] This general obligation may be supported by express provisions in the agreement concerning budgets and specific promotional efforts to be undertaken by the record company. But, even compliance with such specific requirements does not immunize record companies against claims that their promotional efforts have been inadequate.[14] Nevertheless, an implied covenant of good faith and fair dealing can be overcome with express language granting discretionary authority about how rights might be exercised, particularly when that discretionary authority is supported by actual consideration, such as guaranteed payments.[15]

## Recording Budgets and Advances

Record companies generally fund the costs of producing the recordings they obtain. For recordings produced on speculation prior to the entry of a recording agreement that are acquired under the terms of the agreement, a payment is generally made to the artist to reimburse them for the cost of producing the recordings. This payment is characterized as an advance against potential future royalties. For recordings produced during the course

---

13. Wood v. Lucy, Lady Duff-Gordon, 118 N.E. 214 (1917).

14. *See, e.g.*, Contemporary Mission, Inc. v. Famous Music Corp., 557 F.2d 918 (2d Cir. 1977); Simon v. Starbucks Corp., No. 09-09074 (C.D. Cal. Jan. 17, 2012) (order granting motion to dismiss the appeal).

15. *See, e.g.*, Third Story Music, Inc. v. Waits, 41 Cal. App. 4th 798 (Ct. App. 1996).

of the recording agreement, the record company generally approves a budget for the production of the recordings which it funds and which either it or the artist will administer. In either event, the amounts paid by the record company will be recouped by the record company from royalties that might otherwise be payable to the artist before the artist receives any further payments.

The amount of the production budget for recordings under the recording agreement may be a set figure or may be determined according to a formula that takes into account earnings from the immediately prior recordings from the artist that the company released. This variable amount is generally collared with a minimum and a maximum figure. The budget may or may not include amounts meant to be retained by the artist in the form of personal advances if the full amount of the budget is not expended.

It is important to recognize that amounts paid by the record company in the form of advances and recording costs are not obligations to be repaid by the artist to the record company in the event they are not recouped from exploitation of the recordings. While it is possible for the record company and the artist to enter loan agreements, advances and amounts paid for recording costs will not create indebtedness by the artist to the record company. It is also important to note how recording costs are defined in a recording agreement. Costs other than as anticipated may be embraced in such a definition, thereby increasing the recoupable amount faced by the artist. For example, the definition of recording costs could include hospitality or travel expenses the recording artist may anticipate are the responsibility of the record company.

## Royalties

Royalties have historically been the subject of Byzantine provisions of recording agreements. It is not enough to understand a quoted royalty rate for an artist—one must carefully examine the way such a rate is adjusted, modified, and qualified to reasonably determine an anticipated payment for the use of a recording. Some of the royalty provisions discussed below are becoming anachronistic as physical products are replaced by digital transmissions. However, it is not uncommon for an attorney to be asked to provide advice concerning the terms of old agreements, which include provisions discussed below.

## Royalty Basis

The first royalty provision to be determined is what the royalty rate will be based on: the suggested retail selling price of the product, the wholesale price, actual net revenue, or some specially defined basis. While the suggested retail selling price of products was often used in the past as a royalty basis, the reduced significance of this pricing model, and the fact that digital retailers today are more instrumental in determining suggested retail selling prices, has caused royalty systems to more and more move away from this basis. The wholesale selling price may be a published price, or it may be a variable price based upon actual receipts. The term "published price to dealers," or "PPD," may refer to the published wholesale price or to a constructed price determined by definition in the agreement. In any event, since wholesale or PPD prices may be a significant discount from a suggested retail price, the royalty rate should correspondingly adjust. For example, if the wholesale price is one-half the suggested retail selling price, the royalty rate as applied to the suggested retail selling price would have to be doubled if based on the wholesale price in order to yield the same result.

It is also important to understand the percentage of sales upon which royalties will be calculated. One historical practice in recording agreements was to base royalties on 90 percent of record sales, which was justified on the claim that many records broke in shipment. While that justification no longer exists, the practice became baked into many royalty systems and may appear, almost zombie-like, in current agreements. If the provision cannot be negotiated out, then the rate should simply be adjusted upward.

## Royalty Rates

Basic royalty rates for recording agreements vary across a wide range, depending on the success level of the artist, projected sales for the music genre involved, or the policies of the particular record company. Generally, a base rate applicable to so-called top-line recordings will be determined under the agreement, and that rate will serve as the reference point for rate adjustments applicable to products other than "top-line" recordings. Royalty rates are also deemed to be "all-in," meaning that all royalty participants involved with a particular recording are meant to be included within the single rate. Thus, if a royalty rate for an artist is 12 percent, and the producer of a recording featuring that artist is entitled to receive a 3 percent royalty rate, the artist's effective royalty rate for such recording is reduced to 9 percent.

Royalty rates do not have to remain static during the term of an agreement. Rates could escalate during option extension period, for recordings that achieve certain sales levels, or for recordings appearing on certain configurations, such as "best-ofs."

## Licensing Income

The royalty rates described above are applicable to products sold by the record company. Of course, the record company can also authorize others to exercise any of the rights held by the record company under license agreements which result in licensing income to the record company. Historically, licensed uses of recordings for such things as compilation albums or soundtracks generally occurred after the record company realized more profitable proceeds from the sale of their own products. Licenses would be permitted if the licensed uses did not cannibalize the company's own sales. Licensing revenue was a secondary source of income, and most recording agreements provided that 50 percent of such licensing income would be paid to the recording artist.[16]

With the advent of digital music services and retailers, the once-secondary source of income is now poised to become primary, which has caused much disagreement. The issue is this: is the relationship between a record company and a digital music retailer such as iTunes or Amazon, which stores a digital music file on its own server and creates and transmits a copy of that file to its customers when purchased, one of a wholesaler and retailer or of licensor and licensee? If the relationship is one of wholesaler and retailer, then

---

16. Not all earlier recording agreements addressed the issue of licensing, which has led to litigation concerning the record company's right to do so under the language of the applicable agreements. *See, e.g.,* Thomas v. Gusto Records, Inc., 939 F.2d 395 (6th Cir. 1991), *cert. denied*, 502 U.S. 984 (1991); Greenfield v. Philles Records, Inc., 780 N.E.2d 166 (N.Y.S. 2002).

the royalty provisions based on the wholesale or retail price of the file will apply. If the relationship is one of licensor and licensee, then the percentage of licensing proceeds provisions of the agreement would apply. These hypotheticals illustrate the material difference. Assume that the royalty rate under an artist's agreement is 20 percent of the wholesale price, which we will also assume, for simplicity purposes, is not adjusted for any of the reasons to be later discussed. The typical "wholesale" price of a single recording sold as a digital download is 70 cents. Therefore, the royalty payable to the artist under the wholesaler-retailer arrangement would be 14 cents. If that same transaction is characterized as one between a licensor and a licensee, the royalty would be 50 percent of 70 cents, or 35 cents, which is greater than two-and-one-half times more than the other arrangement.

As of this writing, multiple lawsuits have been brought by artists whose recordings were produced under contracts that did not anticipate digital sales by others as becoming the principal source of income for the record companies owning those recordings. The results of those lawsuits have been mixed.[17]

Current recording agreements generally seek to characterize sales through digital transmission under the authority of the record company as sales subject to the regular royalty scheme set up for the sale of physical products, and to distinguish such sales from more traditional licenses such as for soundtracks or compilations. The issue with respect to legacy agreements, however, is not expected to be settled soon, given the large financial amount at stake.

## Container Charges

Most recording agreements will contain a provision reducing the base for the calculation of royalties by a percentage that will vary according to the

---

17. *See* Allman v. Sony BMG Music Entm't, 2008 WL 2477465 (S.D.N.Y. 2008) (the court found that the transaction between the record company and the online sellers of downloads was one of sale and resale, and royalty formulas applicable to sales rather than licenses applied). *But see* F.B.T. Prods., LLC v. Aftermath Records, 621 F.3d 958 (9th Cir. 2010), *cert. denied*, 131 S. Ct. 1677 (2011) (recording agreement unambiguously provided that the sale of downloads and mastertone ringtones resulted in licensing income subject to the higher royalty provisions of the agreement); *see also* James v. UMG Recordings, Inc., 2012 WL 1376977 (N.D. Cal. 2012); Clifford v. Concord Music Group, Inc., 2012 WL 380744 (N.D. Cal. 2012).

configuration in which the recording was sold. For example, the royalty base might be reduced 12.5 percent for vinyl albums, 20 percent for cassette tapes, and 25 percent for compact discs. The reasons given in justification of such reductions are varied. Some argue that each configuration has its own profit margin that requires application of a royalty rate tailored to that configuration. Others argue that the price of a physical recording includes the cost of the packaging in which the recording is sold, and the portion of the price so paid for that packaging should not be included in the base upon which the artist's royalty is calculated. Whatever the reason or the validity of the argument, container charges are standard features of recording agreements, and all assessments of royalty rates have to take them into account. Fortunately, contemporary recording agreements generally do not apply a container charge to digital transmissions of recordings. However, that does not mean that the language of an agreement offered today, or the legacy language of an agreement entered prior to the anticipation of digital transmissions, might not permit such a reduction.

## Format, Territory, and Channel of Trade Adjustments

Recordings have been sold in a variety of formats and circumstances that produce differing margins for the record companies and thus certain royalty rate adjustments. For example, record companies often reduce the price of certain recordings after the initial demand for such recordings has been satisfied and price becomes a material purchase incentive. These reduced price line categories are generally referred to as "mid-price" and "budget," and the royalty rate applicable to such releases may be reduced by between 25 percent and 50 percent, respectively. Royalties are also sometimes reduced for new product formats characterized as "new configurations," on the grounds that the development, manufacturing, and marketing costs of such new configurations produce lower margins commanding lesser royalty payouts. The same argument sometimes applies to high-end so-called audiophile recordings having a specialized market. New configuration provisions appear less frequently in contemporary contracts and should be narrowly defined to prevent their application to a new format that becomes prevalent.

Sales of products in foreign territories and through channels of trade other than regular retail, such as by mail order, carry additional costs that affect royalty rates. The rate for foreign territories will generally be reduced from between 10 percent and 50 percent, depending on the territory, and rates for nontraditional channels of trade may be reduced between 25 percent and 50 percent. As digital transmissions, which do not bear the same incremental territory or channel of trade costs, surpass physical products in sales volume, the applicability of such provisions will fade.

## Free Goods

Promotion of a recording is generally an organized and coordinated effort to build commercial demand during a certain period. Record companies want to know that the promoted recording will be available for purchase when that demand is being created, since records are often an impulse purchase, or a purchase based upon an interest that can quickly diminish or disappear. Record companies therefore want to have sufficient records available to meet anticipated demand. As a result, the practice grew in the industry of incenting retailers to purchase recordings by giving the retailers a certain number of records free for every amount that they purchased, rather than a discount on the purchase price. Records distributed for free also had the advantage of generally being non-royalty bearing. This practice has become fairly standardized, with the percentage of album products purchased becoming standardized at 15 percent. Therefore, the royalty payments made to artists are reduced by this 15 percent to reflect the free nature of this distribution. Records distributed as so-called free goods are not the same as records distributed for promotional purposes for free, to such persons as reviewers or broadcasters, although royalties are not payable on promotional records either.

## Digital Royalties

With the conversion of physical sound carriers—CDs, tapes, vinyl, etc.—into digital files as the principal method of sales exploitation, a great number of the foregoing terms that adjust royalty calculations are not applicable. For example, digital files bear no container charges, it is not necessary to offer free goods to a digital retailer, and there are no differing cost structures among different channels of trade that might compel a royalty adjustment. Further, while digital royalty rates might still be distinguished by format (a higher bit rate or other technical feature) or by price point category (newer hit releases as opposed to catalog material), there generally are not variable costs associated with differing digital format or price point categories justifying a royalty rate adjustment—the adjustment is made in the royalty base (price), not the rate. The hope too would be that the sale of recordings in digital formats would permit greater transparency in accounting and reporting as sales and financial systems become more efficient and comprehensive.

## Royalty Calculation Example

When advising an artist as to the royalty provisions of a proposed recording agreement, it is a good idea to apply the royalty scheme set out in the agreement to some hypothetical situations to see the actual output in dollars and cents. Doing so not only establishes correct expectations for the return to the artist, but may also reveal inconsistencies or ambiguities in the agreement that should be corrected. It also provides grounds for further negotiation with the record company if the output is unreasonably low.

For example, assume a base rate for top-line recordings of 20 percent applied to a compact disc with a wholesale price of \$7. A typical royalty scheme, taking into account the factors identified above, would be as follows: .20 X \$7 × .75 (the container charge) × .85 (the 15 percent free goods reduction) × .90 (the amount of sales the royalties are paid on), resulting in a royalty of 80.3 cents per disc. If royalties of 5 percent are due to the producer of the hypothetical recordings, the artist's portion of royalties would be reduced by an additional 25 percent, or to approximately 60 cents per disc.

Several years ago, when I was with a television production company that was negotiating royalty agreements with participating artists for the release of products featuring the programs our company was producing, we elected to make our recording agreements more transparent by eliminating the container charges, new configuration reductions, producer royalties, and other adjustments that customarily appear. The royalty rate of course was lower, since it was not being reduced by all the customary factors. Expecting to receive compliments for our efforts from the attorneys representing the artists, I instead received an almost universal condemnation of the rate as being too low. Instead of creating goodwill by simplifying the negotiation,

I had to overcome negative initial impressions created by an analysis of the agreement that went no further than the review of a single number. In the end, after lengthy explanation, the rate was accepted, but not having received any "love" for our efforts at transparency was yet another example of the entrenched effect of legacy recording agreements. And a good illustration of why it is important to actually test the royalty formula with hypotheticals to determine their merit.

## Accountings and Audits

Royalty accountings under recording agreements are generally rendered on a semiannual basis, usually between sixty and ninety days after the close of each half calendar year. Because recordings in physical formats are sold to retailers on a full returns basis (meaning the retailer may unconditionally return unsold recordings), the record company will establish a reserve against anticipated future returns before remitting payments to the artist. Reserves are generally in the range of 20 percent to 25 percent of records shipped to retailers and liquidated with a reasonable period, perhaps eighteen months. The accounting provisions also might state that the accuracy of each statement will be deemed accepted if specific objection is not given within a certain period of time after the statement is rendered, perhaps two to three years. This becomes an enforceable contractual "statute of limitations" to litigation claims, so is very important to observe in practice.[18]

The record company will generally treat all recordings produced pursuant to the terms of the agreement under a single account, meaning that the costs of all records produced under the agreement are cross-collateralized against each other. This means that the earnings from a successful recording will not be paid out until the costs from all less successful recording are recouped. Language may appear in the recording agreement also permitting the record company to recoup costs "from this *or any other* agreement" between the artist and the record company. This language would permit, for example, recoupment of recording costs from earnings derived from

---

18.  Allman v. UMG Recordings, 530 F. Supp. 2d 602 (S.D.N.Y. 2008).

a music publishing agreement between the artist and the record company. Such cross-collateralization language between agreements is objectionable and should be struck.

As with the music publishing agreements, the recording artist should have the right to audit the books and records of the record company to ensure the accountings are proper. The considerations raised earlier in Chapter Three applicable to audit provisions in music publishing agreements—when and where the audit may take place, how long it may take place, the frequency of audits, what may be reviewed, any cost shifting in the event a discrepancy is discovered, confidentiality, and whether there is any sharing of any audit report—apply to recording agreements as well. As also mentioned in the discussion concerning music publishing agreements, failure to make required royalty payments may not give rise to an action for rescission unless the failure to pay is almost total.[19]

# Approvals

Creative endeavors require a myriad of important decisions, many of which may create tensions between the interests of the artist and those of the record company as they each seek to control the creation and marketing of the artist's recordings. These areas may include the selection of compositions to be recorded, the producer, the studio, and participating musicians, the budget for master production, when recordings are considered complete and accepted, remixes or edits of recordings, artwork, the label the artist will be released on (assuming the record company has more than one label), how the artist is depicted in advertising and promotional material, directors and storylines for music videos, and the use of recordings for certain purposes by third parties under license or in connection with premiums. At a minimum, the artist should be consulted concerning major decisions concerning the production and exploitation of recordings. As a practical matter, the artist is very much in control of the creative process involving the

---

19. Peterson v. Highland Music, Inc., 140 F.3d 1313 (9th Cir. 1998), *cert. denied*, 525 U.S. 983 (1998); Robinson v. Sanctuary Record Groups, Ltd., 826 F. Supp. 2d 570 (S.D.N.Y. 2011).

recording of the masters, as the forced performance by an artist is unlikely to be commercially viable, if the recording takes place at all. However, a record company may change recordings after delivery unless it is denied that opportunity without the artist's approval. While the record company will want to exploit recordings to their full commercial potential, the artist may not wish their recordings to be used in association with certain areas previously mentioned with respect to composers: alcohol, tobacco, firearms, certain food products, with religious, political, or other issue-oriented messages, or audiovisual works of a certain genre.

## Controlled Compositions

A controlled composition is generally defined as a musical composition that is written, owned, or otherwise controlled by the recording artist or the recording artist's publishing company. The controlled composition provisions of the recording agreement include a license from the recording artist to the record company permitting the record company to exploit recordings of each controlled composition. This is critical from the record company's perspective, as the company does not want to expend resources for the production of recordings, only to have their ability to exploit such recordings frustrated by a refusal by the recording artist, in their capacity as the songwriter, to issue a first-time mechanical license or synchronization licenses, for which compulsory licenses are not available. The controlled composition clause insures that, if the recording artist records his or her own composition, the company's ability to exploit that recording will be unimpaired, both with respect to the initial release of the recording and others.

The more critical function of a controlled composition clause is to reduce the record company's license costs, which can be achieved in a number of different ways. First, the record company may seek a discount from the statutory rate for compulsory mechanical licenses. A discount to 75 percent of the statutory rate is common, and deeper discounts for mid-line and budget releases may also be sought. Also, since the statutory rate also increases for recordings that are longer than five minutes, the controlled composition clause may seek to apply the minimum rate (or the discounted rate), no matter what the length of the recording may be. The clause may also provide that multiple versions of a particular recording appearing on the same product would be paid as one. The language may also seek to establish as the rate going forward for all time the statutory rate in existence at the time the agreement was entered. Since the statutory rate is periodically adjusted through Copyright Office proceedings, such language should be resisted.

The controlled composition provisions may further seek to establish a cap on the aggregate amount the record company will pay for publishing on albums or other configurations. This cap is generally calculated as a multiple of a certain rate otherwise applicable to an individual recording. For example, the cap for an album might be established by multiplying the then-applicable statutory rate by a number meant to approximate the expected number of tracks on an album. This number is negotiable but generally falls in the range of ten to thirteen. Efforts to use any discounted statutory rate as the basis for determining the cap should be resisted, as the effect of such a low cap can be material, particularly when non-controlled compositions are included on a release. Since non-controlled compositions are likely to be available only on the basis of a full statutory rate, their inclusion at that rate as a portion of an aggregate amount determined on the basis of a discounted rate may drive the effective rate for a controlled composition to little, if anything.

The problems with controlled composition clauses for artists has been somewhat mitigated by Congress. In 1995, the Digital Performance Right in Sound Recording Act declared that a controlled composition clause shall not be enforceable for digital downloads of recordings released pursuant to a contract entered after 1995.[20] As digital downloads continue their ascent to dominance over physical products, the impact of controlled composition clauses will diminish.

---

20.   17 U.S.C. § 115(c)(3)(E) (2011). *See generally* Jay Rosenthal, *The Recording Artist/Songwriter Dilemma: The Controlled Composition Clause—Enough Already!*, LANDSLIDE A PUBLICATION OF THE ABA SECTION OF INTELLECTUAL PROPERTY LAW, Mar./Apr. 2011.

# Merchandising

Merchandising generally refers to taking a product or service from a company and selling it to a consumer. For our purposes, however, it refers to a more specific activity, which is the marketing of products or services that have been branded or otherwise associated with a musical individual or entity, usually under license from the individual or entity. Merchandising implicates a number of different rights, depending upon what is used to create the desired association. For example, a T-shirt might simply display the name of an individual performer, in which case the performer's right of publicity is implicated. If the performer appears under a collective name, use of the name, especially in a distinctive logotype or design, would implicate trademark rights. If a photo of a performer is used, or a graphic image, the copyright in such photograph or graphic would be implicated. Conceivably, all three interests could be combined in a single property, i.e., a photograph of a performer that is used as a service mark by the performer for their musical performance or recording services. Merchandising can be a very lucrative part of an individual performer's income. The group Kiss, perhaps the most aggressive and successful of all merchandising performers, has reportedly issued over 5,000 licenses for products ranging from condoms to caskets.[21]

The merchandising provisions of recording agreements have grown from initial modest terms that permitted the record company to use album cover artwork on selected apparel items and posters to the granting of all rights to use a performer's identity and trademarks across all product categories. The expansion of such rights has followed the growth of merchandising capabilities by record companies, particularly major labels that have either launched their own merchandising divisions or purchased merchandising companies. Whether a recording artist grants merchandising rights to a record company and the scope of such rights, if any, should depend on the ability of the record company to actually implement such rights. Granting a record company rights beyond its ability to exercise simply interposes the company between the artist and the actual party producing the product,

---

21. *Kiss and Sell*, Billboard, Oct. 3, 2009, 24.

generally without delivery of value by the record company or real benefit to the artist.

The more critical terms of the merchandising provisions of a recording agreement are control and royalties. Who controls what words and/or images will be applied to products or services, and what products or services might be marketed? Who determines the licensees of the words and/or images, if the record company does not produce and sell the product itself, and what will be the terms and conditions of such licenses? What personal services might be required of an artist in connection with the promotion of a licensed merchandising product? Does the recording artist retain any rights to produce their own merchandise, perhaps for sale in connection with personal appearances? What flexibility will the artist have to participate in sponsorships or endorsements within the context of the merchandising rights held by the record company?

Since the function of trademarks is to identify source, sponsorship, or approval, quality control is the key term to any trademark license agreement. Unsupervised uses by third parties do not serve to identify the trademark owner and create the risk that a trademark owner will no longer be able to retain rights in his or her mark. Therefore, to the extent that a merchandising agreement implicates a trademark right (and most music-related products will), the agreement must establish a standard for quality. The agreement must also identify procedures to ensure that the standards will be met, such as the submission of prototypes for approval and periodic inspections. The agreements also should contain language acknowledging that all the goodwill created by the promotion and sale of the licensed product inures to the benefit of the artist as owner of the marks. This may be critical in supporting applications to register artist-owned trademarks, or to maintain such registrations, that are based on licensed uses rather than uses produced directly by the artist.

The financial terms of the merchandising provisions generally provide payment to the artist of 50 percent of proceeds received by the record company from the exploitation of merchandising rights, net of manufacturing costs, sales agents, and perhaps a percentage of sale revenue to represent the recapture of overhead costs. The artist will want the agreement to provide that the revenue earned through merchandising is not cross-collateralized with the recoupable costs that might be due from the recording or publishing activities under the agreement. Care should also be taken to limit the merchandising rights to the term of the recording agreement. The record company of course will require the ability to use the artist's identity to promote recordings produced under the agreement after the artist is no longer an exclusive recording artist with the label, but there is no companion requirement that the label be required to produce new merchandising products. Further, the artist may be required to grant exclusive merchandising right to a successor label, which the artist cannot do if the prior record company held nonexclusive rights.

## Videos

The first major label recording agreement that I negotiated was over fifty pages in length, and was accompanied by a side agreement of perhaps another ten pages. Despite the lengthy agreement, the following is the entire provision that addressed the production of musical audiovisual works:

> You shall, upon our request, appear on dates and at film studios or other locations designated by us upon reasonable notice to you for the filming, taping or other permanent fixation of audiovisual reproductions of your performance.

It wasn't as if music videos were unknown then. It also turned out that a music video from the group involved was one of the first twenty videos broadcast on the day MTV launched its service in 1981. The primitive attention given to music videos in the not-so-distant past demonstrates how far the medium has advanced, as music videos of course are now standard features of recording agreements.

Musical audiovisual works are generally treated in the same manner as sound recordings. They are works made for hire and are generally subject to the same royalty scheme as sound recordings (with some exceptions). The scope of exclusivity the record company has with the recording artist is generally limited to the production of works featuring musical performances, as opposed to dramatic performances, and to the sale of products reproducing such performances. One-half of the costs of producing music videos are generally treated as recoupable from royalties otherwise payable for the sale of audio-only recordings but fully recoupable from any royalties earned from music video proceeds. While the royalty rates for audiovisual works may not be the same as those provided for audio-only recordings, the royalty adjustments applicable to audio-only recordings, such as container charges, fee goods, and territory and channel of trade reductions, generally apply. License receipts will generally be shared equally between the record company and the artist. However, the allocation may be of a net figure enabling the record company to recover certain required costs it may have incurred to fulfill its delivery obligations under the license, such as transcoding costs. The rates will be all-in, meaning all royalty participants will be paid from the single negotiated rate.

Issues of control and commitment also mirror those affecting audio-only recordings. Will the record company commit to the production and release of a music video, and if so, at what budget? Who will select the director, writer, editor, guests, and recordings used? Will any sponsor support be available or permitted? Since there is no compulsory license for synchronization rights, the record company will generally obtain rights to controlled compositions through the provisions in the agreement otherwise applicable to audio-only recordings.

Market and technology forces have created new tensions affecting how audiovisual works are addressed in recording agreements. First, the means by which audiovisual works are produced and distributed have become inexpensive and decentralized, giving commercial options and capabilities to many more parties, including the recording artist themselves. Second, distribution platforms for entertainment properties have converged. Companies that originally produced works only for broadcast (which the record companies would not control) now routinely seek the right to distribute such programming by means of DVDs and online and mobile devices, which in the past would be the general domain of the record companies. Finally, the growth and acceptance of branded entertainment—music as a sponsored activity—has created new opportunities and requirements for those artists that participate. Sponsors seeking to use music to deliver a commercial message generally will insist upon having exclusive rights for certain periods in custom audio or audiovisual content as a draw to their promotional campaign. This material may conflict with the exclusivity provisions of the artist's recording agreement.

What does this mean? First, the definition of the scope of exclusive rights in audiovisual works that is held by the record company is critical. What rights might a performer want to hold back? Streaming or downloading of recordings of live performances from the performer's own website or social media platform? Ability by the performer to authorize live performances at events such festivals to be streamed or archived by the event promoter, or to authorize television broadcast performances by the performer to be distributed as DVDs or electronic transmissions? Ability to authorize fan recordings to be produced and circulated, or to produce specific audiovisual works for fan club distribution? Ability to fulfill sponsorship commitments for exclusive content to be exploited, if not owned, by the sponsor? If the performer anticipated a certain type and number of outside projects, perhaps the recording agreement could contain a provision preapproving a certain number of outside projects that fell within defined boundaries. If such projects are not carved out, they will be handled on a case-by-case basis.

Second, if audiovisual works are produced and exploited outside the bounds of the exclusivity provisions of the recording agreement, where does the money earned from such works go? Is it paid to the artist, to the record company, or to both? Can a distinction be made as to whom receives any advance paid in connection with an outside audiovisual project and who receives royalties that might be generated? Does it make any difference as to whom is paid whether the artist's royalty account is recouped or unrecouped? Each of these factors may come into play in sorting out whether the project will be authorized.

# 360 Deals

The role and economic model for record companies is changing as a result of the economic challenges they face from the dislocation of physical product sales. Also, the traditional roles record companies controlled of providing artist discovery, capital, promotion, and distribution have become more widely distributed and available from other parties. Selling products is still key, but new roles and new revenue streams are evolving. For example, music is more and more a means by which a commercial message may be delivered—the means by which an audience is convened, attention obtained, and an impression created. As a supplier of that music, record companies act in the new role as service providers to other industries and marketers. In like manner, record companies understand they have a platform from which commercial messages may issue, which is valuable to brands seeking to affiliate with the values associated with talent and properties owned by the record companies. Finally, record companies have broadened their business capabilities, both in artist management[22] and in ancillary areas that exploit their recording artists, and the results of the talent of those recording artists, to create new revenue streams.

All of these new developments have caused record companies to reassess the contractual relationships that they have with their talent. The term "360 deal" has been used to describe the expanded form of recording agreement that embraces multiple new rights areas.[23] While record companies have annexed publishing and certain merchandising rights in the past, they are now seeking rights in all merchandising, an artist's "official" website, fan club, social media platforms, personal appearances, and other areas the company will actively manage and control. Further, record companies have sought certain "passive" income, or the right to receive a percentage of the artist's income from entertainment-related activities that are not produced or managed by the record company, both during and after the term of the recording agreement. The rationale presented to the artist is that if the record company is going to invest significant resources, at great risk, in developing the identity and market value of an artist through their promotional efforts, the record company should receive a return on that investment from whatever areas the recording artist will receive revenue as a result of that

---

22. *See, e.g.*, Ray Waddell & Ed Christman, *Giant Steps*, BILLBOARD, Oct. 1, 2011, at 4.

23. Ian Brereton, *Beginning of a New Age? The Unconscionability of the "360-Degree' Deal,"* 27 CARDOZO ARTS & ENT. L.J. 167 (2009); Zac Locke, *The New (Record) Deal*, 15 UCLA ENT. L. REV. 105 (2008); Michael Rudell & Neil J. Rosini, *"360" Agreements Reflect Industry's Economic Shift*, ENT. L. & FIN., Oct. 2008.

identity and market value.[24] This is not an argument unavailable to record companies in the past, but it is an argument with greater resonance today, when the risks of investing in the music industry are so much greater.[25]

The expanded provisions of 360 deals have not settled into customary terms or practices, but some general comments can be made. First, if the recording artist permits the record company to operate the artist's "official" website, that operation should only be in effect for the term of the exclusivity provisions of the recording agreement. The artist should continue as the owner of the URL for the website, with the record company operating the site with the artist's permission. Further, the artist should receive all data collected in connection with the operation of the website, such as e-mail and postal mail addresses, purchasing history, and other fan/customer activity. This is achieved by sharing that information with the artist during the term of the agreement, but if that is not possible, then the information should be separately maintained so that it can be delivered to the artist at the conclusion of the agreement. Finally, use of the artist's identity and trademarks should be under proper licenses to the record company to insure that the goodwill created through the operation of the website inures to the benefit of the artist. The same comments would hold true for the operation of an artist's fan club, social media platform, or Twitter, Pinterest, Tumblr, or any similar account.

Second, it is likely that an artist's principal source of revenue, at least for the near future, will not be from the sale or other exploitation of sound recordings. It seems anomalous that an agreement nominally dedicated to the production of sound recordings would control other areas of a performer's career that are likely to be more revenue producing than sound recordings, but that is the value proposition offered by a 360 deal. A recent study by an artist advocacy group[26] found that for musicians who perform,

24. The International Federation of the Phonographic Industry has estimated that the cost of breaking a new pop artist in a major market is approximately $1 million. *See Record Labels Invest $4.5 Billion in New Music*, IFPI (Nov. 12, 2012), http://www.ifpi.org/content/section_news/investing_in_music.html.

25. *See* Jeff Leed, *The New Deal: Band as Brand*, N.Y. TIMES, Nov. 11, 2007, *available at* http://www.nytimes.com/2007/11/11/arts/music/11leed.html?pagewanted=all&_r=0.

26. *Artist Revenue Streams*, FUTURE OF MUSIC COALITION, http://money.futureofmusic.org/ (last visited May 10, 2013).

live performance income was their essential revenue stream. Further, live performances provide leverage for other sources of income from the on-site sale of music and merchandise. The point of these observations is that how one approaches the negotiation of the expanded rights of a 360 deal will depend on the anticipated relative revenue from the various rights being granted to the record company. There is little point in obtaining a greater royalty rate for sound recordings in consideration of granting a percentage of personal appearance income when the revenue from such sound recordings will be relatively less important to the artist. It would be better to retain more of the personal appearance income and accept the lesser royalty rate.

Third, a record company should only be granted enhanced active or passive rights in an artist's talent under a 360 deal when the company has both corresponding operational capabilities to directly manage such rights and makes commitments ensuring value will be created for the artist through the expenditure of record company resources. There is little point in granting a right to a record company that has no means to directly exercise it. To do so only means that the record company will be interposed between the artist and a third party the artist could have contracted with directly, with perhaps little value added by the record company for the value extracted.

The record company commitments for expanded rights under a 360 deal could take the form of confirmed budgets, payments, or release or promotional commitments. The agreement could also establish defined triggers, such as the commercial release of a certain number of albums or the achievement of certain sales or chart positions, which must be achieved before passive income rights vest. The point is that rights should not be granted without assurances that there is an exchange of value and not just a shift in the revenue payee to offset the record company's risk.

Finally, there are multiple points of negotiation with respect to the expanded rights of a 360 deal. In addition to the scope of the actively exercised rights granted to the company, the scope of noncontract revenue subject to a passive percentage interest by the record company needs to be carefully considered, together with the issue of what that percentage might be, what the rate is based on, how long it is paid, and whether it varies over time or with respect to certain revenue sources. Are there separate advances paid for specific rights, and are any rights categories cross-collateralized with other accounts under the agreement? What approvals are required with respect to actively managed rights? With respect to the record company's passive percentage interest, does it have the right to audit the books and records of the artist in the same way that the artist has the right to audit the books and records of the record company? All these questions should be weighed in the balance with the capabilities and commitments of the record company to determine whether a 360 deal is appropriate for the artist.

## Alternative Recording Agreements

At the same time that major record companies are increasing the scope of their capabilities and obtaining a broader range of rights to exploit, the decentralization away from the record companies of the means by which recordings may be produced, distributed, and sold has broad implications for artists looking for alternatives. Tools are available for artists to control many more of the functions previously controlled by the record companies. But just as there is the potential for greater direct reward, there is greater responsibility and risk. Opportunities for arrangements alternative to those generally followed by the major labels do exist for artists preferring the independent label route.

One alternative arrangement is a license agreement between the artist and the record company. Under this scenario, the artist finances the production of the recording and delivers the finished recording to the record company. The record company exploits the rights in the recording that are defined in the license agreement for the period of time and in the territory that are also defined. The record company will generally pay an advance for such rights (which would generally be less than the recording costs incurred by the artist to produce the recording) and a royalty. The royalty could be calculated in the same manner as described above for a recording artist agreement, or it could be arranged on an alternative basis. Alternatives include a set fee if the rights to be exercised by the record company are narrowly restricted to only a few configurations. At the end of the license term, all rights to the recording revert to the artist. The artist is also in a position to license the recording to multiple licensees on a territory-by-territory basis if that is a more favorable arrangement. A license arrangement also does not commit the artist to an exclusive recording arrangement with the record company, although some companies will, as a condition to licensing and promoting a recording, request one or more options to obtain further recordings if the initial licensed recording is successful. Royalty rates are generally higher for licensed recordings than recordings produced under artist agreements, as the risk to the record company is much less. The record company does not have to advance as much cost, and it is able to assess the commercial prospects of a completed recording as opposed to advancing funds for the production of recordings not in being, with all the attendant risks of unfavorable or untimely results.

Another alternative arrangement offered by some independent labels is a profit sharing deal. The arrangement could be in the form of a license of master recordings, co-ownership of the master recordings between the artist and the record company, or a more traditional artist agreement. The principal distinguishing feature of such agreements is that instead of royalties, the artist and the record company share profits derived from the exploitation of the recordings on some defined basis. The key term to be negotiated in such an agreement is of course the definition of shared profits. Usually, the recording costs incurred in producing the record, the manufacturing costs of products (including artwork), advertising and promotional costs (perhaps pursuant to a mutually approved budget), and distribution fees are netted against gross revenue received by the record company. A company overhead charge calculated as a percentage of gross revenue might also be netted against gross revenue. As net profits are realized, they are distributed to the artist in the negotiated portion allocated to the artist, which could remain constant or vary as certain milestones are achieved.

Another alternative arrangement offered by some independent labels is a service provider agreement. Under this agreement, the recording is produced by the artist at the artist's expense and delivered to the record company for manufacture, distribution, promotion, and sale. However, instead of receiving a royalty or a share of the profits, the artist reimburses the record company for the cost of manufacturing the recording. The artist also pays a service fee to the record company for managing the release of the recording. This fee could be a set amount for certain defined responsibilities over a period of time, an actual cost figure uplifted by a certain percentage, a certain percentage of gross revenue, or a blend of any of these factors. The artist realizes his or her return on the profit represented by the remaining sales proceeds. While the record company has a lesser potential return with such an arrangement, its risk is significantly reduced as it has little outlay. The company also recovers its fee and costs from the revenue from the sale of the recording, after which it remits any funds to the artist.

## Producer Agreements

The role of a producer of sound recordings has changed over time as recording technology has advanced. The initial functions of record producers were more along the lines of what is generally performed today by A&R personnel—they identified artists to be recorded by the record company, they helped select compositions to be recorded, and they supervised the recording sessions, which included aligning the performers in front of the primitive sound horns and recording equipment to capture the best sound. As recording technology advanced, the process became more technical. Lab coats were not an infrequent apparel item for sound engineers pictured in photographs of early recording sessions,[27] but the role of the producer mostly remained that of a talent spotter and wrangler. It was their responsibility to capture what a performer sounded like, and make it technically satisfactory for the production of records that could be manufactured and played back. It was with the advent of tape recording, however, that the role of producer as a creative force really came into being.[28]

Prior to the development of tape as a recording medium, recordings captured actual linear performances in a singular process. Nothing could be added to or taken from the recordings, and they were of performances

---

27. *See, e.g.,* PETER MARTLAND, SINCE RECORDS BEGAN: EMI THE FIRST 100 YEARS 138 (Batsford 1997).

28. *See* GREG MILNER, PERFECTING SOUND FOREVER: AN AURAL HISTORY OF RECORDED MUSIC (Faber & Faber 2009) (background on the introduction of recording tape technology in the United States).

occurring in real life.[29] Tape changed everything. Tape permitted editing and multitracking of sound over sound, or, more accurately, sound side-by-side with sound. Tape also permitted manipulation of the recording and playback process to create special effects. In short, tape opened the door for innovation and creative contributions by producers. Today, very little of what we hear in recordings is an accurate capture of the actual sound of a performance. Most popular recordings today are built up through multiple inputs over a period of time that in their final result in no way reflect the capture of anything that actually happened in real life. The creation of such recordings is the role of a producer today, and it has become a very important role, in some cases even more important than the role of the credited performer.

Producers may be engaged either directly by the artist, if the artist is in charge of creating the recording, or by the record company. In either case, it is critical that the agreement with the producer treat the contributions of the producer in the same manner as the contributions of a recording artist are treated in a recording agreement. The contributions should be defined as works made for hire, or, alternatively, assigned to the artist or the record company, respectively. The producer's role in the production of the sound recording will be recognized as copyrightable, and the producer will be considered at least a co-owner of the copyright in the sound recording if a written agreement is not in place addressing that ownership.[30]

The fee producers are paid for their production services generally acts as an advance against royalties, or "points," payable to the producer when the recording is exploited. If the producer is engaged by the artist, the royalty arrangement can be on any terms the parties agree. If the producer is engaged by the record company, however, their royalties are generally calculated and paid in the same manner as the royalties for the recordings produced by the producer are calculated and paid for the artist. The

---

29. Notwithstanding this statement, experiments were conducted as early as 1930 to produce multitrack recordings through the mechanical means of recording individual parts and then recording the simultaneous playback of such recordings, e.g. PAUL HINDEMITH, ORIGINALWERK FÜR SCHALLPLATTE: INSTRUMENTAL TRICKAUFNAHME, (1930) [excerpt], *included in* MARK KATZ, CAPTURING SOUND: HOW TECHNOLOGY HAS CHANGED MUSIC (University of California Press 2004).

30. Diamond v. Gillis, 357 F. Supp. 2d 1003 (E.D. Mich. 2005).

principal difference with respect to producer royalties, however, is that producers start to accrue royalties from the sale of the first record—they are not subject to the recoupment of recording costs as the recording artist is. However, the key word is "accrue." While royalties may start to accrue for the producer upon the sale of the first record, those royalties are held by the record company and not paid to the producer until the recording costs attributed to the recording produced by the producer are recouped. At the point of recoupment, all accrued royalties are paid, net of any advance that may have been paid to the producer for such recordings. The key negotiating point to watch for is the rate at which the recording costs will be deemed "recouped." Will it be the full artist royalty rate, which favors the producer, or the artist's royalty rate, net of the royalty payable to the producer, which favors the record company, since application of a lesser rate will require greater revenue before recoupment occurs.

Another key provision of producer agreements is credit. Credit for the production of recordings is critical to the success of a producer's career, as his or her standing within the industry and ability to command prestigious assignments and fees may turn on how they are associated with successful projects. As discussed earlier, credit will only be enforceable to the extent it is contractually obligated. Therefore, the credit provisions of a producer's agreement should identify the wording of the credit that will be accorded the producer for both original recordings and remixes, the relative size of the credit, and when and where the credit will be accorded. In addition to the producer's name, the producer may want credit to be accorded to the producer's production company, either by name, logo, or both. Failure to accord credit as agreed to may result in significant damages for the record company.[31]

---

31. Popovich v. Sony Music Entm't Inc., 508 F.3d 348 (6th Cir. 2007) ($5.6 million judgment for failure to affix producer logo affirmed); *Composer is Awarded $241,000 in Damages Due to Omission of His Artist Credit on Single Record*, ENT. L. R. 1983 5(6) (Barry De Vorzon claim regarding song "Nadia's Theme"); Stan Soocher, *Lack Of Logo Placement At Center Of Ruling Over Meat Loaf Album Packaging*, ENT. L. & FIN., Jan. 2008.

## Production Company Agreements

The importance of the role producers currently play in the creation of sound recordings is reflected in the variety of ways record companies arrange their relationships with producers. With the exception of an independent label that might be headed by a producer or organized around the output of a particular recording studio, most producers today operate independently from record companies. Few record companies engage staff producers anymore. Producers often work on a project-by-project basis, as described above, but their work can also involve entering agreements with undeveloped recording artists to produce and shop recordings to record companies or even more complex and exclusive joint venture arrangements with record companies.

It is not uncommon for an artist's first recording agreement to arrive in the form of an offer from a production company rather than a record company. The key difference between a production company and a record company is that the principal role of the production company is the production of recordings. The production company does not have the structure or resources to actually market and sell the recordings—those roles are undertaken by the record company to which the recordings produced by the production company are delivered. An independent production company may consist of an individual producer with a recording studio or access to studio facilities, or may be the co-venture partner of a major label with a significant staff and other resources. What is common within this range of capabilities is the fact that the production company does not actually release the recordings it produces but relies upon its relationships with record companies to do so.

An offer to an artist from a production company may feature many of the provisions that are otherwise found in an offer from a record company, particularly with respect to the scope of rights acquired and how royalties are calculated. This is because the production company is either modeling its business arrangements after those customary arrangements adopted by record companies or anticipating becoming a record company itself at some time in the future. The production company may also anticipate assigning the production agreement with an artist to a record company, which the production company anticipates will want to succeed to terms they would have obtained if they had originally signed the artist directly. But because the production company, at least initially, will be relying upon others to actually release and market the recordings, the offer presented by the production company may reference either existing or anticipated record company agreements in several key provisions.

## Development Agreement

Production companies without a distribution or other form of agreement with a record company or the resources or interest in releasing and marketing the recordings itself will generally have interest in developing an artist as a recording artist and shopping the recordings and/or the artist to a record company. The agreements such a production company may offer are speculative. Whether the recordings produced under the agreement are ever commercially exploited depends upon the production company's success in interesting others to acquire the recordings. Under such circumstances, the royalty provisions of the production company offer to the artist are likely to be structured as a percentage of the revenue received by the production company from the buyer or licensee of the recordings. Further, the scope of rights obtained by the production company—merchandising, publishing, etc.—are likely to be defined as those necessary to conform the agreement to the requirements of the buyer or licensee of the recordings.

If the development offer from a production company is speculative, what are the issues the artist should be concerned with? First, the period of time the producer has to actually produce and then shop the recordings should be carefully defined. This period is likely to be exclusive, as the producer does not want to devote resources to the production and marketing of the recordings and be vulnerable to circumvention. In like manner, the artist does not want to be tied to an agreement which bars the artist from other offers if the development work of the production company is not rewarding. A development and shopping period of nine to twelve months is not unreasonable. The agreement should also address how ancillary rights might be handled during the period of the production agreement. Although the producer may not be in position to exploit any ancillary rights, it may need the ability to convey such rights to a buyer. One solution would be to permit the artist to continue to exploit such rights but to not grant rights to any third party that might restrict or impair the production company's ability to grant such rights to a buyer or licensee.

The development agreement should also address issues related to the production of recordings. For example, how many recordings are to be produced, who is responsible for the payment of the costs of producing the recordings, and what is the status of the recordings if the development agreement ends without a buyer or licensee being found? In the development of an artist, many possible paths may be explored, which may be affected by the responses received by the production company to the initial recording efforts from prospective buyers. From the artist's perspective, such early recordings, if they become available, may reflect unfavorably or cause confusion with their later efforts.

The extent the artist will be involved in the transaction with a buyer or licensee of the recordings produced under the production agreement is very important. Will the artist have the ability to approve the buyer or licensee, or any terms of the transaction? Will the production company continue as an intermediary between the artist and the record company buyer/licensee, or will the artist sign a new agreement with the buyer/licensee? If the intention of the buyer/licensee is to enter a long term agreement with the artist, then the artist will have significant control as the transaction is not likely to be completed under such circumstances without the assent of the artist.

The financial implications to the artist of a production company continuing as an intermediary between the artist and the record company are significant. First, the recording cost recoupment arrangement between the artist and the production company may be broader and more inclusive than the arrangement between the production company and the buyer/licensee. This could delay or otherwise unfavorably impact payments to the artist from the production company. There may also be a cash flow issue that could affect the production company's ability or willingness to pay royalties. For example, the artist's account with the production company may be recouped, but the production company's account with the buyer/licensee might not be. This may be caused by any number of circumstances, including the possibility that the production company's account with the buyer/licensee is cross-collateralized with the account of other artists delivered by the production company. A cash flow issue could also occur if the production company gets into a dispute with the buyer/licensee for reasons unrelated to the artist and, as a result, the buyer/licensee withholds payments to the production company or stops promoting or selling the artist's recordings.[32]

Retaining the production company as an intermediary between the artist and the buyer/licensee also has financial impact if the production company experiences financial distress. The party marketing the artist's recordings may be financially healthy, but the amounts otherwise payable to the production company for remittance to the artist could be attached by the creditors of the production company and never see their way to the artist. Further, to the extent funds might be available to the production company, they may be exhausted by payments made to creditors or other artists, which in effect creates a form of unintended cross-collateralization. Finally, the artist's recordings could be embroiled in a bankruptcy or other insolvency proceeding or conflict involving the production company, notwithstanding success that might be achieved by the buyer/licensee with such recordings. Bankruptcy proceedings may even extinguish the obligation to pay royalties on a go-forward basis by the successor in interest to the recording and publishing assets of the production company.[33]

Other nonfinancial implications occur when the production company continues as an intermediary between the artist and the buyer/licensee. Artistically, the artist may wish to work with producers who are not affiliated with the production company. This may be difficult or impossible if the artist remains signed to the production company as opposed to directly with the buyer/licensee. Also, even if the production company has a distribution/marketing agreement with a record company, the production company could lose that arrangement or change to a different record company in a manner disadvantageous to the artist. Finally, a producer may claim rights to aspects of the artist's career in addition to those connected with sound recordings alone, particularly if the producer was instrumental in developing the overall artistic presentation of the artist.[34]

---

32. *See* TVT Records v. The Island Def Jam Music Group, 412 F.3d 82 (2d Cir. 2005).
33. Thompkins v. Lil' Joe Records, Inc., 476 F.3d 1294 (11th Cir. 2007).
34. *See, e.g.,* Rob Fusari Prods. LLC v. Team Love Child LLC, No. 650179 (N.Y. Sup. Ct. 2010).

## Established Production Company

At a certain point in the successful career of a producer, a record company may want to have an exclusive arrangement with the producer in the same way they have exclusive arrangements with artists. This arrangement could take the form of delivery/output for a specific number of recordings during a certain period of time or even a form of joint venture with the record company. In a joint venture, the record company becomes a co-owner of the production company and its recordings.

An agreement between a production company and an established outlet for the distribution and marketing of its recordings is clearly a different prospect than the development arrangements discussed above. Yet, these arrangements still present some of the same issues, particularly with respect to the payment of royalties. If a production company has an established distribution arrangement, it will remain an intermediary between the artist and the record company. The artist is being brought into the transaction as part of the agreement between the production company and the record company. The production company also has certainty it can offer concerning key contractual issues, such as the ownership of recordings produced by the production company, the rights the production company is required to obtain from any artist signed to the production company, and the existence of a royalty structure. Because the established production company is not in a position to be dislodged as an intermediary, the provisions of the production agreement with the artist should be carefully assessed to determine the outcome of the occurrence of any of the adverse financial circumstances mentioned above with respect to a development agreement. This may require inquiry into the terms of the production company/record company agreement or specific undertakings by the record company on behalf of the artist.

# Chapter Six
# **Personal Representatives**

The music industry, like the entertainment industry generally, is characterized by the presence of intermediaries. These representative intermediaries include agents, managers, attorneys, business managers, and others. There are several reasons for this.

First, musicians quite often are away from home for great periods of time, traveling from performance to performance or otherwise engaged in activities demanded by their careers. This disrupts the ability to conveniently confer about matters that require attention, or to obtain execution of certain agreements. Also, artists may not want to give attention to certain business matters for a variety of reasons, including the distraction such matters can give to creative activity, so intermediaries are engaged to handle such matters to relieve the artist of that burden. Artists may also believe the intermediary will be able to relate more knowledgably with business matters to a better result.

Second, performers generally are engaged on a project-by-project basis. They are not employed as regular employees on the payroll of a company over a length of time. This means that the conditions of their work, and their compensation, must be repeatedly negotiated many more times than the employment conditions and compensation applicable to a regular employee. Representatives are specialized in understanding the terms of engaging talent and assume a time-consuming responsibility that would otherwise distract talent from what talent does best.

Third, at their most successful level, the results of a performer's talent create a large and complicated business requiring the contributions of many advisors and assistants. One would assume that a business that grossed, as an example, $1 million or even $500 thousand, would have a staff of employees to handle the myriad administrative and operational details that the business created. With a performer, the business may consist solely of the individual performer and the results of his or her talent, such as personal appearances, recordings, song writing, and other activities. Talent representatives and assistants for a performer are all part of the management team that any executive in a regular business would have to carry out the business of the company. In the talent's case, the business is the talent's career.

Fourth, since talent is engaged on a project-by-project basis, representatives play the dual role of being a scout for opportunities and a filter of proposals. To sustain a career, talent needs a consistent deal flow of financial and career-enhancing opportunities. These opportunities may include a local club performance, the opening performance with a popular artist, or a key merchandising deal. Agents and managers make it their job to identify and promote such opportunities. Conversely, representatives are in a position to deflect or vet proposals that are made to talent that might otherwise be distracting or difficult to avoid. This can also take the form of being the "bad cop," whereby the representative is the person delivering bad news or expressing difficult views, from which the talent may disassociate him- or herself in an effort to create goodwill, avoid friction, and allow professional relationships to exist in a creative environment.

# Agents

The relationship between agents and talent is generally thought to arise under circumstances of good faith and goodwill. Yet, many collapse under circumstances that cause some people to liken it to the relationship between Faust and Mephistopheles:

I will bend myself to your service in this world, to be at your beck and never rest nor slack. When we meet again on the other side, in the same coin you shall pay me back.[1]

While the relationship between an artist and an agent may be just as exclusive and, perhaps, just as stubborn to terminate, the requested commission seldom equals the consuming tribute exacted of Faust, nor does the relationship share that bond's term, impliability, and scope.[2]

The principal role of an agent is to find work for his or her clients. This activity is generally something that is controlled by state or local statute, as agency work in the past has generally been characterized by many abusive practices. In Illinois, for example, employment agencies are required to obtain a license from the Illinois Department of Labor, which involves an application, the posting of a bond, the use of forms that have been approved by the state, and an annual fee. Securing or attempting to secure employment for persons seeking employment without a license is a misdemeanor in Illinois. More importantly, failure to be properly licensed when engaged in agency activities can be a bar to recovery of fees that might otherwise be payable to the agent for their successful efforts, or the grounds for a disgorgement of fees already received. We will address this more fully in the section about personal managers.

Agency relationships with talent are usually exclusive, as agents want to be the exclusive beneficiary of any promotional efforts that they may make on behalf of the talent they represent. However, some agencies work on a nonexclusive basis, particularly those who sell into a market where the identity of the performers may not be critical, such as weddings, private parties, or corporate events. In such cases, a performer may be affiliated with more than one such agency, which will reach out to performers as appropriate to meet client requests.

Agencies generally work on a contingency basis, generally receiving between 10 percent and 15 percent of the compensation payable to the

---

1. JOHANN WOLFGANG VON GOETHE, FAUST (Louis MacNeice trans., Oxford University Press, New York, 1951).

2. "The agreement between Mephistopheles and Faust is against public policy." United Aircraft Corp. v. Boreen, 284 F. Supp. 428, 447–448 (E.D. Pa. 1968).

talent for the engagements arranged by the agent. Compensation for the talent, including deposits for performances, is generally paid to the agent, which then deducts its fees and remits the balance to the talent. The scope of an agent's responsibility may be a negotiated term. This is particularly important for performers with career opportunities in entertainment areas other than music, such as book publishing or television or film appearances, where more specialized agents may offer better representation.

The time period of an agent's representation is a negotiated term that has greatest importance when the relationship is exclusive. Because of the personal nature of the relationship between talent and an agent, some talent may want to negotiate a provision which allows the talent to terminate the agreement upon his or her election after a certain notice period. If that provision is not obtainable, then the talent's right to terminate could be tied to a certain performance achievement by the agent, such as a minimum dollar amount of compensation earned during a defined period. If the talent is drawn to the agency because of the presence of a certain individual who the talent prefers to work with, the talent might obtain a key-man provision, permitting the talent to terminate the agency agreement if the key individual was no longer available to work with the talent.

The legal relationship between an agent and talent will depend on the express provisions of the agency agreement and upon their respective circumstances in the relationship. Agency agreements typically contain a power of attorney provision permitting the agent to execute agreements on behalf of the talent and to negotiate certain instruments, such as checks. Since the agent is the business office of the talent for purposes of finalizing agreements and collecting payments, permitting the agent to sign contracts for the talent's performances and deposit payments is generally necessary and desirable. Granting a power of attorney beyond these functions is generally not advisable.

Whether the relationship between the agent and the talent is one of a fiduciary is determined on the basis of the respective circumstances of the parties at the time. The fact that the agent is a representative of the talent does not in and of itself create a fiduciary relationship. There must be the repose of trust and confidence by the talent in the agent beyond a conventional business relationship. One approach to this point is to address it in the agreement between the agent and the talent. Some suggested language concerning the remittance of payments to the talent is the following:

> Any portion of the compensation for Artist's services which may become due to Artist shall, if not paid immediately on the receipt thereof by Agent, belong to Artist and shall be held in trust for Artist until payment is made; the ownership of said trust fund by Artist shall not be questioned whether the monies are physically segregated or not.

The efforts the agent must expend on behalf of the talent when the relationship is exclusive are generally the agent's commercially reasonable efforts. Since such efforts are difficult to assess in retrospect and will of course differ from the subjective perspectives of the parties, the agreement between the agent and talent could establish specific initiatives or goals to help quantify this effort. From the talent's perspective, the responsibility could also be elevated to require the agent's "best" efforts to obtain engagements under the best possible terms and conditions. Below is suggested language along these lines to include in the agency agreement:

> Agent agrees to conduct all transactions with respect to Artist diligently and in good faith and at all times to give Artist full information and truthful explanation of all matters relative to Agent's activities under this agreement, including but not limited to the persons with whom Agent is in contact during the Term in connection with Artist. Agent agrees to report to Author immediately of any offers that Agent obtains.

One development that has occurred in the last few years is the appearance of online services to help musicians obtain paid performance opportunities. Websites such as GigMasters, ReverbNation, and Sonicbids offer the ability for musicians to identify venues appropriate for their music and promote themselves to potential buyers. The relationship between the talent and the online services will be defined by the respective site's service agreements, but generally the services should be viewed as tools to facilitate engagement agreements. The online services are not active agents soliciting and promoting talent but instead are creating a more efficient market by provid-ing the means by which buyers and talent may communicate and connect among themselves. These services generally operate on a subscription basis with various tiers of service available, and may charge an additional fee for engagements they have successfully facilitated.

Another online form of agency that has recently arisen is the music licens-ing services offered by websites such as Taxi, Musicdealers, Pump Audio, You License, Musync, Jingle Punks, and Rumblefish. These services generally represent the recordings of their clients to music users on a nonexclusive basis under business models that vary from site to site. The services are often referred to as "retitling" libraries for the reason that in order to dis-tinguish and track the usage of recordings they have licensed apart from licensed uses of the same recording that may have been arranged by oth-ers, the agency will retitle the recordings they represent with titles that are unique to their service. As a result, one's work may appear in the market under various titles, with usage calculated on an individual project basis as opposed to what may be a more favorable aggregate basis.[3] Of course, this may be a happy problem for the owner of a recording, who may be very pleased that his or her recordings are being used multiple times.

## Personal Managers

The principal role of a personal manager is to guide the careers of the tal-ent they manage.[4] The responsibility is broader than that of an agent. The following is typical language from a music manager agreement published by the National Conference of Personal Managers:

> As and when requested by me during and throughout the term hereof, you agree to perform for me one or more of the services as follows:

---

3. Ron Mendelsohn, *Ron Mendelsohn on Signing with a Non-Exclusive Retitling Library*, FILM MUSIC MAGAZINE (June 18, 2010), http://www.filmmusicmag.com/?p=5673.
4. For a very helpful review of the provisions of manager contracts for musicians, see Kent Newsome, *Designing Management Contracts for Musicians*, 21 ENT. & SPORTS LAW. 1 (Summer 2003).

advise and counsel in the selection of literary, artistic, and musical material; advise and counsel in any and all matters pertaining to publicity, public relations and advertising; advise and counsel with relation to the adoption of proper format for presentation of my artistic talents and in the determination of proper style, mood, setting, business, and characterization in keeping with my talents; advise, counsel, and direct in the selection of artistic talent to assist, accompany, or embellish my artistic presentation; advise and counsel with regard to general practices in the entertainment and amusement industries and with respect to such matters of which you may have knowledge concerning compensation and privileges extended for similar artistic values; and advise and counsel concerning the selection of theatrical agencies, artists' managers, and persons, firms, and corporations who will counsel, advise, seek, and procure employment and engagements for me.[5]

You may notice that the above description of services does not include soliciting employment for the artist. The manager may in fact counsel a performer to *not* accept proposed engagements when the manager believes such engagements might not be beneficial to the performer. Further, in some cases, as we will see, soliciting employment for an artist client without also being licensed as an employment agency can create serious problems for a manager.

Recent developments in the music industry have made the role of personal managers more centric. The traditional functions of record companies that solidified their central role in the development of musical artists—talent discovery, capital, distribution, and marketing—have been challenged by the availability, and relative inexpense, of technological tools that more widely distribute such functions within the means of more artists. Platforms such as social media provide means to create fan followings of artists, recordings can be made within reasonable budgets, and digital distribution is available through a variety of alternative means. While marketing remains a significant obstacle for artists unaffiliated with a record company, the tools are

---

5. *Music Manager Agreement*, NATIONAL CONFERENCE OF PERSONAL MANAGERS, INC., at 1 (2009).

there for artists to be more self-sufficient and independent. This creates greater opportunity, and responsibility, for managers to manage these tools and relationships. An example at the top end of the industry, the Eagles recorded their own last album and released it through their own distribution setup through Wal-Mart. At the center of all these arrangements was their management company, which managed the central business entity that was the Eagles/the group.

The skill set required of managers today has also changed. The availability of tools that permit artists to conduct and operate the business of exploiting rights as the result of their talent, as opposed to turning such rights over to other companies to exploit and remit a royalty payment to them, means that the manager is required to take on different operational functions. The job of operating the business of, for example, merchandising or record distribution instead of managing the relationship between the band and the company that performs such functions requires different talents, which should be considered when the selection of management services is being made.

The agreement a manager may have with an artist deals with some of the same issues that are present in an agency agreement. Management agreements are invariably exclusive, as the role of the manager is not as easily parsed between entertainment areas and the efforts of the manager are meant to create value across all entertainment forms. Because the relationship is more personal, the ability to terminate the agreement if the relationship breaks down or a key person becomes unavailable takes on greater significance. The measure of a manager's performance may also be quantified in some objective fashion along the lines discussed in connection with agents, such as the undertaking of specific tasks or the achievement of certain financial goals as a condition for continuing the agreement.

Because of the personal aspect of the managerial relationship, managers generally have fewer clients. In some cases, they have only one. The compensation managers receive is generally a contingent payment based upon the entertainment income of the artist and generally ranges from 20 percent to 25 percent. Of course, there are exceptions, such as Colonel Parker's reported 50 percent commission as the manager for Elvis Presley. The manager's commission is usually higher than an agent's because with fewer clients, the commissionable base for the manager is less than an agent's. Also, the manager is taking an overall greater risk, as he or she is responsible for providing management services even when the artist is not engaged in remunerative activities.

The more personal and encompassing responsibilities of a manager often means that the manager will become involved with the overall financial affairs of the talent, with many payments being made by the manager on behalf of the talent. While such arrangements may have the appeal of expediency, the manager should not be given complete control over the talent's financial affairs. Instead, the financial activities of the manager should be subject to periodic review by other members of the talent's team, such as the talent's business manager or attorney. The consequences of reposing complete, unmonitored financial trust and authority in one's manager have often been devastating to performers.[6]

The commission payable to a manager may be negotiated in several ways. The commission may vary depending on the amount of the commissionable base, going either up or down after hitting certain income milestones, or not applying at all until a certain minimum is reached. Funds received by an artist that are dedicated to the production of certain works, such as sound recordings, should be carved out of the commissionable base. Certain investment income that is unrelated to the artist's career should also be exempted. One important issue to resolve is the extent to which the manager will earn a commission on the revenue received by the artist during the term of the manager's agreement that is derived from agreements in existence prior to the commencement of the management agreement. In like manner, the extent to which the manager will continue to receive a commission after the management agreement is over for agreements entered during the term of the management agreement must be resolved. Generally, managers will continue to receive commissions on such agreements, but the post-term commission might be reduced, or "sunsetted," in anticipation of that same revenue being commissionable by a successor manager.

The relationship between a manager and an artist is not per se a fiduciary relationship but may develop into one. One significant case which addressed

---

6. *See, e.g.,* Natural Wealth Real Estate, Inc. v. Cohen, 2008 WL 511761 (D. Colo. 2008).

this issue was *Reznor v. J. Artist Management, Inc.*,[7] which involved claims asserted by Trent Reznor of Nine Inch Nails against a former manager, including a claim for breach of fiduciary duty. In *Reznor*, the court found that, under New York law, a fiduciary relationship exists when one person "is under a duty to act for or to give advice for the benefit of another upon matters within the scope of the relation."[8] In denying cross motions for summary judgment on the issue of fiduciary duty, the court concluded that, at the time Reznor and his former manager entered their management agreement, a jury could find that the relationship was informal enough to be a conventional business arrangement. But the court also concluded that a jury could find that as the relationship progressed, the manager became a trusted advisor such that a fiduciary relationship was created that bound the manager to a standard of fairness, good faith, and loyalty. As with the agency agreement, specific language in the agreement between the manager and the artist could address this issue, although states are split on the question of whether one may disclaim a fiduciary duty by contract.[9]

Another interesting case that addresses the responsibility of an artist's manager post-termination of the management relationship is *ABKCO Music, Inc. v. Harrisongs Music, Ltd.*,[10] which involved a dispute between George Harrison of the Beatles and his prior manager Alan Klein. During Klein's tenure as Harrison's manager, he handled matters relating to a copyright infringement action brought against Harrison by the publisher of the song "He's So Fine." The lawsuit resulted in a finding of liability against Harrison. After Klein's management agreement ended, but before damages had been determined in the lawsuit against Harrison, Klein covertly acquired ownership of the song "He's So Fine" and thus a stake adverse to Harrison in the litigation. When all was revealed, Klein was forced to give up his interest in the song based on his violation of his duties to Harrison to not use what he had learned as Harrison's manager against Harrison. While one

---

7. Reznor v. J. Artist Mgmt., Inc., 365 F. Supp. 2d 565 (S.D.N.Y. 2005).
8. *Id.* at 574.
9. BNP Paribas Mortg. Corp. v. Bank of Am., N.A., 2012 WL 2026063, 9 (S.D.N.Y. 2012) (duty may be disclaimed); Hands on Video Relay Servs., Inc. v. American Sign Language Servs. Corp., 2009 WL 8691614 (E.D. Cal. 2009) (duty exists apart from contract).
10. ABKCO Music, Inc. v. Harrisongs Music, Ltd., 722 F.2d 990 (2d Cir. 1983).

certainly hopes one's manager will be a savvy advocate, the case brings to mind Aesop's fable about the snake at the bosom, which repays kindness with a fatal bite: "You knew I was a snake when you took me in."

One area of persistent tension in the manager-artist agreement is the extent to which a manager will seek employment for the artist, and what the consequences are for the manager if he or she does. As mentioned earlier in connection with agents, the solicitation of employment without a proper license may violate various state laws. The violation of such laws has forced certain managers who sought employment for their artists to return commissions they had previously received for their efforts. In some cases, returning commissions has resulted in restitution of several million dollars.[11]

If managers are aware of the severe consequences for not being licensed as an employment agent, why do more managers not simply obtain a license? California provides some good reasons why not. To comply with California's licensure requirements for operating as an agent, the agent must submit his or her contracts with the talent and fee schedules, post and maintain a bond in the amount of $50,000, and maintain records of his or her efforts for inspection by the state.[12] Most managers do not accept these restraints.

The scope of permissible employment seeking activity in which a manager may be engaged will depend on the state in which the manager is operating. In California, a manager is permitted to seek recording agreements for artist clients without a finding that they are an unlicensed employment agent.[13] In New York, managers may seek employment opportunities for artist clients that are only "incidental" to their management efforts.[14] In Illinois, the licensure provisions of the Department of Labor for employment agents has been interpreted to apply to placement services to the general public, not to managers.[15] The Illinois licensing requirements have also been held to not be applicable to attorneys seeking employment opportunities for their clients.[16]

---

11. The following cases were decided by the State of California Labor Commission: Pryor v. Franklin, No. TAC 17 MP114 (1982); Hall v. X Mgmt., No. TAC 19-90 (1991).

12. *See generally* CAL. LAB. CODE §§ 1700–1700.47 (1994).

13. CAL. LAB. CODE § 1700.4 (1994).

14. N.Y. Gen. Bus. Article 11, § 171(8) (2004).

15. Zinn v. Parrish, 644 F.2d 360 (7th Cir. 1981).

16. Musburger v. Meier, 394 Ill. App. 3d 781 (1st Dist. 2009).

Recent developments have reduced the punitive risk managers take when seeking employment for their artist clients. In 2008, the California Supreme Court decided in the case of *Marathon v. Blasi*[17] that a near-reflexive policy of disgorgement of all fees by an unlicensed manager that sought employment for his or her clients was not supportable. Instead, the Court stated that the doctrine of severability could be applied so that the prohibited aspects of the management agreement (procurement) could be severed from the permitted (advice, counseling, and the like). Thus, the Court said, "For the personal manager who truly acts as a personal manager, however, an isolated instance of procurement does not automatically bar recovery for services that could lawfully be provided without a license."[18]

A second development was the opinion in the Supreme Court case of *Preston v. Ferrer.*[19] In *Preston,* the Court was required to determine whether an arbitration provision in an agreement trumped state regulation of the activity that was the subject of the agreement. The Court found that an arbitration agreement between parties engaged in commercial activity subject to state regulation removed jurisdiction from the state agency empowered to enforce the regulation. By so holding, the Court handed managers a powerful tool to avoid having their disputes with artist clients heard within a framework of unfavorable precedent, which in the case of California was the California Department of Labor. From the perspective of a manager, arbitration provisions are now viewed much more favorably.

Another area that often arises in manager-artist agreements is the treatment of minors. Minors may have significant careers as musical artists and require the services of managers and agents. Most states have procedures in place for the approval of agreements with minors to make them enforceable and not subject to disaffirmance by the minors.[20] While the signature of a parent on behalf of a minor will not create an enforceable agreement, it can enable the manager or agent to recover from the parent whatever damages they suffer as a result of a disaffirmance. Further, even though an

---

17. Marathon v. Blasi, 42 Cal. 4th 974 (Cal. 2008).
18. *Id.* at 998.
19. Preston v. Ferrer, 552 U.S. 346 (2008).
20. *See, e.g.,* CAL. LAB. CODE § 1700.37 (1994); CAL. FAM. CODE § 6751; Illinois Artistic Contracts by Minors Act (820 ILCS 20/); N.Y. ARTS & CULT. AFF. § 35.03.

entertainment contract with a minor may be disaffirmed, the termination of the agreement may not foreclose the enforcement of the agreement for purposes of collecting fees due under the agreement from when it was in place.[21]

Conflict resolution is an additional area that bears attention in an agreement between a manager and artist. First, the artist should have strong rights to audit the books and records of the manager to determine the accuracy and completeness of statements and payments made to the artist, both during the term of the management agreement and for a period thereafter. The venue and jurisdiction provisions for where dispute resolution will occur are also key. Finally, arbitration should be considered as an alternative to litigation for two reasons. First, the parties could agree to the use of an arbitrator familiar with the entertainment industry, which may expedite the proceeding and perhaps lead to a determination more acceptable to the parties. Second, arbitration maintains the confidentiality of the proceedings, and the parties' financial information.[22] Organizations that offer mediation and arbitration services in the area of music disputes are listed in Appendix A.

## Business Managers

A business manager is generally responsible for the financial caretaking of the artist's business matters.[23] The business manager does not provide counsel about the direction of the artist's career, but instead would provide accounting services and perhaps insure that payments are tracked and collected, bills are paid, and the business of the artist runs efficiently and productively. Business managers are quite often accountants and may provide tax planning, return preparation, investment advice, statement review, auditing of royalty accounts, preparation of financial statements and other

---

21. Scott Eden Mgmt. v. Kavovik, 563 N.Y.S. 2d 1001 (N.Y. Sup. Ct. 1990), *aff'd*, 197 A.D.2d 569 (1993).

22. For an article discussing the benefits of mediation to resolve entertainment disputes, see Richard S. Reisberg, *Why Entertainment Disputes Are Well Suited for Mediation*, Corp. Counsel, Aug. 2005, at A4–5.

23. *See generally* Glenn Peoples, *Money Never Sleeps*, Billboard, Apr. 2, 2011 at 20–21.

financial reports, and management of certain vendor relationships such as insurance. Business managers are particularly key in planning and managing personal appearance tours and dealing with settlements with promoters, payroll, and tax obligations in the multiple states where appearances occur. The fee arrangements with business managers will depend on the scope of services provided, and the revenue generated by the artist. It is not uncommon for business managers of established high-income artists to charge 5 percent of the artist's income. Because of the financial aspects of the business manager's responsibilities and the special expertise he or she typically brings to the role, the business manager relationship will generally be considered a fiduciary relationship.[24]

---

24. ABKCO Music, Inc. v. Harrisongs Music, Ltd., 722 F.2d 990 (2d Cir. 1983).

# Chapter Seven
# Personal Appearances

In a world where creative expression is increasingly distributed and consumed in a solitary experience by means of digital transmission, the communal experience of witnessing a live personal performance of a musical artist takes on greater meaning and reward.[1] The following are some of the issues relating to a broad range of circumstance involving live performances.

## Busking

Busking, or performing in a public place, usually for the purpose of soliciting compensation, is almost as old as music itself. And regulation of busking has been around almost as long. The Roman Republic, in the Laws of the Twelve Tables, barred the performance of defamatory song upon pain of death.[2] Mayor LaGuardia banned street musicians entirely in New York City in 1935, which lasted until Mayor Lindsey lifted the ban in 1970.

---

1. Digital distribution has also made it possible for performing artists to syndicate live personal performances to individual subscribers through the assistance of such websites as www.Stageit.com and www.Evinar.com.

2. Cohen, David and Ben Greenwood. (1981). *The Buskers: A History of Street Entertainment*. London: David and Charles, page 14.

Other municipalities have long sought to control public performances for various reasons.

The regulation of busking is generally premised on the need to protect public safety and avoid nuisance. These state interests must be balanced with the First and Fourteenth Amendment rights of the performer. Generally, the time, place and manner regulations effecting expressive conduct may be enforced if they are reasonable, content neutral, narrowly tailored to serve significant government interest, and leave open ample alternative channels of communication.[3] Local regulation for street performers reasonably related to issues of sound volume, access to public ways, entrances and exits, traffic flow, and conduct affecting the function or management of public places may be enforced.[4] However, licensing schemes that principally have as their origin the protection of merchants complaining of lost business have had a difficult time surviving challenges.[5]

## House Concerts

The presentation of musical performances in private homes is not a new idea. Until the emergence of recorded music in the late nineteenth century, of course, the performance of music in the home with and for guests was a common occurrence. However, the idea of home concerts has resurrected itself in contemporary form and has become a popular form of social entertaining, although not one without its own set of legal issues.

House concerts implicate local regulation when they begin to take on the features of commercial activity. When that occurs, local zoning laws may start to apply. An occasional presentation of musical performances in one's home for one's private guests would not draw regulation. However, the frequency of the events, how they are advertised and promoted, particularly if to a general audience, and whether and how an admission

---

3. Ward v. Rock Against Racism, 491 U.S. 781, 790 (1989); Friedrich v. Chicago, 619 F. Supp. 1129, 1142. (N.D. Ill. 1985).

4. Carew-Reid v. Metropolitan Transp. Auth. 903 F.2d 914 (2d Cir. 1990).

5. *See, e.g.*, Perry v. Los Angeles Police Dep't, 121 F.3d 1365 (9th Cir. 1997); Horton v. City of St. Augustine, Fla., 2000 WL 35918961 (M.D. Fla. 2000).

charge is collected may cause the activity to be characterized as commercial. If the activity is commercial, it may require commercial licensure or presentation at a venue located in a nonresidential area.[6] If characterized as commercial, it is also possible that such activity could run afoul of applicable condominium, co-op, or housing development bans or restrictions on the engagement of commercial activities in the homes subject to such restrictions. This would particularly be the case if the house concert activities were brought to the attention of one's neighbors as a result of regularly increased traffic, parking congestion, or noise.

House concerts also raise liability issues for those who are the presenters. Home owner's insurance policies may or may not cover premises liability for guests, particularly if the guests are deemed to be commercial patrons of a commercial activity. House concerts also may involve staging, lighting, and sound equipment not normally found in the home, which may create hazards. Finally, serving alcohol may create liability, particularly if the concerts are deemed commercial and/or the alcoholic beverages are sold.

## Public Venues

The range of circumstances under which a musician may publicly perform is broad. The focus of this chapter will be on individual performances, as the issues involved with touring are beyond the scope of this book.

Terms of an agreement engaging the personal services of a musician to perform may be negotiated by the artist's agent or by the artist directly. Basic terms include the following: the identity of the artist engaged, the place of performance, the date, the time of equipment load-in and sound check, and the time and duration of performance. The following sections detail additional terms that should also be addressed.

---

6. Harris v. Township of O'Hara, 2008 WL 2265294 (3d Cir. 2008).

## Compensation

Payment for a personal appearance can take several forms, with multiple variations within each method. Typical forms include flat fee, straight percentage, flat fee against a percentage, or flat fee plus percentage.

A flat fee is a guaranteed set amount, which is not dependent on ticket prices, sales, or any other factor. Payment is generally made by cash or certified check and may be made in installments—a portion paid upon confirmation of the engagement (usually held by the artist's agent if involved) and the balance upon performance.

Percentage compensation is generally based upon admission revenue, excluding tax. The percentage can be applied to all revenue or to revenue in excess of certain delineated costs incurred by the talent buyer. For example, a performer appearing at a music club may receive 85 percent of all admission revenue in excess of the costs of lighting, sound system, and security. Since the amount the performer will receive is unknown until revenue is calculated on the night of performance, payment is generally made in cash.

The risks of a straight percentage arrangement to an artist are many. If cash is used for admission, all the cash may not be reported to the artist, either because of skimming by the talent buyer or his or her employees. Also, the talent buyer (or his or her employees) may admit some people for free as a trade-off, or if the talent buyer believes their portion of the admission revenue is immaterial to the amount the people admitted for free are likely to spend on food or drinks. Because of the potential for abuse, a straight percentage agreement, or "playing for the door," is disfavored although perhaps inevitable for emerging artists performing in smaller venues.[7]

An arrangement paying the greater of a flat fee or a percentage guarantees the artist a minimum fee, which can be increased if admission revenue exceeds a certain negotiated amount. For example, an artist might negotiate an agreement to receive $1,000, plus 30 percent of all ticket revenue in

---

7. As disfavored as "playing for the door" may be, certain other practices are even more unfavorable to artists. For example, some music clubs have as a condition for appearing at the venue the requirement that the performer purchase a certain number of admission tickets, which the performer is then required to resell as his or her compensation for the appearance. Also, the appearance of a performer as a supporting act on a tour may be conditioned on the payment of fees for the privilege of being involved.

excess of 150 tickets sold. The variable fee paid to the artist might also be calculated as a percentage of all admission revenue in excess of an amount permitting the talent buyer to recover his or her costs, including the guarantee. That amount is called the "breakeven" point. Whatever the arrangement, the talent buyer will be required to support his or her costs at the end of the evening when payment to the artist is settled.

Under a flat fee plus a percentage arrangement, an artist is paid a negotiated guarantee. The artist also receives a percentage of the amount by which admission revenue exceeds the sum of the breakeven mentioned above and a certain amount designated as the promoter profit. This sum is called the split point. The promoter profit is frequently calculated as 15 percent of the promoter's breakeven point for the presentation of the event, other than the amount paid to the artist as a guarantee. For example, assume the artist negotiates a $50,000 guarantee, plus 80 percent of all admission revenue in excess of the split point. Also assume that the total admission revenue for the contracted event is $250,000, that the promoter's breakeven (without the guarantee) is $100,000, and that the promoter's profit is agreed to be 15 percent. In such case, the split point would be $165,000 ($150,000 [the breakeven plus the guarantee] plus 15 percent of $100,000), the amount in excess of the split point would be $85,000 ($250,000, less $165,000), and the amount payable to the artist would be $118,000 ($50,000, plus 80 percent of $85,000). These figures are not representative but are used simply for illustration, as each of the variables in the calculation is negotiable depending on the appeal of the artist and the costs involved in presenting the appearance.

## Hospitality and Benefits

Compensation can be paid to an artist by means other than dollars. For example, an artist might negotiate for the payment of travel and accommodation expenses by a promoter, who may have sponsor arrangements with hotels or airlines. An artist's agreement may also describe the type of ground transportation provided and the destinations and times involved with such ground transportation. The artist may also negotiate for the promoter to pay the rental costs of instruments or other equipment necessary for the performance, which is referred to as the "backline." The artist might also receive a certain number of complimentary tickets or the ability to purchase additional tickets in desirable locations.

While some performers are renowned for the extravagant excesses of their demands, the purpose of the hospitality provisions in an artist's agreement is not vanity. The goal of the performing artist is to deliver a great audience experience. The ability of the artist to do that is enhanced when the artist's comfort and sensibility are supported. Comfortable, private, and well-lit dressing rooms with outlets, towels, mirrors, appropriate food and drink, furniture, and utensils are keys to an artist's ability to deliver a good performance.

Proper security is another way a promoter helps both support a good performance and eliminate liability. This includes securing the backstage area, the route to and from backstage, and all equipment, limited sound check access, on-stage protection, audience control, and proper evacuation instruction.

## Billing

How an artist is billed for a performance may be standardized for certain venues, but any special requirements an artist may have should be addressed in a performance agreement.[8] For example, an artist may wish to be identified by a particular typeface or logo in advertisements, publicity, tickets, and venue signage. An artist may also have certain sponsor arrangements that require a reference of the relationship between the artist and the sponsor. The relative type, color, size, and position of billing accorded to multiple performers at an event may also be the subject of negotiation.

## Merchandising

The sale of artist-related merchandise—recordings, apparel, etc.—will be handled differently by different venues. Some artist-friendly venues supply facilities and staff without charge to help the artist sell merchandise. Other venues may charge a so-called hall fee ranging from 10 percent to

---

8. It is also critical that the performer be properly identified when he or she is being presented to a talent buyer for consideration of an appearance. *See, e.g.,* Finley v. River North Records, Inc., 148 F.3d 913 (8th Cir. 1998).

25 percent of revenue. Whatever may be the arrangement, it is important to address in the artist's performance agreement the facilities and personnel that will be provided for merchandising sales, if any, and the fees involved. The artist should also be assured that his or her merchandising arrangements will be exclusive for the event so that the artist's own sales are not in competition with other offerings. A promoter generally does not share in any merchandising revenue unless it owns the venue, in which case it may receive a hall fee.

## Cancellations

The consequences of an event cancellation will turn on the terms of the artist's engagement agreement and when a binding commitment to perform has been made between the parties.[9] If a promoter paid a deposit to secure the performance of an artist, the promoter will generally forfeit that deposit if he or she elects to cancel the appearance prior to the performance date. A cancellation due to the occurrence of a force majeure will generally excuse the parties from liability, but the issue should be addressed specifically in the engagement agreement. Whether an artist's illness constitutes a force majeure also will depend on the language of the agreement. Generally, the risk of nonperformance due to weather is borne by the talent buyer. The artist is engaged to perform "rain or shine," so if an event is cancelled because of bad weather, payment is still due to the artist with it being understood that weather-related risks are insurable by the promoter.[10]

Given the way in which an artist's fortunes may quickly change for the better, some artists may seek provisions in their engagement agreements permitting them to terminate the agreement upon a certain advance notice if the terms of the engagement are no longer favorable.

---

9. *See, e.g.*, Allgood Entm't, Inc. v. Dileo Entm't & Touring, Inc., 2010 WL 3322530 (S.D.N.Y. 2010).

10. Susan Page White, *A Primer on Insurance Coverage for Live Events*, ENT. L. & FIN., Sept. 2012, at 3; *see also* Robert I. Steiner, Richard D. Milone & Elizabeth C. Johnson, *When the Show Can't Go On: Seeking Insurance Recovery for Concert Cancellations*, ENT. L. & FIN., Apr. 2011.

## Technical Riders

Performances require various levels of technical conformity between the needs of the artist and the capabilities of a venue. On a basic level, a venue will need to know a performer's stage plot—what equipment and microphones will be needed and where they will be placed on the stage. The venue and the artist will also need to communicate in advance concerning lights, monitors, cabling, microphones, inputs, and any special effects that are required, such as video projections, staging, or power requirements. Technical riders may also identify the number and type of personnel required at the venue to accommodate the setup and performance, along with their contact information in order to facilitate necessary advance work.

## Exclusivity

Talent buyers generally want to know that the appearance of an artist they are promoting will be exclusive for a period of time within the area from which they draw their audience. The talent buyer does not want to promote the appearance of an artist, only to find out that the artist is also appearing a few days later in the same area.

The provision in an artist's agreement that bars them from appearing within a certain geographic location during a certain period of time is called a "radius" clause. The variables affecting an artist's exclusivity commitment will depend on the prominence of the event and the geographic range of attendees. For example, a major music festival may demand that the artist not appear within a 300-mile radius of the festival location 180 days before the event and ninety days thereafter. The radius clause for a smaller club will be correspondingly less, perhaps fifty to one hundred miles within a thirty-or sixty-day period. For musicians who only perform locally, a radius clause would not be practical unless the compensation for an appearance were significant. In any event, any radius clause commitment given by an artist must be carefully considered to avoid impairing the artist's ability to accept other opportunities.

## Proceeds of Personal Performances

The presentation of a personal performance may result in the creation of valuable property, such as audio or audiovisual recordings or photographs of the performance. The unconsented recording, transmission, sale, or rental of copies of live musical performances is a both a civil copyright violation[11] and a criminal offense.[12] However, artists frequently permit the presenting venue of a performance to record that performance on the artist's behalf and to deliver that recording at the end of the performance in consideration of the reimbursement of the venue's costs. The artist may then use the recording for archival purposes or to offer to their fans.

Photographs of performances are not controlled in the same manner as recordings, but the taking of photographs having an image of a commercially valuable quality may be managed by controlling access to areas from where such photographs might be captured. Rights to photographs taken within the performance area might also be controlled by means of language granting rights in such works to the artist as a condition to the purchase of a ticket, or by means of a waiver signed as a condition to obtaining access to photo-taking areas.[13]

## Ticketing

A ticket is generally considered a license to enter a venue at a specific time on a specific date and sit in a specific seat or remain in a certain area to view what is presented at the time, subject to the terms and conditions and

---

11. *See* 17 U.S.C. § 1101(a), implementation of the anti-bootlegging provisions of the Uruguay Round Agreements Act of 1994, Pub. L. No. 103-465, Sec. 512, 108 Stat. 4809.

12. Unauthorized Fixation of and Trafficking in Sound Recordings and Music Videos of Live Musical Performances, 18 U.S.C. § 2319A (2008); *see also* Kiss Catalog v. Passport Int'l Prods., 405 F. Supp. 2d 1169 (C.D. Cal. 2005) (18 U.S.C. § 2319A enforced against a constitutional challenge).

13. Robert W. Clarida & Robert J. Bernstein, *Aggressive Copyright Positions by Lady Gaga, Burning Man Festival*, ENT. L. & FIN., June 2011.

policies of the venue. It is not a guarantee of subjective satisfaction with what is presented.[14]

Tickets can be categorized as either "hard" or "soft." A hard ticket refers to the customary experience of paying for admission to a venue for the purpose of seeing a performer. The ticket price reflects the ability of the performer to draw an audience, and ticket prices in such instances are generally determined between the promoter and the performer (assuming the performer is sharing in the overall ticket revenue in some manner). A soft ticket refers to the circumstance where admission to the performance may be incidental to admission to other activities, such as a fair, festival, or similar event, and the performer is perhaps being used as a draw to attract audiences for such other activities (and revenue streams). In such instances, the ticket price may be unrelated to the actual drawing power of the performer or even free, and the performer would not be involved in setting the ticket price.

The ticket seller for an event may be determined by the promoter, by the venue, or by the artist. Promoters will generally want to select the ticket seller in order to control the terms of the service, including rebates, to retain data concerning the purchasers of tickets, and to keep confidential information concerning their events from competitors which may own ticketing services. However, since venues often enter exclusive arrangements with ticket sellers, including so-called "white label" services which permit the venue to brand the ticket service as their own, a promoter may be required to use a specific ticket service as a condition to using a particular venue. Services such as ScoreBig, which focus on discounted "name your own price" sales, are used to augment regular sales channels. Services such as Nimbit and Etix also permit artists to sell tickets directly to their fans.

The growth of electronic ticketing has created new ways of conceiving the utility of a ticket. Data associated with a ticket purchaser, such as preferences or prior purchases, can be used to value-load a ticket with night-of-performance offers of food, drink, or merchandise purchase credit

---

14. Brian A. Rosenblatt, *I Know It's Only Rock and Roll, But Did They Like It?: An Assessment of Causes of Action Concerning the Disappointment of Subjective Consumer Expectations Within the Live Performance Industry*, 13 UCLA ENT. L. REV. 33 (2005).

for redemption at the venue, which become activated when the ticket is scanned at admission. Radio-frequency identification can also be used with wristbands to eliminate the need for cash at an event, to facilitate pre-purchase of products or services to be redeemed at the event, or to track the movement of the wristband wearer within the event to gather marketing information. Paperless tickets have also impacted the secondary market for tickets,[15] as, unlike a physical property, the transferability of an electronic ticket to an entertainment event can be controlled much as the transferability of an airline ticket is controlled. In response, ticket resellers such as StubHub and TicketsNow have launched efforts such as the Fan Freedom Project[16] to maintain the secondary market in tickets without interruption.

---

15. *See generally*, Eric Schroeder, Josh Fisher, John Orbe & John Bush, *A Brief Overview on Ticket Scalping Laws, Secondary Ticket Markets, and the Stubhub Effect*, 30 ENT. & SPORTS LAW. 1 (Nov. 2012).

16. FAN FREEDOM PROJECT, http://www.fanfreedom.org (last visited Jan. 20, 2013).

# Chapter Eight
# **Distribution**

Perhaps the most significant changes brought to the music industry by digital technology have occurred in the area of distribution. Although the manufacturing, warehousing, transporting, advertising, and sale of physical goods is still key to making recorded music available to consumers and is a significant source of record company revenue, digital distribution has created multiple new revenue streams and business models. As of this writing, digital distribution models have overtaken physical products as a percentage of overall record company revenue. We will first discuss issues involving distribution of physical products and then address the new issues brought on by digital distribution.

## **Distribution of Physical Products**

Decades ago, most records were distributed through a network of independent distributors throughout the country who promoted and distributed recordings regionally to both retail accounts and jukeboxes.[1] With the

---

1. For a fascinating history of many of the important independent record labels of the 1950s and 1960s and their distributors, see JOHN BROVEN, RECORD MAKERS AND BREAKERS (University of Illinois Press 2009).

consolidation of music labels beginning in the 1960s, the major labels each developed their own respective national distribution operations. Independent distributors continued to operate with independent labels, but with an increased ability to service accounts nationally rather than regionally.

Today, distribution of physical products is concentrated with the operations connected to the major recording companies. Each major label (Sony Music Entertainment, Universal Music Group, and Warner Brothers Records) maintains a distribution operation for its own respective recordings, together with certain other selective record labels. Each major label also maintains a distribution operation for other independent record labels. Warner Brothers Records has Alternative Distribution Alliance (ADA), Sony has RED Distribution, and Universal retains an interest in Fontana Distribution through its minority interest in Ingrooves, the recent purchaser of Fontana.

A number of independent distributors are also available as distribution options for physical product, including general distributors such as Entertainment One Distribution, Super D, and Alliance Entertainment and specialty distributors such as Central South Distribution (gospel), Beatport (dance), or Fat Beats Distribution (vinyl releases).[2] Finally, an intermediate player in the distribution setup is the so-called one-stop, such as Baker & Taylor, which aggregates finished goods from a broad range of record companies and other distributors and provides the convenience to retailers of obtaining product from multiple sources in a single order, or to smaller accounts that might not qualify to be open directly with certain distributors.

Distribution arrangements for physical products generally take one of two forms. Either the record company delivers finished product to the distributor or the distributor is in charge of manufacturing the product in addition to distribution (a "P&D" deal).[3] Which option a label selects will depend on the administrative means of the record company and the costs charged

---

2. The American Association of Independent Music maintains a list of its independent distributor members at http://a2im.org/contents//?taxonomy=t_sitewide&term=distributor.

3. The rights granted from the record company to the distribution company should only include the right to distribute recordings, and only for the term of the distribution agreement. For the story of a record label that conveyed ownership of its recordings under what it believed was a distribution agreement, see ROB BOWMAN, SOULVILLE U.S.A.: THE STORY OF STAX RECORDS (Schirmer Books 1997).

by the distribution company for the service of arranging manufacture relative to arrangements made directly. While the record company pays a fee to the distribution company for the manufacturing service, it may be money well spent if the record company does not have the resources or experience to administer the manufacturing process within the delivery, quality, and quantity requirements of the distributor.

## Distribution Functions

The functions performed by the distributor of physical products includes warehousing the product, production of catalogs and other sales support material, coordination of marketing efforts such as price and positioning of product within a retail store and co-op advertisements, solicitation and fulfillment of sales through its sales and shipping teams, processing of returns, billing and collections, preparation of regular accounting reports, and payment of amounts due. The distributor generally bears the risk of bad debts because it is the entity with a direct relationship with accounts and is in the position to assess the credit risk of the account. In essence, it is the job of the distributor to get the record into the retail account, and it remains the job of the record company to create demand through marketing and promotion that will result in a sale of that record from that account.

## Distribution Process

The distribution process generally involves the commitment by the record company to a release date for a record, or "street" date,[4] at least three or four months in advance.[5] This permits the distribution company to prepare sales material, including catalogs and sell sheets, and for sales personnel to solicit sales and arrange for any special promotional efforts that might be undertaken. Those special efforts may include favorable payment dating to encourage retail customer acceptance of an order. There will be specific

---

4. The record industry has selected Tuesdays of each week as the date new releases will first be made available for sale. *See* Frannie Kelley, *Why Albums Are Released on Tuesdays in the U.S.*, NPR Music (Sept. 8, 2010), http://www.npr.org/blogs/therecord/2010/09/08/129725205/why-albums-are-released-on-tuesdays.

5. It seems to happen more years than you would guess—it is not unusual for us to be approached around Thanksgiving by someone wanting to know how to obtain distribution of a seasonal recording. The answer is to wait until the following summer.

deadlines for delivery by the record company of finished goods, or, if the distribution agreement is a P&D deal, artwork and manufacturing parts. Records are then shipped to accounts in anticipation of the release date. The record companies do not want "street date violations," or the sale of records prior to the release date. Such sales will not only cause retailers to be unhappy about perceived lost sales to gun-jumpers, but such sales also fall outside the reporting period for industry sales charts and thus lessen the impact of cumulative first week sales.

Billings to accounts are generally paid within ninety days, and terms can be settled either by cash or by the value of previously distributed product that is returned.[6] The distributor will then in turn pay the label, generally sixty to ninety days after the close of each monthly period, after deduction of its distribution fee (a percentage of the receipts). The accounting also will be subject to a reserve for anticipated returns, which should generally be liquidated within nine to twelve months. The distribution company will also charge certain additional costs, such as re-stickering or otherwise refurbishing returned product, for excess inventory, or for cutting out or scrapping non-moving inventory.

Under the distribution agreement, the record company will have its own responsibilities. First, the company will be required to release a certain minimum number of recordings during each calendar period of the agreement's term. Each product delivered must be properly coded and packaged (if the agreement is not a P&D deal). The company will also be required to fund the price and positioning programs and co-op advertisements arranged by the distributor (which will generally range between $1.00 and $2.50 per CD) and to execute its marketing and promotional programs. The company is also likely to be required to provide periodic financial statements, sales projections, and proof of insurance to the distributor.

## Scope of Distribution Agreement

The scope of the distribution arrangement for physical products is one of the principal issues negotiated in a distribution agreement. Generally,

---

6. Most physical recorded product is sold on a fully returnable basis. Some products, such as vinyl releases, may be sold on a non-returns basis.

distribution rights will be exclusive and for all formats and configurations, including physical and digital. However, carve-outs from the exclusivity provisions may be appropriate in certain situations. This may occur if some recorded products may have commercial appeal in distinct channels of trade that may be serviced by other distributors. For example, the sale of gospel or contemporary Christian releases in the Christian bookstore market is a market that is often carved out of a general distribution agreement. Also, unless the record company has no administrative ability to handle such functions, the record company should reserve the right to directly license its masters to non-retail users of recorded music such as Mood, formerly Muzak, (background music) or TouchTunes (digital jukeboxes). The record company should also preserve the right to make its products available for premium use or licensing for compilations or synchronization uses.

It is also important to understand how the exclusivity provisions of the distribution arrangement affect the principal owners or officers of the record company, particularly if any such persons may play a creative role in connection with recordings distributed under other arrangements. For example, if a person affiliated with the record company is a recording artist or a producer, must all recordings with which they are involved be distributed under the distribution agreement?

Another issue that is often negotiated in a distribution agreement is whether the record company or distribution company will have any rights to "upstream" a particular recording artist or recording if success is achieved that requires the dedication of resources beyond those of the original record company. The "upstream" conversion may involve moving the distribution of a recording from the independent arm of the distribution company to the major-label equivalent level, or it may even involve moving the artist from the independent label to a major label affiliated with the distribution company, with the original record label retaining a production credit and financial participation. The consequences of any such conversion to an independent record label should be carefully considered. While the greater resources brought to a recording or artist may result in a level of success beyond the capabilities of the original record label, the loss of the artist may have other consequences for the long-term aspirations of the label.

## Warranties and Representations

Other significant areas for negotiation are the warranties and representations that the label will be making to the distribution company, the scope of indemnification committed by the record company, and the amount and type of insurance coverage that may be put in place to support such indemnification. Distribution of a copyrightable work is a separate right of the copyright holder, and any party in the distribution chain can face liability for distributing infringing product, whether they created it or not.[7] Because the distribution company generally plays no role in the creation of the product that it distributes, it must rely upon its distributed labels to deliver products free from adverse claims. A distribution company might also have greater concern about this potential liability when dealing with smaller record companies that may not have the business affairs capabilities enjoyed by larger, more experienced, and fully staffed labels. As a result, most distributors will not make the same mistake one record company made several years ago. It took on distribution of a record company that not only was the subject of multiple IRS liens and garnishment actions, but whose mechanical licenses with the Harry Fox Agency (HFA) had also been terminated for lack of payment. This left the company not only out the advance it had paid, but also in the crosshairs of both the IRS and the HFA and eventually drawn into the distributed company's bankruptcy proceeding. The recommended practice is not only to insist on credit, lien holder, and publishing status checks for potential distributed labels, but also to insist on being named as an additional insured in appropriate insurance policies obtained by and paid for by the record company before committing resources against a new relationship.

## Advances

Another important area of negotiation is advances. The amount of the advance, if one is available, that is paid by a distributor will generally be based on sales projected from the prior sales experience of the label and

---

7. Columbia Broad. Sys., Inc. v. Scorpio Music Dist., 569 F. Supp. 47 (E.D. Pa. 1983), *aff'd*, 738 F.2d 421 (3d Cir. 1984); UMG Recordings, Inc. v. Disco Aztecha Distribs., Inc., 446 F. Supp. 2d 1164 (E.D. Cal. 2006).

the artists expected to be released by the label. Of equal concern is how the advance may be recouped by the distributor. If the distribution company is entitled to recoup an advance it might pay from 100 percent of the revenue otherwise payable to the record company, the record company may experience a cash flow problem for operating funds, particularly if the record company was required to expend a significant portion of any advance it received to fund recording projects. One solution is to permit the distribution company to recoup an advance from no more than a certain percentage of the revenue otherwise payable to the label, thereby guaranteeing the label with a monthly payment. For example, the agreement might provide that the distribution company would only retain up to 50 percent of the revenue payable to the record company, with the record company assured it would receive at least half of sales revenue.

Another issue with advances may be how repayment might be secured by the distributor. The record company may have, or may want to seek, an operating line of credit from a bank that would insist on an overall blanket security interest in the assets of the record company. To permit such a line of credit to be extended, the distributor would need to limit its security interest to the label's inventory and receivables, and then perhaps in a second position to the bank, leaving the remaining assets, including the label's intellectual property rights, available to secure other financing.

## DIY Distribution

Artists that elect to self-distribute their recordings to their fan base have several options to support that path. Services such as Nimbit and Topspin facilitate the sale and fulfillment of physical products from artists to their fan base. The services can integrate with an artist's own website to fulfill sales generated from the site or simply handle the purchase transaction, with the artist then fulfilling the orders themselves. These services also handle other products on behalf of the DIY artist, such as merchandise and tickets.

## Digital Distribution

The development of the means to record, distribute, and transmit sound digitally has caused greater disruption and dislocation than any other event since sound began to be recorded. Reproduction and distribution of sound recordings is no longer centralized, expensive, detectable, and controlled—it is now ubiquitous, inexpensive, undetectable, and private. Consumers have the means, and the power, to duplicate, transmit, alter, and compile digital recordings. With this power, consumers have elevated their values and needs, including speed of access, comprehensiveness, reduced costs, portability/ubiquity, and convenience, over the control interests of music owners. Music licensing has also been challenged. For example, territorial limitations have disappeared, content is always accessible, once-secure content can be endlessly modified, and channels of distribution and sale are being invented faster than transactions can be completed.

As a business matter, most distributors of physical music recording products also have the ability to distribute such recordings in digital formats to companies such as online music retailers (iTunes, Amazon), digital music services (Pandora, Spotify), mobile devices (Cricket, Nokia, Samsung), digital cable and satellite television services (Music Choice and Mood), and satellite radio services (SiriusXM) and insist on obtaining exclusive rights to distribute recordings in both physical and digital formats. Even if a smaller record company or an artist elects to self-distribute its recordings to digital music services and retailers, as a practical matter it will need to enter an agreement with a digital music distribution aggregator, such as The Orchard, CD Baby, Tunecore, BFN Digital, Catapult, Reverbnation, or I Am Digital Media. Single artists and most smaller labels will not have the administrative capabilities to manage the distribution relationships with many digital music users across multiple platforms. Further, most key digital music users will not enter direct agreements with artists or smaller companies but will instead direct them to an aggregator for access to the platform the user provides.

Aggregators assist client artists and labels in the encoding of their recordings and the formatting of the metadata associated with such recordings. The aggregators then deliver the resulting files to the digital music users with which they have entered blanket agreements. Digital aggregators will also work with artists and labels to help promote the artist's and label's recordings within the platforms of the music users. The fee arrangements for aggregators range from set fees to percentages of revenue.

For the artist with an established direct connection to their fan base who prefers to market his or her products directly to that fan base instead of through music services or retailers, services such as Bandcamp, Nimbit, Reverbnation, and Topspin are available to facilitate such distribution without the involvement of aggregators.

## Digital Distribution Revenue

The television series *South Park* has been a cultural touchstone for a broad range of topics for many years, and of course digital distribution of entertainment content could not escape its attention. The following are the thoughts of Kyle Broflovski, one of the principal characters from the show, on the current financial rewards of digital distribution:

> You know, I learned something today. We thought we could make money on the Internet. But while the Internet is new and exciting for creative people, it hasn't matured as a distribution mechanism to the extent that one should trade real and immediate opportunities for income for the promise of future online revenue. It will be a few years before digital distribution of media on the Internet can be monetized to an extent that necessitates content producers to forgo their fair value in more traditional media.[8]

There is much truth in Kyle's observations, but the range and growth of revenue platforms for digital music remain impressive.[9]

---

8.  *South Park: Canada on Strike* (Comedy Central television broadcast Apr. 2, 2008).

9.  *See generally* Paul Resnikoff, *Exclusive: Streaming Revenues Now Surpass $1 Billion Annually in the US . . .*, DIGITAL MUSIC NEWS (Mar. 27, 2013), http://www.digitalmusicnews.com/permalink/2013/20130327streamingbillion; Todd Brabec & Jeffrey Brabec, *Online Music Licensing*, 29 ENT. & SPORTS LAW, No. 2, 2011 at 1.

## Webcasting

Since 1897, the owners of musical compositions have been entitled to compensation when recordings of their composition are publicly performed. Yet, neither the owners nor producers of those recordings, nor the performers featured in the recordings, were able to receive any payment for such public performance until the passage of the Digital Performance Right In Sound Recordings Act (DPRA) in 1995. The DPRA added § 106(6) to the Copyright Act, giving the owners of sound recording copyrights the right to publicly perform such sound recordings by means of digital audio transmissions (which at the time were principally digital cable transmissions).[10] This followed the passage of the Audio Home Recording Act of 1992,[11] which created a royalty system for recording devices and blank digital audio tapes. Three years later in 1998, Congress passed the Digital Millennium Copyright Act (DMCA),[12] which among other provisions amended Section 114 of the Copyright Act to provide a compulsory license of the sound recording public performance right for non-interactive digital audio transmissions,[13] or webcasting.

With the statutory performance right in sound recordings in place, in 2000 the Recording Industry Association of America (RIAA) created an organization called SoundExchange to act as the central clearing house for the issuance of licenses to digital music users availing themselves of the compulsory licensing provisions of the DPRA and DMCA. SoundExchange was spun off as an independent organization in 2003. Under the authority granted by the Copyright Act, SoundExchange has been authorized to participate in rate setting proceedings and conduct negotiations with all interested parties to determine the rates charged for the compulsory licenses provided in the DPRA and DMCA.[14] Rates are ultimately determined by

---

10. Digital Performance Right in Sound Recordings Act of Nov. 1, 1995, Pub. L. No. 104-39, Sec. 1, 109 Stat. 336 (codified as amended at 17 U.S.C. §§ 106, 114–115).

11. Audio Home Recording Act of 1992, Pub. L. No. 102-563, 106 Stat. 4237 (1992) (codified as 17 U.S.C. §§ 1001–10 (1992)).

12. Digital Millennium Copyright Act of 1998, Pub. L. No. 105-304, Sec. 405(a), 112 Stat. 2860 (codified as 17 U.S.C. §§ 101, 104, 104A, 108, 112, 114, 117, 512, 701, 1201–1205, 1301–1332).

13. 17 U.S.C. § 114(d)(2).

14. Amy Miller, *SoundExchange Counsel Faces Royalty Skirmishes*, ENT. L. & FIN., Dec. 2008.

the Copyright Royalty Board,[15] although negotiated settlement agreements between SoundExchange and certain groups of webcasters have been authorized and implemented.[16] The service features of the DPRA and DMCA compulsory licenses have been carefully drawn, and SoundExchange may only issue licenses for services that comply with the requirements of such features. For example, services operating under authority of a compulsory license must be non-interactive and must observe limitations on how often recordings by artists or from certain albums may be performed within a particular time period.[17] Music services that are interactive may not obtain a license for such services from SoundExchange but must obtain licenses directly from the record labels. The current rates for webcaster compulsory licenses may be found at 37 C.F.R. 380(A) and at SoundExchange.

SoundExchange distributes license proceeds based upon data it collects concerning the actual usage of recordings in the music services it licenses. After deduction of its service fee, SoundExchange then distributes 50 percent of the revenue directly to the owners of the sound recording copyright in the recordings it represents, 45 percent of the revenue directly to the featured artists appearing on the recordings, and 5 percent to performers' unions for the non-featured musicians and vocalists. The amounts paid to the artists by SoundExchange are not subject to any recoupability provisions that might be

---

15. The Copyright Act of 1976 originally established the Copyright Royalty Tribunal as a permanent body to set royalty rates for mechanical, cable television system secondary transmission, and jukebox compulsory licenses, and to distribute and settle controversies over the distribution of compulsory license royalty fees paid by cable television system and jukebox owners. In 1993, Congress passed the Copyright Royalty Tribunal Reform Act of 1993, Pub. Law 103-198, 107 Stat. 2304, to replace the Copyright Royalty Tribunal with copyright arbitration royalty panels (or CARPs). In 2004, Congress passed the Copyright Royalty and Distribution Reform Act of 2004, Pub. Law 108-419, 118 Stat. 2341, which abolished the system of arbitrators and replaced it with three full-time Copyright Royalty Judges. *See* 17 U.S.C. §§ 801–805. The original method by which the Copyright Royalty Judges are selected was found to violate the Appointments Clause of the U.S. Constitution, but this method was modified in a manner to remedy the constitutional issues. *See* Intercollegiate Broad. Sys., Inc. v. Copyright Royalty Bd., 684 F.3d 1332 (D.C. Cir. 2012).

16. Webcaster Settlement Act of 2009, Pub. L. No. 111-36 (amended 17 U.S.C. § 114); 74 Fed. Reg. 34796–34802 (July 17, 2009).

17. 17 U.S.C. § 114(j)(13) (2011). Disputes have also occurred over whether the features of certain digital music services exceed the eligibility requirements for the statutory compulsory webcasting licenses created by the DMCA. *See, e.g.*, Arista Records, LLC v. Launch Media, Inc., 578 F.3d 148 (2d Cir. 2009), *cert. denied*, 130 S. Ct. 1290 (2010).

included in their respective recording agreements. SoundExchange reported that it distributed $426,000,000 in digital performing royalties in 2012.[18]

It is critically important for all recording artists and record labels to register with SoundExchange to obtain the compulsory license proceeds that it collects. When record labels register, it is also key that they keep registration of their releases current with SoundExchange so that performances of the recordings can be properly logged and allocated. If performances of recordings or featured artists that are reported to SoundExchange cannot be matched to registered parties, SoundExchange will retain royalties for such artists or sound recording copyright holders for up to three years until a match can be found.[19] It has been our experience that featured artists who have been unaware of the role of SoundExchange have received significant payments when they have finally registered with the organization. Of course not all parties will receive accrued payments of that amount, but the stakes are significant and increasing. There is no reason not to register to receive payments to which the artists and record companies are entitled.

## Music Services

Music services can embrace a range of features but generally are considered to include the ability to receive some combination of a streamed performance of a recording upon demand,[20] downloaded music files that may be permanent or that may time out on a subscription basis, or some form of remote storage of music files to facilitate access across multiple devices and locations.

Many well-known digital music "services" have involved efforts by companies to offer digital music files without licensing sound recordings from the copyright owners. This has led to some equally well-known litigation.

---

18. *SoundExchange Ends Record-Setting Year with $462 Million in Total Distributions*, SoundExchange (Jan. 16, 2013), http://www.soundexchange.com/2013/01/16/soundexchange-ends-record-setting-year-with-462-million-in-total-distributions/.

19. Michael Huppe, *You Don't Know Me, But I Owe You Money: How SoundExchange Is Changing the Game on Digital Royalties*, 28 Ent. & Sports Law, No. 3, 2010 at 3.

20. Stephen M. Karamarsky, *Internet Music Stream vs. Download*, Ent. L. & Fin., Aug. 2007.

Lawsuits involving peer-to-peer offerings—Napster,[21] Aimster,[22] Grokster,[23] and Limewire[24]—all tested the limits of fair use and permissible conduct under the DMCA and were successful for the copyright owners.[25] In addition to pursuing infringement claims against peer-to-peer software providers, the recording industry mounted a campaign of lawsuits[26] against individual users of such software.[27]

Another example of an unlicensed music service was MP3.com, which offered an unlicensed "locker" service, whereby one could listen to streamed recordings of songs appearing on CDs supposedly owned by the user. The company's fair use defense was rejected,[28] and the assets of the company were eventually purchased by Universal Music Group. The prior owner of MP3.com returned with a different form of unlicensed "locker" service several years later, and while certain features of the service were approved when litigated, liability nevertheless was found against both the company and its founder.[29]

Currently, litigation is pending involving the music site Grooveshark[30] and the music service ReDigi, whose service facilitating the resale of digital music files was recently found to violate the copyright rights of content owners.[31] Criminal proceedings have also been commenced against the file

---

21. A&M Records, Inc. v. Napster, Inc., 239 F.3d 1004 (9th Cir. 2001).

22. *In re* Aimster Copyright Litig., 334 F.3d 643 (7th Cir. 2003), *cert. denied*, 540 U.S. 1107 (2004).

23. Metro-Goldwyn-Mayer Studios, Inc. v. Grokster, Ltd., 545 U.S. 913 (2005).

24. Arista Records, LLC v. Lime Group LLC, 784 F. Supp. 2d 398 (S.D.N.Y. 2011).

25. *See* Arista Records, LLC v. Usenet.com, Inc., 633 F. Supp. 2d 124 (S.D.N.Y. 2009) (Usenet operators held liable for infringement occurring within newsgroups); *see also* Columbia Pictures Indus., Inc. v. Fung, 96 U.S.P.Q.2d 1620 (C.D. Cal. 2009) (liability found for operation of site to collect, receive, index, and make available descriptions of content, including so-called dot-torrent files, and to provide access to open-access BitTorrent trackers).

26. *See, e.g.,* Sony BMG Music Entm't v. Tenenbaum, 660 F.3d 487 (1st Cir. 2011), *cert. denied*, 132 S. Ct. 2431 (2012); Capitol Records, Inc. v. Foster, 86 U.S.P.Q.2d 1203 (W.D. Okla. 2007); BMG Music v. Gonzalez, 430 F.3d 888 (7th Cir. 2005), *cert. denied*, 547 U.S. 1130 (2006).

27. Robert W. Clarida & Robert Jay Bernstein, *How Courts Are Defining "Distribution" in Peer-to-Peer File-Sharing Lawsuits*, ENT. L. & FIN., May 2008.

28. UMG Recordings, Inc. v. MP3.com, Inc. 92 F. Supp. 2d 349 (S.D.N.Y. 2000).

29. Capitol Records, Inc. v. MP3tunes, LLC, 821 F. Supp. 2d 627 (S.D.N.Y. 2011).

30. UMG Recordings, Inc. v. Escape Media Group, Inc., 37 Misc. 3d 208, 948 N.Y. 2d 881 (2012).

31. Capitol Records, LLC v. ReDigi Inc., 2013 WL 1286134 (S.D.N.Y. 2013).

storage service Megaupload and its principals, both in the United States and New Zealand.[32]

Today there are a number of licensed music services which offer access to millions of musical recordings on a subscription and non-subscription basis, including Rhapsody, Spotify, Muve, Rdio, eMusic, Slacker, and MediaNet.[33] Unless established through direct licenses with sound recording copyright owners, the rates payable by a music service for the use of musical compositions by means of interactive streaming of sound recordings and conditional, or limited, downloads are described at 37 C.F.R. 385(B). The formula for determining payments is beyond complicated, but it essentially involves alternative calculations based upon revenue, numbers of subscribers, and per-use minimums. Payments for the use of master recordings in music services began very modestly[34] but are currently being reported to range between .12 cents and 1.5 cents per play, depending on the service, whether the service is advertiser-based and free to the user or subscriber-based, or whether the service is on a mobile application.[35]

Also in 2012, a group of music industry professional organizations, record labels, and services negotiated a proposed set of rates and terms for the use of musical compositions in a broad range of digital music services as part of a rate setting proceeding initiated by the Copyright Royalty Judges pursuant to the requirements of the Copyright Act.[36] As of this writing, the proposed rates were published for comment[37] but have not yet been adopted. They nevertheless provide guidance to the range of financial terms to be

---

32. Ben Sisario, *7 Charged as F.B.I. Closes a Top File-Sharing Site*, N.Y. TIMES, Jan. 19, 2012, *available at* http://www.nytimes.com/2012/01/20/technology/indictment-charges-megaupload-site-with-piracy.html.

33. The fact that it has obtained licenses for millions of recordings and compositions for its service did not immunize MediaNet from the infringement claims of certain small publishers. *See* Appalseed Prods., Inc. v. MediaNet Digital, Inc., 2012 WL 2700383 (S.D.N.Y. 2012).

34. Patrick Smith, *Fair Play? A Million Spotify Streams Earned Gaga $167*, PAIDCONTENT (Nov. 23, 2009), http://paidcontent.org/2009/11/23/419-fair-dos-a-million-spotify-streams-earned-gaga-167/.

35. Ben Sisario, *As Music Streaming Grows, Royalties Slow to a Trickle*, N.Y. TIMES, Jan. 28, 2013, *available at* http://www.nytimes.com/2013/01/29/business/media/streaming-shakes-up-music-industrys-model-for-royalties.html?_r=0; Paul Resnikoff, *The Most Infamous Music Infographic, Updated for 2012 . . .* , DIGITAL MUSIC NEWS (July 30, 2012), http://www.digitalmusicnews.com/permalink/2012/120730infamous.

36. 17 U.S.C. § 801(b)(1) (2011).

37. 77 Fed. Reg. 29259–29270 (May 17, 2012).

expected from digital music services having the features described in the proposed regulations. The rates reported for the use of master recordings in so-called cloud services, or storage lockers, range between 53 percent and 58 percent of the service's revenue.[38]

## Permanent Downloads

Permanent downloads, or digital phonorecord deliveries in the nomenclature used in the Copyright Act, are perhaps the best known form of digital music. iTunes and Amazon are two of the largest digital retailers. On the music publishing side, the mechanical license rate[39] for a permanent download is the same as for a track on a compact disc: the greater of 9.1 cents or 1.75 cents per minute of playing time or fraction thereof.[40] As mentioned earlier, there are various compression formats used to prepare audio files for sound recordings, as there are various bit rates used to determine the quality of the files. Also, some files sold by digital retailers may be accompanied by digital rights management (DRM) software, which may restrict use of the files in some manner, such as the number of times the file may be used to burn a compact disc, shared with others, or other features.[41] Currently, the payment made by digital music retailers for a "standard" permanent download retailing for 99 cents is 70 cents. The retail price of the permanent download, and thus the amount paid by the retailer, may be greater for current "hit" product or high resolution files, or less for legacy material.

Also as mentioned earlier, there is a significant issue about how royalties are to be calculated for the sale of permanent downloads.[42] Most legacy recording agreements provided that income from the licensing of recordings by the record company to others would be divided equally between the

---

38. Ed Christman, *This Year's Model*, BILLBOARD, June 11, 2011, at 6.

39. The performing rights organizations representing the music publishing interests had also argued that downloads of music files implicated the performance right in the songs included in the files and thus claimed license fees were due for download sales. The ASCAP rate court, however, disagreed in U.S. v. ASCAP, In the Matter of the Application of AOL et al., 485 F. Supp. 2d 438 (S.D.N.Y. 2007), *aff'd*, 627 F.3d 64 (2d Cir. 2010), *cert. denied*, 132 S. Ct. 366 (2011).

40. Royalty Rates for Making and Distributing Phonorecords, 37 C.F.R. 385.3(a) (2011).

41. Ali Matin, *Digital Rights Management (DRM) In Online Music Stores: DRM-Encumbered Music Downloads' Inevitable Demise As a Result of the Negative Effects of Heavy-Handed Copyright Law*, 28 LOY. L.A. ENT. L. REV. 265 (2009).

42. Edward F. McPherson, *F.B.T v. Aftermath: Eminem Raps the Record Industry*, 29 ENT. & SPORTS LAW, No. 1, 2011 at 10.

record company and the recording artist. Such licenses typically occurred after a market for a recording had been established through the sale of phonorecords manufactured and sold by the record company for which the recording artist would be paid a much lower percentage of revenue.

The sale of downloads and ringtones by parties other than the record company caused disagreement about how the relationship between the record company and such sellers should be characterized. Was the relationship one of wholesaler-retailer? If so, a royalty rate would be applied to the price paid by the online seller for the download or ringtone. Or was the relationship one of licensor-licensee, in which case the recording artist would be entitled to one-half of the price paid by the online seller. The difference in the amount paid to the artist is significant. If the relationship were characterized as one of licensor-licensee, the resulting royalties are generally between two and three times the amount paid under the wholesaler-retailer model. Record companies and digital retailers seem to have settled on a wholesaler-retailer model in their own relationships, which is illustrated by the fact that record companies pay the publishing costs for permanent downloads. However, the interpretation of the relationship between the record companies and their legacy artists continues to unfold.

### Ringtones and Ringbacks

Although the market for ringtone sales has declined from its peak a few years ago, ringtones remain a significant source of revenue for sound recording copyright holders. The fee to the music publisher for the composition embodied in a ringtone is 24 cents per copy,[43] while the payment for music publishing for a ringback, which is a performance of the embodied composition rather than a download, is licensed through the performing rights organizations ASCAP, BMI, and SESAC.[44] Payments for the use of the master recording in a ringtone are approximately 40 percent of the retail price.[45]

---

43. Royalty Rates for Making and Distributing Phonorecords, 37 C.F.R. 385.3(a) (2011).

44. Publishers also sought without success to establish that the playing by a mobile phone of a ringtone when it received a call was a public performance of the composition featured in the ringtone. *See in re* Cellco Partnership, 663 F. Supp. 2d 363 (S.D.N.Y. 2009).

45. *See generally*, Steven Masur & Ursa Chitrakar, *The History and Recurring Issues of Ringtones*, 24 ENT. & SPORTS LAW, No. 1, 2006 at 1.

## Satellite Radio and Cable Music Services

The royalty rate paid by satellite radio service provider Sirius XM Radio for the use of sound recordings is 9 percent of gross revenues for 2013; 9.5 percent for 2014; 10 percent for 2015; 10.5 percent for 2016; and 11 percent for 2017, which was determined through a rate proceeding before the Copyright Royalty Board in the Copyright Office[46] and is paid through SoundExchange. However, Sirius XM is currently seeking to obtain direct licenses with record companies for their service through the music licensing company Music Reports, Inc.[47] Sirius XM also has brought suit against SoundExchange and the American Association of Independent Music asserting antitrust and tortious interference claims based upon the licensing practices of SoundExchange and AAIM.[48]

Cable music service Music Choice is characterized as a "preexisting" subscription service and may avail itself of a compulsory license to use sound recordings under Section 114(d)(2) of the Copyright Act. The royalty rate paid by Music Choice through 2013 under its compulsory license for this service is 8 percent of revenue, which rises to 8.5 percent for 2014 through 2017.[49] This royalty is paid through SoundExchange. Music Choice is also required to pay an advance of $100,000 for each year of its compulsory license.

---

46. *In the Matter of Determination of Rates and Terms for Preexisting Subscription Services and Satellite Digital Audio Radio Services*, No. 2011-1 (Copyright Royalty Judges, Feb. 24, 2013), *available at* http://www.loc.gov/crb/proceedings/2011-1/rates/Public-Majority-Final-Determination.pdf.

47. Trefis Team, *Sirius XM And SoundExchange Square Off in the Battle Over Royalty Rates*, FORBES, Apr. 10, 2012, http://www.forbes.com/sites/greatspeculations/2012/04/10/sirius-xm-and-soundexchange-square-off-in-the-battle-over-royalty-rates.

48. Sirius XM Radio, Inc. v. SoundExchange, Inc., 12 CV 2259 (S.D.N.Y. filed Mar. 27, 2012).

49. *In the Matter of Determination of Rates and Terms for Preexisting Subscription Services and Satellite Digital Audio Radio Services*, No. 2011-1 (Copyright Royalty Judges, Feb. 24, 2013), *available at* http://www.loc.gov/crb/proceedings/2011-1/rates/Public-Majority-Final-Determination.pdf.

Chapter Nine
# Tax Considerations
# for the Musician

*By Heather Ryan Liberman*

Willie Nelson,[1] Lauryn Hill,[2] and Lil Wayne[3] are all world-renowned for their musical talent *and* their tax indiscretions. As illustrated by these musicians' experiences, the consequences of failing to properly file taxes range from financial penalties to imprisonment.[4] Beyond failure to file, improper calculations or inaccurate tax advice can mean the difference between having a surplus or a deficit in the musician's bank account. To avoid such disastrous outcomes, counsel must be sought from accountants who are skilled

---

1. Willie Nelson reportedly owed over $6 million in back taxes and $10 million in penalties. Nelson released numerous albums in the effort to pay back the taxes and auctioned off his ranch, which he was eventually able to repurchase. But note that, although Nelson's tax problems were highly publicized, it was the musician Harold Jenkins, professionally known as Conway Twitty, who set tax precedent when Twitty was challenged by the IRS for deductions related to repayment of investors in a failed business, even though he was not obligated to make these payments. In issuing its order, the court concluded with a composition entitled, "Ode to Conway Twitty," which states in part:

"Twitty Burger went belly up
But Conway remained true
He repaid his investors, one and all
It was the moral thing to do.
His fans would not have liked it
It could have hurt his fame
Had any investors sued him
Like Merle Haggard or Sonny James.
When it was time to file taxes
Conway thought what he would do
Was deduct those payments as a business expense
Under section one-sixty-two.
In order to allow these deductions
Goes the argument of the Commissioner
The payments must be ordinary and necessary
To a business of the petitioner.
Had Conway not repaid the investors
His career would have been under cloud,
Under the unique facts in this case
*Held*: The deductions are allowed."
*See Conway Twitty, R.I.P.: Balladeer, Tax Law Hero*, 79 J. Tax'n 127 (Aug. 199).

2. Lauryn Hill failed to file her federal income taxes from 2005 to 2007 and owes the IRS more than $2 million. As a result, she was sentenced to three months in federal prison.

3. Phil Dotree, *Lauryn Hill and 3 Other Musicians with Tax Problems*, Yahoo! Contributor Network (June 8, 2012), http://news.yahoo.com/lauryn-hill-3-other-musicians-tax-problems-213100241.html.

4. Rapper Jeffrey "Ja Rule" Atkins was sentenced to 28 months in prison for failing to pay more than $1.1 million in federal taxes for five years. *See Daily Tax Report*, 138 DTR K-1, July 19, 2011.

in various accounting methods[5] and attorneys with specialized knowledge of state and federal laws.[6]

Although a detailed analysis of general tax law and accounting are outside the scope of this chapter, income, deductions, and choice of entity will be discussed in great length.

## A Musician's Gross Income

A musician may derive his or her gross income from a range of sources. To stay organized, the musician's income should be tracked, recorded, and categorized. This is important because income may be characterized as capital or ordinary, and active or passive. The differences between these tax treatments, as well as other tax concerns, including deferred compensation, foreign income, and emerging income streams will be discussed in the following sections.[7]

## Ordinary Income vs. Capital Gains

A musician's income is characterized as either ordinary income or capital gains. The majority of the musician's income is ordinary income, which is

---

5. For an overview of accounting methods, including cash basis, accrual, and income-forecast methods, see PAM GAINES & CATHY MCCORMACK, FINANCIAL MANAGEMENT FOR MUSICIANS (Intertec Publishing 2009); see also Abkco Indus., Inc. v. Commissioner of Internal Revenue, 56 T.C. 1083 (1972) (accrual method of accounting improper when contingent royalties too speculative).

6. For an excellent resource to understand the intersection of tax and entertainment law, see SCHUYLER MOORE, TAXATION OF THE ENTERTAINMENT INDUSTRY (CCH, 9th ed. 2008).

7. While the musician has a certain set of tax considerations, so do the entities that support the musician, such as a record label. Although a detailed explanation of these considerations are outside the scope of this chapter, it is worth noting that a record label must capitalize and amortize the costs to record music and create videos, unless the recording or video was created solely for purposes of advertising, in which case the costs can be deducted as an advertising expense. Similarly, advances can be capitalized as recording costs and amortized using acceptable methods. There have been circumstances where advances have been amortized over the course of recoupment, rather than the life of the license. For a more thorough explanation, see Moore, *supra* note 6.

taxed at regular income tax rates as high as 39.6 percent.[8] One example of ordinary income is income derived from copyrights in sound recordings, or payments from a live performance.[9] In contrast, capital gains income receives lower tax rates when an asset meets certain standards and is held for a specified amount of time.[10] Capital gains income is realized upon the sale of capital assets, which include assets held for investment, stocks, or real estate. Capital assets do not include inventory or property held for sale in the ordinary course of business, or certain self-created assets.

Specific examples of capital gains and ordinary income are described below.

## Capital Gains: Musical Compositions

Although self-created assets are typically excluded from capital assets, the Songwriters Capital Gains Tax Equity Act, which was originally only a temporary tax break for songwriters,[11] was permanently enacted in 2007.[12] The Act allows the taxpayer (songwriter) to elect to receive capital gains treatment on the income derived from the sale of the copyright in a musical composition, if the copyright was held for more than twelve months.[13]

---

8. Alexander Lindey, *Tax Considerations*, 6 LINDEY ON ENTERTAINMENT, PUBL. & THE ARTS § 17:4 (3d ed.) (2013).

9. This income stream maintains that characterization even if transferred to another person as a gift. *See* Capital Asset Defined, I.R.C. § 1221(a)(3) (2010); Basis of Property Acquired from a Decedent, I.R.C. § 1014 (2010).

10. Tax Imposed, I.R.C. § 1(h)(1)–(4) (if the taxpayer is in the 10 percent or 15 percent bracket, the tax on capital gains is zero). Please be aware that tax law is always fluctuating. Exact tax rates should be researched by a qualified professional.

11. Significant lobbying by the Nashville Songwriters Association International convinced Congress to institute the temporary carve-out in § 1221(a)(3) for Songwriters. *See* Rodney Mock & Jeffrey Tolin, *I Should Have Been a Rockstar; Deconstructing Section 1221(A)(3)*, 65 TAX L. 47 (2011).

12. Tax Relief and Health Care Act of 2006 (P.L. 109-432, Dec. 20, 1906) removed the original December 31, 2010, expiration date.

13. The IRS has not issued a pronouncement on whether the one-year timeframe begins upon notice or actual reversion of copyrights in musical compositions for which the transfer has been terminated under § 203 of the U.S. Copyright Act. *See* Michael Morris, *Songwriters and Music Publishers Continue to Score Tax Breaks*, J. MULTISTATE TAX'N & INCENTIVES, June 2009; *see also* Denise M. Stevens, *Songwriters Gain from Change in Tax Law*, ENT. L. & FIN., July 2006.

To elect the preferential treatment, the taxpayer must include each musical composition sold or exchanged during the taxable year on Schedule D. The filing is due prior to the date of the income tax return for the taxable year of the sale.[14] Yet, even if a songwriter sells his or her song catalog and elects capital gains treatment, the ongoing royalty and fee income generated from the copyright in the same musical compositions receives ordinary income treatment.

The Act also allows purchasers of a song catalog to amortize acquisition costs over a five- year period, in lieu of the typical lengthier timeframe, which is based on the life of the income-producing asset. However, this election has limitations that should be reviewed and analyzed prior to purchasing a song catalog.[15]

## Ordinary Income: Compensation for Services Rendered vs. Royalties

As previously mentioned, the majority of the musician's income is ordinary income. Ordinary income may be characterized as compensation for services rendered, royalties, or contingent sale proceeds. Each of these categorizations impacts the tax treatment of the income.

One way to determine whether the income is compensation for services rendered or royalties is by answering the question: who has control? When the musician does not have control, as in a work for hire relationship, the income is probably compensation for services rendered. In contrast, income is probably deemed royalties when the musician has control, such as merchandising income because it is usually the license of rights owned by the licensor.[16]

### Compensation for Services Rendered: Touring Income

Touring income is taxed as compensation for services rendered.[17] In addition to federal taxes, touring may invoke state taxes as well as foreign taxes

---

14. Rules and Regulations, *Time and Manner for Electing Capital Asset Treatment for Certain Self-Created Musical Works*, 26 C.F.R. pt. 1 (2011).

15. Depreciation, I.R.C. § 167(g)(8)(E) (2007).

16. Moore, *supra* note 6.

17. *Rolling Stones Protest Taxes, Cancel Gigs*, 89 J. Tax'n 64 (1998).

when the musician is touring abroad.[18] To properly advise the musician client, it is critical to be aware of tax treaties between the United States and the countries in which the musician is accruing income. Many of the treaties include an "artists and entertainers clause" that excludes artists and entertainers from the treaty.[19] Whether the clause exists in the treaty will help to determine whether musician will be subject to local taxes in the country at issue.

### Royalties: Publishing Income

Unlike touring income or payments under musician recording agreements, a musician's publishing income,[20] whether under a publishing, co-publishing, or administration agreement, is typically characterized as "royalties" or "sale proceeds."[21] This distinction is because musical compositions are typically not works for hire.[22]

## Unqualified Deferred Compensation: Advances

A musician's representatives should also be aware of the existence and impact of unqualified deferred compensation on a musician's taxable gross income. Unqualified deferred compensation is prevalent in the recording industry and requires attention by the experienced practitioner to avoid potential pitfalls.[23] Unqualified deferred compensation occurs when a payment is made to a musician in a tax year after the services are rendered.

---

18. Income collected in the United States by foreign citizens is outside the scope of this chapter. However, for more information, see Aninda Dhar, *Foreign Music Acts and United States Taxation*, 26 CARDOZO ARTS & ENT. L.J. 151 (2008); *see also Instructions on How to Apply for a Central Withholding Agreement*, INTERNAL REVENUE SERVICE, 2012, http://www.irs.gov/pub/irs-pdf/f13930.pdf.

19. *See* Moore, *supra* note 6.

20. *See* Irving Berlin Music Corp. v. United States, 487 F.2d 540 (Fed. Cir. 1973), *cert. denied*, 419 U.S. 832 (1974).

21. Importantly, when a payment is considered a royalty or sale proceeds, the income is sourced to the location where the work is exploited, *e.g.*, if an artist writes a composition in Chicago, that work is subject to U.S. tax law when exploited in the U.S.

22. Note that a PRO typically withholds taxes prior to the distribution of this income.

23. The deferred compensation is unqualified under Section 409A if it does not meet the qualifications for pension or profit sharing plans.

For example, advances,[24] profit participations, residuals, or other similar payments are usually characterized as unqualified deferred compensation.[25]

Taxation of unqualified deferred compensation is very particularized and changed dramatically under the American Jobs Creation Act of 2004, which amended several sections of the Internal Revenue Code.[26] For example, IRC Section 409A changes the previous version of the Code by:

(1) requiring service providers to meet deadlines for elections;[27]

(2) limiting events that allow a deferred compensation distribution to be taken;[28] and

(3) prohibiting acceleration of payments.[29]

If any of these new requirements are not satisfied, the service provider must pay tax on all amounts deferred for all years at the regular tax rate of up to 35 percent plus penalties at 20 percent and interest.[30] However, relief for certain inadvertent and unintentional failures to comply with Section 409A is available pursuant to IRS Notice 2010-6.[31]

In addition to relief, an independent contractor may be exempt from the requirements of Section 409A if the contractor provides services to at

---

24. If the record label provides the musician with a recording advance, the musician is only taxed on any excess money not spent on the recording that the musician is authorized to keep. The same principles apply if the record label provides the musician with an advance to create a music video. *See* Moore, *supra* note 298.

25. Bradford S. Cohen, *The Taxation of Deferred Compensation in Standard Service Agreements*, L.A. LAW., May 2010, *citing* Treas. Reg. § 1.409A03(b); *see also* James A. McCarten, *Music City Tax-Ache: Avoiding the Heartache of Section 409A's 80 Percent Tax Rate*, TENN. B. ASS'N NEWSLETTER 1 (2009).

26. Robert Jason & Olga Loy, *Federal Tax Reform Includes Traps for Deferred Compensation Deals*, ENT. L. & FIN., Mar. 2005.

27. The deadlines depend on whether the compensation is performance-based or not.

28. Distribution may occur upon the following: date of the service provider's separation from service, service provider's death or disability, a fixed time, a change in ownership of the employer, or the occurrence of an unforeseeable emergency.

29. However, payment thirty days prior to the due date does not constitute an acceleration. *See* Treas. Reg. § 1.409A-3(d).

30. The service provider may be able to avoid the penalty if he or she can show a "substantial risk of forfeiture." A substantial risk of forfeiture under Section 409A exists if: entitlement to the payment is conditioned on the performance of future services by the service provider or the occurrence of a condition related to a purpose of the compensation, and the possibility of forfeiture is substantial. *See* Treas. Reg. § 1.409A-1(d)(1).

31. INTERNAL REVENUE SERVICE, INTERNAL REVENUE BULLETIN NO. 2010-3 (Jan. 19, 2010) *available at* http://www.irs.gov/pub/irs-irbs/irb10-03.pdf.

least two other unrelated service recipients and the payment from neither service recipient totals more than 70 percent of the independent contractor's revenue for the year.[32]

## Emerging Income Streams: Crowd-Funded Income

Additional income streams may be available to musicians who follow non-traditional or DIY models. Crowd-funding, also known as fan-funding, is one common avenue for musicians to raise financing for use in connection with any number of purposes, including reserving studio time, arranging a tour, or releasing an album.

As discussed in Chapter Four, the crowd-funding company, Kickstarter, is one of the most widely used platforms for musicians to raise money from the masses. Although Kickstarter is commonly used, the tax implications of crowd-funding may not be commonly known by musicians. First and foremost, the pledges from the public are taxable income, unless the pledge is considered a donation and the band is a 501(c)(3),[33] or if the pledge falls under an exempt "capital contribution" under the JOBS Act.[34] Notwithstanding the foregoing exemptions, it is more likely than not that the pledge income is taxable. Further, the musician should be aware that when an album is pre-sold to the purchaser in exchange for a monetary pledge, some states argue that the exchange creates sales tax obligations to the musician.

There are also issues surrounding Kickstarter and the availability of deductions. Those concerns are raised in the following section.

---

32. James A. McCarten, *Music City Tax-Ache: Avoiding the Heartache of Section 409A's 80 Percent Tax Rate*, Tenn. B. Ass'n Newsletter 1 (2009).

33. Glenn Peoples, *Business Matters: Are Kickstarter Pledges Taxable Income?*, Billboard (Aug. 1, 2011), http://www.billboard.biz/bbbiz/industry/digital-and-mobile/business-matters-are-kickstarter-pledges-1005300092.story.

34. The Jumpstart Our Business Act "JOBS Act" was signed into law on April 5, 2012. Although the JOBS Act provides an exemption from securities registration requirements for crowd-funding and permits companies to sell up to $1 million of securities each year to an unlimited number of investors that may not be accredited, the Securities Exchange Committee has not yet implemented the rules of the Act and warns against relying on this exemption. *See Information Regarding the Use of the Crowdfunding Exemption in the JOBS Act*, U.S. Securities & Exchange Comm'n (Apr. 23, 2012), http://www.sec.gov/spotlight/jobsact/crowdfundingexemption.htm.

## Taxation of the Musician's Income

Taxes applicable to a musician may include any combination of the following: self-employment tax if he or she is an independent contractor;[35] payroll tax if an employee;[36] sales/use tax on the sale of CDs, tapes, and other merchandise; business license fees; personal property tax; franchise and excise tax; and other federal, state,[37] local, and foreign taxes.[38] Further information about tax rates and income brackets are outside the scope of this chapter but are available through the relevant tax authorities.

## Deductions

Upon meeting certain thresholds, musicians have unique opportunities to offset their non-W-2 income with deductions,[39] such as "qualified creative expenses."[40] This section reviews the hurdles a musician faces in deducting creative expenses, known as the hobby-loss challenge, and provides a non-exhaustive list of those deductions that are available.

---

35. An independent contractor's income is reported to the IRS on Form 1099 and there are no withholdings. Specific tax considerations surrounding independent contractors are outside the scope of this chapter.

36. An employee receives a W-2.

37. Issues surrounding whether Sheryl Crow's performance in an aircraft invoked state taxes for each state flown through from Chicago to Los Angeles, *see Taxing Sheryl as the Crow Flies*, 101 J. Tax'n 128 (Aug. 2004).

38. *See* Moore, *supra* note 6.

39. The availability of certain deductions and credits should be analyzed by an accountant and tax lawyer. Be aware that certain instances of deductions and credits have constituted "tax shelters." A "tax shelter" can be defined as "an investment which has a significant feature for federal income or excise tax purposes either of the following attributes: (1) deductions in excess of income from the investment being available in any year to reduce income from other sources in that year, or (2) credits in excess of the tax attributable to the income from the investment being available in any year to offset taxes on income from other sources in that year." *See* United States v. Music Masters, Ltd., 621 F. Supp. 1046 (W.D.N.C. 1985), *aff'd*, 816 F.2d 674 (4th Cir. 1987) (sound recording lease program was an abusive tax shelter because valuations of sound recordings were grossly overstated, rendering ineligible any deductions and credits to investors).

40. Rules Relating to Property Produced by the Taxpayer, 26 C.F.R. § 1.263A-2(a)(2)(ii)(A)(1) (2012).

## Hobby-Loss

Unfortunately, even musicians who are dedicated to writing, recording, and performing their art may not be able to benefit from certain deductions. This is because the IRS categorizes a musician as either a hobbyist or a professional, and only the latter may take most of the available deductions.[41]

Although the IRS presumes that a musician is engaged in a business or trade, the musician is deemed a hobbyist unless his or her activities have yielded a profit during three of five consecutive years ending with the tax year at issue.[42] One mechanism to demonstrate profit is to regulate the time and receipt of income and the time and occurrence of expenses.[43] However, this is not recommended without advice from a tax expert.

If deemed a hobbyist, the musician can only deduct the expenses of the hobby up to the amount of income produced by the hobby. For example, if a musician does not yield net profits during three of the consecutive five years leading up to the year in question, and only earned $1,000 in the last year, only $1,000 can be deducted.

Yet, a musician can overcome the hobbyist characterization if the musician can demonstrate a "profit motive."[44] A profit motive is established by the facts and circumstances surrounding a musician's activities, as indicated by assessing the following nine factors:

(1) Manner in which the taxpayer carries on the activity;[45]
(2) Professional expertise of the taxpayer;
(3) Time and effort expended by the taxpayer in carrying on the activity;
(4) Expectation that assets may appreciate in value;
(5) Success of the taxpayer in similar activities;
(6) Taxpayer's previous income or losses with respect to activity;

---

41. Lindey, *supra* note 8.

42. *See* Doak Turner, *Financial Management for Musicians' Author Offers Tax Tips for Songwriters, Workshop Hosted by Songwriters Guild Office, Nashville, TN*, MUSIC DISH, Mar. 4, 2005, http://www.musicdish.com/mag/index.php3?id=9397.

43. Lindey, *supra* note 8.

44. Wesley v. Commissioner, 2007 WL 968731 (U.S. Tax Ct. 2007), *citing* Commissioner v. Groetzinger, 480 U.S. 23 (1987).

45. *Id.* Musician claiming deductions for installation of recording equipment does not satisfy the profit motive analysis when the musician failed to keep regular records of expenses and presented only a few receipts for studio time that occurred eight years prior to the year at issue.

(7) Amount of earned profits;

(8) Financial status of the taxpayer, e.g., wealth and independent income; and

(9) Whether activities are for personal pleasure or recreation.[46]

If a musician is considered a "professional" after analyzing the factors, there may be deductions available for ordinary and necessary expenditures, which are explained in the following section.

## Ordinary and Necessary Business Expenditures

Deductions for ordinary and necessary business expenditures may be available to offset income generated by a self-employed musician filing Schedule C,[47] or an LLC or Corporation. Remember, these deductions are not available to offset W-2 income.

Ordinary and necessary business expenditures include, but are not limited to, instruments, workspace, repairs, travels for business purposes, promotional expenses, legal, and accounting fees.[48] To be deductible, these expenditures must be reasonable.[49] Obviously, the determination of what

---

46. Activities Not Engaged for Profit, I.R.C. § 1.183-2(b); *see also IRC Audit Technique Guide*, http://www.irs.gov/Businesses/Small-Businesses-&-Self-Employed/Audit-Technique-Guides-(ATGs).

47. In order to keep track of the musician's expenses, it may be useful to create a worksheet with columns for the following to support claimed deductions: continuing education, such as voice training and rent for rehearsal space; promotional expenses, such as audition tapes, business cards, professional headshots, and website development and hosting; supplies and expenses, such as union and professional dues, insurance, interest on business loans, postage, repairs for instruments, and sheet music; travel to auditions, business meetings, continuing education or other professional activities; and equipment purchases. The worksheet and receipts will be useful when it is time to file taxes.

48. Although the MSSP guidelines include fees paid to musician's managers, Stevie Nicks's attempt to deduct $119,291 paid to her personal manager was challenged by the IRS on the grounds that the expense was not business, but rather, personal. *See Ordinary and Necessary Business Expenses for Entertainers: What's Reasonable*, 87 J. TAX'N 63, 1997, *citing* Docket No. 22733-96, filed October 22, 1996.

49. *See* Teschner v. Commissioner, TCM 1997-498 (U.S. Tax Ct. 1997). The court found that Rod Stewart's backup musician was an employee and not able to deduct expenses for silk underwear or the costs of meals allegedly paid for as a punishment by Rod Stewart for the musician's late arrival to the tour bus. *See also More on "Ordinary and Necessary" Business Expenses for Entertainers*, 88 J. TAX'N 126 (1998).

is reasonable is very fact specific and outside the scope of this chapter.[50] Regardless, the musician and his or her counsel should be aware of the non-exhaustive list of possible deductions below.

### Home-Office Workspace

It is not unusual for musicians to teach music lessons out of their home, or allocate space within their home for rehearsals. When done properly, a musician may be able to deduct their home office studio as their principal place of business.[51] A home office could be the taxpayer's principal place of business where:

(a) the office is used for administrative or management activities of any trade or business; and

(b) there is no other fixed location where the taxpayer conducts substantial administrative or management activities of such business or trade.[52]

### Instruments

Rather than capitalizing and depreciating a musical instrument, the cost of a certain amount of professional equipment may be deducted during the year of its purchase. Additionally, musicians may deduct the depreciation of musical instruments, even those that have actually increased in value.[53]

---

50. For example, if the expense is a business necessity, a musician may be able to deduct the cost of using his or her car to transport musical instruments between home and the business.

51. Drucker v. Commissioner, 715 F.2d 67 (2d Cir. 1983) (concert musicians successfully argued that their home office studios used for individual practice became their principal place of business for purposes of deductions).

52. *See* Disallowance of Certain Expenses in Connection with Business of Home, I.R.C. § 280A(c); *see also* Charles M. Flesch, *Employed Artists' Home Office Deductions in the Aftermath of Weissman v. Commissioner: The Second Circuit's New Limited Exception for Taxpayer-Employees*, 4 CARDOZO ARTS & ENT. L.J. 337 (1985).

53. *See* Liddle v. Commissioner, 65 F.3d 329, *aff'd*, 65 F.3d 329 (3d Cir. 1995); Simon v. Commissioner, 68 F.3d 41 (2d Cir. 1995); *Musicians May Take Tax Deductions for Depreciation of Musical Instruments, Even Though Instruments Do Not Have "Determinable Useful Lives" and May Have Increased in Actual Value, Federal Appellate Courts Rule in Two Cases*, ENT. L. REP., June 1996, http://elr.carolon.net/BI/V18N01.PDF.

## Clothing

Musicians may be able to deduct clothing as an ordinary and necessary business expense. The availability of this deduction depends on if the clothing is (1) required or essential in the taxpayer's employment, (2) not suitable for general or personal wear, and (3) not so worn.[54] An example of a costume probably not suitable for everyday wear is the gown made of meat that Lady Gaga wore to the 2010 MTV Video Music Awards.[55]

However, musicians must be careful when trying to deduct clothing and costumes, because the IRS explicitly states:

> Taxpayers in the entertainment industry sometimes may incur expenses to maintain an image. These expenses are frequently related to the individual's appearance in the form of clothing, makeup, and physical fitness. Other expenses in this area include bodyguards and limousines. These are generally found to be personal expenses as the inherently personal nature of the expense and the personal benefit far outweigh any potential business benefit. No deduction is allowed for wardrobe, general makeup, or hair styles for auditions, job interviews, or "to maintain an image.[56]

As with many other IRS inquiries, whether clothing is deductible is very fact specific, and requires sufficient evidentiary support.[57]

---

54. Where a musician claims that clothing was for performance in concerts, receipts from department stores for gowns and earrings were insufficient, when such clothing items are typical in women's wardrobes and could be worn outside of performance. *See* Tilman v. United States, 644 F. Supp. 2d 391 (S.D.N.Y. 2009); *see also Miscellaneous Deductions*, IRS PUBLICATIONS, http://www.irs.gov/publications/p17/ch28.html (last visited May 10, 2013).

55. Zack Greenburg, *Lada Gaga's Potentially Meaty Tax Deduction*, FORBES, Apr. 20, 2011, http://www.forbes.com/sites/zackomalleygreenburg/2011/04/20/lady-gaga -meaty-tax-deduction/.

56. *Business Expenses – Entertainment Tax Tips*, IRS PUBLICATIONS (Dec. 2012), http://www.irs.gov/Businesses/Small-Businesses-&-Self-Employed/Business-Expenses -Entertainment-Tax-Tips.

57. Musician's clothing, and maintenance thereof, were deductible as ordinary and necessary business expenses when the clothing was formal evening wear worn only while performing as a lounge singer deductible when he maintained trunks of "off-season" clothing. *See* Fisher v. Commissioner, 23 T.C. 218 (T.C. 1954), *aff'd*, 230 F.2d 79 (1956).

## Passive Loss Deductions

A musician should be aware of the limitations on deducting losses that arise when generating passive income. Passive losses can only offset income[58] that is derived from the conduct of a trade, business, or transaction entered into for profit in which the taxpayer does not materially participate.[59] Note that material participation is established by regular, continuous, and substantial basis in the operations of the activity.[60] For example, when a musician creates musical copyrights, the royalties collected by the musician for the exploitation of those copyrights constitutes material participation.[61] This distinction highlights the importance of maintaining organized records and seeking counsel from experienced accountants and attorneys.

## Charitable Deductions

A musician may claim deductions under IRC § 170(m) if he or she donates musical copyrights to a charitable organization.[62] This type of donation may be fruitful for the musician because during the ten years following the donation, the musician may deduct a percentage of the income generated by the charity for the exploitation of the copyright. The table below illustrates the percentage of the income generated by the donation that the artist is able to deduct:

| Taxable Year of Donor Ending After Date of Contribution | Applicable Percentage |
| --- | --- |
| 1st | 100 |
| 2nd | 100 |
| 3rd | 90 |
| 4th | 80 |

---

58. *See* Passive Activity Losses and Credits Limited, I.R.C. § 469 (2005) [hereafter Passive Activity Losses].

59. *Id.* at § 469(c)(1); *see* Reg. §§ 1.1362-2(c)(5)(ii)(A)(2)-(3). *But see* I.R.C. § 469(e)(1). Certain royalties are considered passive income.

60. Passive Activity Losses, *supra* note 350 at I.R.C. § 469(h)(1).

61. Schuyler Moore, *Entertainment Industry Affected by Several Tax Developments*, 73 J. Tax'n 176 (1990), *citing* Temp. Reg. 1.469-2T(c)(7)(i).

62. *See generally* Bradford S. Cohen & Kyle Neal, *Star Power Celebrity Involvement in Charitable Causes Raises Both Tax and Business Affairs Issues*, L.A. Law., May 2011.

| Taxable Year of Donor Ending After Date of Contribution | Applicable Percentage |
|---|---|
| 5th | 70 |
| 6th | 60 |
| 7th | 50 |
| 8th | 40 |
| 9th | 30 |
| 10th | 20 |
| 11th | 10 |
| 12th | 10 |

63

Another way that musicians donate to charities is through live performances or lending their name to social causes. Although these activities may benefit the charity, they may be financially detrimental to the musician if the IRS determines that the musician's compensation is unreasonable or if the event is for private inurement. These questions arise when an insider of the organization benefits from the musician's performance.[64]

## Abandoned Property

A deduction may be available to musicians or music-related businesses for losses sustained in connection with the abandonment of intangible assets when the abandonment occurred by an identifiable event.[65] Although relinquishment of legal title is not necessary to support a finding of abandonment, intent and affirmative act of abandonment are needed.[66] A musician may also take a deduction for valueless copyrights, but that is likely much more difficult to demonstrate.[67]

---

63. Charitable, etc., Contributions and Gifts, 26 U.S.C. § 170(m)(7).

64. Blake Behnke & Mark Weinberg, *When Celebrities and 501(c)(3)s Collide—The Perils and the Pathways*, 23 TAX'N EXEMPT 12 (2011).

65. Bradford S. Cohen & David P. Schwartz, *Accounting: Determining Entertainment Industry Deductions for Creative Properties Deemed Abandoned or Worthless Remains Difficult Despite IRS Guidance*, 135 DTR J-1 2004.

66. *See* Lockwood v. Commissioner, 94 T.C. 252 (1990) (leaving master recordings on a shelf without preservation constituted abandonment).

67. *Capitalization of Motion Picture, Master Recording, and Video – Entertainment Tax Tips*, IRS PUBLICATION, http://www.irs.gov/Businesses/Small-Businesses-&-Self-Employed/

## Crowd-Funding Considerations

Crowd-funding raises unique issues related to deductions. First, unlike the usual model where an album is recorded and then sold before the band earns income, many bands raise Kickstarter income before stepping foot into a recording studio. If the band does not incur any expenses during the year it receives Kickstarter income, then it will be foreclosed from taking deductions for those expenses. Therefore, to minimize tax exposure the band should incur expenses during the year the Kickstarter income is received.[68] However, deductions still may be available if the band pre-pays for certain goods or services, but there are separate pitfalls associated with that practice.[69]

Second, if the Kickstarter financing is less than the actual cost of recording, producing, mixing, mastering and releasing an album, it may be possible to offset all of the Kickstarter income.[70] But bear in mind, that when a taxpayer produces or creates a product, including a sound recording, and the taxpayer incurs a large portion of the expense before the product is ready to produce income, the IRS states that "the taxpayer is usually required to capitalize those expenses and recover (deduct) them over the period of time that the product is producing income."[71]

Finally, if the Kickstarter income is greater than the cost of the album, then the band may elect to depreciate the Kickstarter funded sound recordings and deduct a portion of the projected income within the first year of sale of the album.[72]

---

Capitalization-of-Motion-Picture,-Master-Recording,-and-Video---Entertainment-Tax-Tips (last visited May 10, 2013) [hereafter Entertainment Tax Tips].

68. A band may elect to use the income forecast method of accounting to depreciate any sound recordings created with Kickstarter financing. *See Kickstarter Tax Tips*, BILLBOARD, June 23, 2012.

69. *Id.* For example, if a band pre-pays for the services of a producer and that producer falls out of vogue in the industry, the band may have wasted its money.

70. Amy Feldman, *Crowdfunded Business May Owe Taxes, Too*, REUTERS, Aug. 13, 2012.

71. Entertainment Tax Tips, *supra* note 67.

72. *Kickstarter Tax Tips, supra* note 68. To depreciate the sound recordings, the band may choose to follow the income forecast method of accounting.

# Tax Credits

Another way in which a musician's tax liability may be reduced is through using tax credits. Although most tax credits have the same savings regardless of the musician's tax bracket, they may otherwise vary. For example, some are nonrefundable, meaning they do not produce a refund in the event losses exceed payment. The following section describes some of the tax credits available to musicians.

## Production Credits

Depending on the state, budget, and type of project, production credits may be available to musicians.[73] For example, in 2007, Louisiana instituted a 25 percent tax refund for in-state expenditures related to the production of sound recordings when a minimum amount of money is spent on the project.[74] In Alabama, there is a 25 percent to 35 percent tax credit for recording a soundtrack with a $50,000 minimum-spending requirement. With the same minimum, Indiana offers a 15 percent refundable credit for audio projects, and Michigan offers a film production credit program that includes a 40 percent refundable tax for sound recordings. In Georgia, the production incentives provide up to 30 percent tax credits for productions, including music videos.[75]

## Foreign Tax Credits

In the publication *International Royalties Tax Reporting Guide*, ASCAP provides information that may reduce a musician's tax liability.[76] ASCAP's guide explains that royalties reported on a member's 1099 are "grossed

---

73. For example, in 2012, the governor of Oklahoma proposed tax reform that would eliminate credits for tourism and film and music facilities. *See* Nancy J. Moore, *Daily Tax Report State Tax & Accounting, Oklahoma: Governor Proposes Major Cut in Personal Income Tax Rates*, 024 DTR H-3, 2012.

74. *See* Louisiana Economic Development Sound Recording Tax Incentive Program, L.S. R.S. 47: 602, 51:6023.

75. *See* Georgia Film, Music & Digital Entertainment Office, http://www.georgia.org/industries/entertainment-industry/Pages/default.aspx (last visited Jan. 21, 2013).

76. *International Royalties Reporting Guide*, AMERICAN SOCIETY OF COMPOSERS AUTHORS & PUBLISHERS, 2011, *available at* http://www.ascap.com/~/media/Files/Pdf/members/payment/IntlTaxReporting.pdf.

up" to include taxes withheld by foreign affiliated societies. This process may allow the musician to claim the taxes paid to foreign governments as foreign tax credits.[77]

## Tax Exemptions

Tax exemptions are yet another way that musicians may reduce their tax liability. For example, in Texas, producers of audio masters receive the benefit of sales and use tax exemptions.[78] The exemption allows the producer to claim a 100 percent exemption from sales and local taxes on certain equipment purchased, rented or repaired during the studio master recording process. Included in this list are acoustic guitars, amplifiers, analog multitrack recorders, analog two-channel recorders, cassette decks, and CD recorders and players.

Clearly, this exemption can be extremely beneficial to musicians and producers. Just as with tax credits, it is critical for a musician's representative to stay up to date on the existence of and changing requirements for tax exemptions.

## Audit

The IRS is aware of attempts by musicians to reduce tax liability through deductions, credits and exemptions. Accordingly, IRS agents are provided with examination guidelines specific to the music industry.[79] The guidelines

---

77. Foreign tax credits have also been the source of litigation, *see* Evans v. Famous Music Corp., 807 N.E.2d 869 (N.Y. 2004). In *Evans*, Henry Mancini, Johnny Mercer, and others sued the publishing company, Famous Music. Although Famous paid the composers monies actually received from foreign sources, less the taxes paid to foreign governments, Famous did not split the tax credit with the composers. The Court of Appeals of New York held that the publishing company was not obligated to share its tax savings from the foreign tax credits.

78. *See Sales and use Tax Exemptions Available for Producers of Audio Master Tapes*, Texas Music Office, http://governor.state.tx.us/music/guides/salestax (last visited May 10, 2013).

79. *Market Segment Specialization Program, Music Industry, Department of the Treasury*, IRS Publications, Mar. 1994; *see also Market Segment Specialization Program, Entertainment*

are split up based on the type of musician or music business being examined, including songwriters, publishers, live performers, producers, managers, and videographers. For each of these categories, an IRS agent is given direction on how to verify whether the claimed deductions are permitted, including what questions to ask to understand the source and amount of the musician's income.

For example, the agents will ask songwriters for PRO royalty statements, publishing agreements, and agency agreements controlling the collection of mechanical and synchronization royalties. In contrast, agents will ask publishers about the sale of copyrights or catalogs and the employment status of performers, producers, nonunion musicians, and arrangers. The IRS also examines live performers as "stars" or "others" depending on the musician's primary source of income. If the musician has multiple jobs to sustain the music career, he or she will be in the "others" category and examined accordingly.

After an audit, the IRS will make a determination about whether there is a deficiency. If necessary, the IRS will file a lien against the musician's assets to secure their interest as a creditor.[80]

## Choice of Entity

Although self-employed musicians may qualify for the deductions, tax credits, and exemptions discussed above, the musician may derive those same benefits *and* limit personal liability if he or she chooses to establish a legal entity.[81] Deciding what entity is best for a musician or music related business

---

*Industry, Department of the Treasury*, IRS PUBLICATIONS, 1995.

80. *See also Songwriter's Assignment of Public Performance Royalties to Creditors has Priority Over IRS Tax Lien, Even Though Creditors Did Not Record Assignment in Copyright Office, Federal Appellate Court Rules*, 19 ENT. L. REP., Feb. 1998, *available at* http://elr.carolon.net/BI/v19n09.pdf. *But see* Broadcast Music, Inc. v. United States, 104 F.3d 1163 (9th Cir. 1997) (unrecorded assignments of a taxpayer's rights to receive royalty income from the performance of a copyrighted work are not unperfected and the rights may transfer prior to the attachment of a federal tax lien).

81. When a member of an entity did not create the music copyright, any income from royalties is considered passive income and can only be offset by passive losses.

requires careful analysis of the individual musician's assets and applicable taxes.[82]

This section provides an overview of the pros and cons of establishing a de facto partnership, limited partnership, C-corporation, S-corporation, or limited liability company (LLC).[83] The chart below is a general introduction to the issues with each entity.

|  | **Formation** | **Operation** | **Tax** |
|---|---|---|---|
| **Sole Proprietorship** | No tax consequences upon formation, without a partner or incorporation the musician defaults to sole proprietorship, and the "doing business as" or dba name should be filed with local/state authorities | Unlimited liability | No entity-level tax |
| **General Partnership** | Generally no tax consequences upon formation | Unlimited liability to partners, any general partner may bind the partnership, and partners share in the profits and losses | Pass through of tax losses and income and partnership doesn't pay taxes, just files an informational tax return and the individual partners report his/her share of profits/losses on the individual return |
| **Limited Partnership** | Partnership agreement establishing which partners are general and limited | Limited liability and management by general partner, so the limited partners cannot bind the partnership | Limited partners must follow the passive income rules |

---

82. *See generally* Bradford S. Cohen, *Income, Estate, and Gift Taxation of Entertainment Assets*, L.A. LAW., May 2012.

83. Although taxation is a major consideration during the process of selecting an entity, there are additional requirements that must be met if the entity is structured as a tax shelter. For example, the entity must have a profit motive and meet the "at-risk" and investment rules established by the IRS.

|  | **Formation** | **Operation** | **Tax** |
|---|---|---|---|
| C-Corporation | File Articles of Incorporation with the Secretary of State, comprised of shareholders and governed by a board of directors, and corporate officers manage the entity | No personal liability as long as corporate formalities are followed, e.g., regular meetings, electing directors and officers, issuing stock, opening a bank account, maintaining sufficient capitalization, which are set forth in bylaws | Pay corporate income tax on the entity's profits; corporation then may elect to distribute remaining monies to shareholders as dividends, which must be reported and taxed as personal income; and may be able to deduct more than S-corporation |
| S-Corporation | Filing an S-corporation election with the secretary of state | Similar to C-corporation | Minimal annual taxes, profits and losses flow through to the shareholders who then report on personal income, and taxed at corporate level if it was previously a C-corporation |
| Limited Liability Company | File Articles of Organization with the secretary of state; Sign an operating agreement | Either member managed or manager managed | Single level of tax, but some states impose a minimum tax on gross revenues |

## Sole Proprietorship

A sole proprietorship is nothing more than a single musician where the band and the individual are one in the same. Since the musician is the employer and the employee, the net profits and losses from the band are reported on the individual's income tax returns.[84] It follows that the owner "materially participates" in the operations of the sole proprietorship and is not subject to the passive loss limitations.

---

84. BRIAN MCPHERSON, GET IT IN WRITING: THE MUSICIAN'S GUIDE TO THE MUSIC BUSINESS (Rockpress Publishing Company 1999).

A sole proprietorship may use the accrual or cash basis method of accounting, except with respect to the sale of inventory.[85] If assets are sold by the sole proprietorship, income received is taxed based on the owner's individual tax rate.[86]

However, under this structure, the individual musician has unlimited personal liability. In the event he or she is sued for copyright infringement related to a sound recording or gets in a car accident on tour, the musician's personal assets are vulnerable.

## Partnerships

### General Partnerships

When two people are doing business together for profit, a de facto or general partnership is created.[87] Typically, a general partnership may use either the accrual or cash basis methods of accounting.[88] Each state has their own laws surrounding partnerships, which should be consulted prior to analyzing a musician's situation.

Generally speaking, musicians working together as a band probably create a general partnership. Although a partnership may be desirable because it doesn't require any filings with the state, a partnership also has numerous default rules that may be detrimental to a musician.[89] First, each musician is an agent of the band and has the ability to bind the partnership. This means that a bassist can book the band for a gig without notifying the remaining band members. This scenario may be problematic when considered along with the next default rule: the partners share in the profits and losses of the band.[90] So, if the drummer cannot come to the gig and the band cannot find a replacement and has to cancel, each musician partner is responsible for any penalties the venue may invoke. To further complicate the relation-

---

85. General Rule for Methods of Accounting, I.R.C. § 446(d).

86. Moore, *supra* note 6.

87. It is highly advisable to consult the act(s) surrounding de facto partnerships in the state where the band is doing business.

88. There is an exception, which requires the accrual method, *see* Limitation on Use of Cash Method of Accounting, I.R.C. § 448(b)(3).

89. John C. Ale & Buck McKinney, *Stumbling Into Partnerships: How Bands, Business Owners and Strategic Allies Find Themselves in Inadvertent Partnerships,* 43 Tex. J. Bus. L. 465 (Fall 2009).

90. *Id.*

ship, if the bassist repeatedly books gigs the band has to back out of and the band wants to kick out the bassist, there may actually be state default partnership rules that prevent the band from being able to do so.

Moreover, each partner is jointly and severally liable for the debts and obligations of the partnership. This means that if one band member racks up a band credit card purchasing band equipment but forgets to make payments to the credit card, all of the members will probably be responsible to repay the debt and accrued interest.

Bands are not the only de facto partnerships, artist/producer development agreements where both the artist and producer jointly share profits from recordings, or joint publishing or distribution deals where a publishing company or record label jointly exploit rights or distribution with bands, are also usually characterized by the IRS as partnerships regardless of whether the parties sign a written agreement stating otherwise (e.g., "nothing contained in this agreement creates a partnership between the parties").[91]

If the band insists on establishing a partnership because it does not want to follow corporate formalities or furnish filing fees to the secretary of state, the band partnership, or any other music related business, should definitely create a partnership agreement. In addition to the general partnership language, the partnership agreement should contain musician-specific clauses, including control, ownership, leaving member, contributions, and amending the agreement.

### Limited Partnership

Limited partnerships are similar to general partnerships but have at least one general partner and additional limited partners. The limited partners have limited liability, authority, and responsibility commensurate with their investment in the partnership. In addition, passive activity losses by the partnership may be offset by passive activity income that is attributable to partners that do not materially participate in the trade or business.[92]

---

91. Moore, *supra* note 6.
92. Passive Activity Losses and Credits Limited, I.R.C. § 469.

## Corporations
### C-Corporations

In contrast to partnerships, corporations are separate legal entities from the shareholders and provide limitation from liability. The shareholders elect the board of directors, who in turn select the corporate officers. When a band establishes a C-corporation, the musicians comprising the band typically elect themselves as the directors and officers of the corporation.

The downside of a C-corporation is that it is taxed twice—once at the corporate level and again at the shareholder level. In addition, while salaries paid to employees are deductible, distributions are not. To compound that shortcoming, upon the death of a shareholder, the heir receives a stepped-up basis in the stock, but the corporation does not.[93]

Corporations must also follow corporate formalities and adhere to record-keeping requirements. These regulations make corporations less desirable for musicians or bands that prefer to set up the entity and do as little as possible to keep it running.

### S-Corporation

S-corporations are nearly identical to C-corporations, except they are not subject to federal income taxes.[94] Instead, the S-corporation passes its taxable income through to its shareholders on a pro rata basis, and those shareholders must report that income on their individual returns.[95]

A clear record of deposits and withdrawals from the S-corporation bank account must be kept to avoid an IRS "bank deposit" analysis of accounts. A bank deposit analysis may reveal that certain withdrawals and transfers do not constitute deductible expenses.[96]

---

93. This means the shareholders can sell the stock and will not realize gain on any amount up to the stepped up basis, which is the value of the stock at the time of death. For a thorough discussion of C-Corporations and S-Corporations, see Cohen, *supra* note 82.

94. Gains on the sales of assets will be taxed at the corporate level if the S-corporation was previously a C-corporation. *Id., citing* Election, Revocation and Termination, 26 U.S.C. §§ 1362(a), 1363(a).

95. Pass-thru Items to Shareholders, 26 U.S.C. § 1366(a)(1).

96. When Larry Johnson, the producer and promoter of the New Kids On The Block attempted to file bankruptcy without filing tax returns for certain years the IRS analyzed whether payments from ASCAP were properly reported by Johnson's S-corporation and whether

Additionally, an S-corporation is limited to one hundred shareholders and one class of stock. The S-corporation must use the accrual method of accounting if the offering meets certain registration requirements or more than 35 percent of the shareholders do not materially participate in the management of the entity.[97]

Another feature of the S-corporation to be aware of is that residuals and the sale of copyrights are subject to income in respect of decedent (IRD) rules. The drawback of IRD is that it does not receive a stepped-up basis and must be reported as income to the beneficiary.[98]

## Personal Holding Companies

Corporations are personal holding companies when 60 percent of their adjusted ordinary gross income is personal holding company income and more than 50 percent of their stock is owned by not more than five individuals.[99] The musician should be aware that personal holding companies are subject to personal holding company tax.[100] To determine whether these additional taxes apply to the musician client, the Code should be reviewed in greater detail.

## Limited Liability Companies

Limited liability companies provide limited liability for the members and managers of the entity and are generally not subject to taxation at the entity level. As a result, capital gains flow through to the entity's members.

---

certain deductions claimed concerning the S-corporation were actually deductible expenses. United States v. Johnson, No. 1:9-cv-0799-JOF (N.D. Ga. Mar. 30, 2000).

97.  Moore, *supra* note 6; *see also* Limitations on Use of Cash Method of Accounting, I.R.C. § 448(a)(3), 448(d)(3); General Rule for Taxable Year of Deduction, I.R.C. § 461(i)(3); Limitations on Deductions for Certain Farming, I.R.C. § 464(e)(2); I.R.C. § 1256(e)(3)(B).

98.  Cohen, *supra* note 82. The recipient of IRD income may deduct part of the estate tax attributable to the IRD income.

99.  Personal holding income includes royalties, but not certain types of copyright royalties. *See* Definition of Personal Holding Company, I.R.C. § 542(a) (2004).

100.  Imposition of Personal Holding Company Tax, I.R.C. § 541 (2012).

The major draw for musicians to establish LLCs is that most creative property, including copyrights, can be contributed to or distributed from LLCs with little to no tax consequences.[101]

### Establishing Multiple Entities

A band may choose to establish multiple entities to separate assets and limit liability. For example, since touring invokes more potential liability, such as automobile accidents, injuries on stage or in the audience, and destruction of equipment,[102] it is probably wise to create a touring entity that is separate from the band entity to insulate certain assets and income-streams.

To illustrate, assume a band maintained one entity housing intellectual property assets, licensing revenue, touring equipment and signed contracts. During a performance, the band's stage was struck by lightning and collapsed on the musicians and audience. To satisfy the band's liability in connection with the destruction, the assets of the entity, including the intellectual property and licensing revenue, may be accessed. In contrast, if the same band establishes two separate entities, the intellectual property and licensing income can be protected from any debts or obligations of the touring entity.

## Conclusion

In conclusion, income, deductions, and choice of entity may have a profound impact on the financial success of a musician. Although a tax professional should ultimately advise the client, a working knowledge of the tax law discussed in this chapter will better equip a lawyer to provide general advice to his or her musician client.

---

101. *See* Cohen, *supra* note 82; *see also* Nonrecognition of Gain or Loss on Contribution, I.R.C. § 721, 731.

102. Jeff Brown, *Business Entity for Touring*, ENT. L. & FIN., Mar. 2005.

# Chapter Ten
# The Musician's Estate

*By Heather Ryan Liberman*

Death does not necessarily end a musician's career. Rather, income streams, goodwill, and performances of video and audio recordings may live on indefinitely. In 2012, Michael Jackson was ranked number one in Forbes Magazine's annual list of the top earning dead celebrities, earning $145 million in that year alone. Also in the top fifteen were Elvis Presley, Bob Marley, John Lennon, and George Harrison, earning a collective $85 million.[1]

These musicians attained posthumous financial success due to factors probably not controlled by lawyers. For example, the musician's fame during his or her life, sensationalized circumstances surrounding the musician's death, the cultural impact of the musician's work, and consumers' ever-changing tastes and trends may all contribute to elevated income. Nevertheless, lawyers should be aware of certain legal issues surrounding

---

1. Zack O'Malley Greenburg, *The Top-Earning Dead Musicians of 2012*, Forbes, Oct. 31, 2012, http://www.forbes.com/sites/zackomalleygreenburg/2012/10/31/the-top-earning-dead-musicians-of-2012/.

musicians and their estates to prevent unnecessary complications and to avoid common pitfalls.[2]

This chapter provides a general overview of the special estate-related considerations musicians and their legal representatives should make, but does not provide estate planning that can be broadly applied. How to draft a will, whether to establish a trust or private foundation, how to select an executor or trustee, navigating the probate process and how to avoid it,[3] and other estate planning and estate tax specifics are outside the scope of this chapter. Consult with an estate-planning expert to carry out specific legal procedures and to determine what devices fit best for your musician client.

This chapter will cover the following topics as they relate to a musician's estate:

(1)  What Comprises a Musician's Estate?
    a.  Inventory, including real, tangible and intangible assets, and existing agreements
    b.  Valuation of assets
(2)  Generating Income for the Estate
    a.  Copyright
    b.  Trademark
    c.  Right of publicity
    d.  Digital assets
    e.  Updating payers, including SAG, AFTRA, ASCAP, and BMI
    f.  Tribute bands

---

2. *See* Andrew Mayoras & Danielle B. Mayoras, Trial & Heirs Famous Fortune Fights (Wise Circle Books 2009).

3. The probate process typically begins with the validation of a will or determination that one does not exist. When one exists, it is submitted to the court for supervision of administration to distribute assets in accordance with the will, discharge creditors and pay taxes. When there is not a will, the estate is subject to the laws of intestate succession, which are determined on a state-by-state basis. Depending on the jurisdiction in which the musician dies a resident, state intestacy laws may provide that the spouse, if any, receives a larger portion of the estate than the children. Note that many musicians, including Amy Winehouse and Jimi Hendrix, have died intestate. For Hendrix, this has caused many legal battles; *see In re* Estate of Hendrix, 134 Wash. App. 1007, 2006 WL 2048240 (Wash. App. Div. 2006).

# What Comprises a Musician's Estate?

A musician's estate is comprised of all of the property the musician leaves after death, including assets and liabilities. Ultimately, the property is transferred to discharge creditors and pay taxes, and then the remaining assets are disbursed to beneficiaries. The musician's debts must be paid first, which means the estate may remain open for a lengthy period of time if the musician amassed sizeable debt during his or her life.[4]

To begin the process of dividing assets, there must be a determination of whether the musician died with a will or trust. This is important because trusts and certain contractual agreements avoid probate. Wills on the other hand go through the probate process, which begins by determining the validity of the will. After concluding the will is valid, the personal representative, or executor, identified in the will begins administering the disbursement of assets. When there is no will, the personal representative of the estate is a court-appointed administrator that carries the same duties as the executor.

The administrator's responsibilities include identifying and valuing the musician's property to ensure that all of the estate assets are properly allocated.[5] Specifically, valuation of the assets is necessary to facilitate payments to creditors, file federal and state estate tax returns, determine the step-up (or step-down) in basis for capital gains purposes, make disbursements to

---

4. Jessica Bozarth, *Copyrights and Creditors: What Will be Left of the King of Pop's Legacy?*, 29 CARDOZO ARTS & ENT. L.J.: 5 (2011); *see also* Susanne Schafer, *Settlement Has Put James Brown Estate in the Black*, ASSOCIATED PRESS (Nov. 1, 2011), *available at* http://acn.liveauctioneers.com/index.php/features/people/5811-settlement-has-put-james-brown-estate-in-the-black (Estate of James Brown was faced with over $20 million in debt before the establishment of a complex settlement); *see also Whitney Houston Heirs Have a Problem: Debt*, N.Y. DAILY NEWS, Mar. 1, 2012 (Houston's heirs may never see royalty payments due to the $100 million advance and loans she took from Sony Music). *But see* Zack O'Malley Greenburg, *Michael Jackson's Personal Debts Paid Off, Just in Time for Bad 25*, FORBES, Nov. 21, 2012, http://www.forbes.com/sites/zackomalleygreenburg/2012/11/21/michael-jacksons-personal-debts-paid-off-just-in-time-for-bad-25/.

5. On December 2, 2011, Lisa Simone Kelly, the administrator of the Estate of Nina Simone and the daughter of the late singer, filed a federal lawsuit against her father for wrongfully obtaining and transferring the assets of the Estate, including master recordings, and diaries. *See* Kelly v. Roker, No. 11-CV-5822 (Cal. Dist. Ct. filed Dec. 2, 2011); *see also* Suzanne Stathatos, *Nina Simone's Daughter Sues Her Own Father Over Jazz Singer's Estate*, SAN FRAN. WKLY., July 11, 2012, *available at* http://blogs.sfweekly.com/thesnitch/2012/07/nina_simone_lisa_simone_kelly.php.

beneficiaries, administer future filing dates (such as trademark and copyright renewals), arrange auctions, invest on behalf of the estate, and ultimately close the estate.

This section will address issues surrounding the estate inventory, and identify approaches for determining the value of the inventory.

## Inventory

An inventory of a musician's assets can be created by speaking directly to the musician during his or her life, or by relying on secondary sources after the musician's death. Regardless of the approach, a musician's inventory consists of tangible property, both real and personal, intangible property, and digital assets. The tangible personal property may include typical estate property, such as household effects or cars, but may also include unique property such as instruments, recording equipment, notebooks or clothing. The musician's unique intangible property may include copyrights in musical compositions, sound recordings, and other works of authorship, trademarks, rights of publicity, and digital assets.

Each of these tangible and intangible assets may be owned by the musician as an individual or as a function of his or her membership in a band. If the musician was in a band with a formal business arrangement,[6] the partnership or shareholders' agreement should outline disbursement of band assets upon the death of a member. When no formal entity exists, the de facto partnership laws of the state should be reviewed.

---

6. Brother Records, Inc. v. Jardine, 432 F.3d 939 (9th Cir. 2005). The Beach Boys are one band that did formally establish an entity. Their entity, Brother Records, is jointly held by Al Jardine, Mike Love, Brian Wilson, and the estate of Carl Wilson. After Carl Wilson's death, Al Jardine and Mike Love refused to tour together, but the remaining members allowed Love to establish a new group and perform as the Beach Boys, as long as the new band paid royalties to Brother Records. Al Jardine also decided he wanted to tour, but used the name "The Beach Boys Family and Friends." Brother Records brought suit against Jardine for trademark infringement and won because Jardine's use of "The Beach Boys" caused consumer confusion as to the people booking Jardine's band as well as the people who attended Jardine's shows.

It is also important to know whether the musician was divorced during his or her life.[7] If so, future income streams may be divided amongst ex-spouses and, depending on the separation agreement, a supported spouse may also be entitled to half of any infringement damages awards[8] or a percentage of the income stream from derivative works.[9] It is important to note that New York and New Jersey recognize "celebrity status" as enhanced earning capacity that is a divisible marital asset in divorce.[10] However, the supported spouse must meet a high threshold to receive any economic benefit for the creative spouse's enhanced financial earnings.

## Valuation of Assets

Once the inventory list is created, the assets should be valued. Valuation of assets can be a very complicated process,[11] and is best left up to professionally qualified actuaries (in the case of a copyright, trademark, or license) or professional appraisers (for real or tangible personal property).[12] These professionals will be experienced in the available valuation approaches and will likely keep in mind estate and gift tax considerations.

That being said, valuation is dependent on many factors, including the amount, timing, reliability and type of income that can be derived from the asset. Additionally, values are influenced by the economy, investor preferences and expectation, the quality of specific industries and the steadiness of assets.[13]

---

7. *See* Judith L. Poller & Elizabeth Warner, *Divorce Distribution of Creative Assets*, Ent. L. & Fin., November 2011; *see also* Maloy v. Maloy, 2008 WL 276018 (Tenn. Ct. App. 2008).

8. *In re* Marriage of Worth, 195 Cal. App. 3d 768 (Cal. Ct. App. 1987).

9. Miner v. Miner, 2002 WL 33955151 (Tex. Ct. App. 2002).

10. Elkus v. Elkus, 572 N.Y.S.2d 901 (N.Y. Sup. Ct. 1991); *see also* Piscopo v. Piscopo, 231 N.J. Super. 576 (N.J. Super. Ct. Ch. Div. 1988).

11. Terry Lloyd, *Valuing Artistic and Creative Works*, 1894 PLI Corp 387, 2011; *see also* Ann-Marie Rhodes, *Valuing Art in an Estate: New Concerns*, 31 Cardozo Arts & Ent. L.J. 45 (2012).

12. The two largest associations of qualified appraisers are the Appraisers Association of America and the American Society of Appraisers.

13. Lloyd, *supra* note 11 at 11.

Valuation will likely follow the market, income, or cost approach. The market approach considers market transactions for identical or comparable assets. However, the uniqueness of creative assets can make it difficult to find a comparable transaction. The income approach uses variables to calculate the future expected benefits as expressed in today's dollars. The variables include the income, rate of return, and growth rate. This calculation is typically based on assumptions, so it is not always the best approach. Yet, there are fewer assumptions about the asset's future earnings if it has a steady history of earnings. The cost approach is less useful for intangible properties, such as copyright and trademark, because the methodology is based on the cost to replace the asset.[14]

While valuation may occur posthumously, authentication and appraisal of unusual tangible assets during the life of the musician may make the assets easier to transfer.[15] Such assets may include a guitar played at a famous concert,[16] books,[17] journals, recording equipment, or clothing. Authentication and appraisal are also important to avoid IRS scrutiny of estate

---

14. Northern Natural Gas v. United States, 470 F.2d 1107 (8th Cir.), *cert. denied*, 412 U.S. 939 (1973); *see also* William Lockwood, *Estate, Tax and Personal Financial Planning*, 4 EST. TAX & PERS. FIN. PLAN. § 35:57 (2012). In addition to following one of the valuation approaches, an appraiser must determine what rules he or she will follow when inserting numerical assumptions into the valuation equation. The purpose for the valuation will dictate which rules to follow. Typically, the IRS follows fair market value, or the value that would be reached between a hypothetical willing buyer and seller. Strategic value is the value to a specific buyer of the asset. Fair value is established by court precedent or statute, which has been used when calculating minority shareholder rights. Fair value is followed by GAAP, or Generally Accepted Accounting Principles, and is a combination of fair market value and strategic value. Going concern is defined as "an intangible that attaches to the tangible assets of some businesses . . . as a value enhancement for the assemblage of a business regardless of a business' profitability." In contrast, goodwill applies only to operating companies, because it is based on earning capacity.

15. The IRS has contested many valuation cases involving unusual assets, *see* Straw v. Commissioner, 62 T.C.M. (CCH) 1056, (1991) (horses); Estate of Miller v. Commissioner, 62 T.C.M. (CCH) 997 (1991) (hunting trophies); Sanz v. Commissioner, 60 T.C.M. (CCH) 1160 (1990), *aff'd*, 983 F.2d 232 (1993) (foreign language text books).

16. Andy Greene, *Experts: Bob Dylan's Long-Lost Newport Folk Festival Electric Guitar Found in New Jersey*, ROLLING STONE (July 11, 2012), *available at* http://www.rollingstone.com/music/news/experts-bob-dylans-long-lost-newport-folk-festival-electric-guitar-found-in-new-jersey-20120711.

17. Omega Auctions presented the "Elvis Presley Collection" for sale on September 8, 2012; Elvis's Bible sold for £59,000 and his shoes sold for £6,900. *See* Omega Auctions, *The Elvis Presley Collection* (2012), http://www.omegaauctions.co.uk/ElvisPresley.php.

and gift tax assessments.[18] A qualified appraisal may also assist the owner of an unusual asset worth more than $50,000 to obtain a "Statement of Value" from the IRS.[19] A musician's Statement of Value only applies to the individual requesting the statement and cannot be used by analogy other individuals with comparable assets.

Once valuation is complete, an estate can begin discharging creditors, paying taxes, making disbursements to beneficiaries, initiating investments, arranging auctions, and donating goods to facilities such as the Rock and Roll Hall of Fame[20] or other museums, subject to any state probate laws.

# Generating Income for the Estate

Generating income for the estate is critical, particularly when the musician amassed substantial debt during his or her life. As previously stated, the estate will not close until debts are satisfied and taxes are paid. While an estate may generate income simply due to the musician or band's fame, it may also earn money as a result of the estate's fiduciary successfully performing its duties.

This section does not exhaust all of the ways in which an estate may generate income, but will discuss the duties of the estate's fiduciary and the role of income-producing assets, such as copyrights, trademarks, rights of publicity, digital assets, and other royalty streams.

## Fiduciary Duties

An executor is the fiduciary when the decedent left a will, and that individual will need court permission to carry out his or her duties. When the decedent passed away without a will, the court will appoint an administrator, who will likely be a friend or family member of the deceased. In contrast, if the

---

18. Frederick K. Hoops, *Unusual Assets*, 2 FAMILY ESTATE PLANNING GUIDE § 34:11 (2012).

19. *Id.*

20. The Rock and Roll Hall of Fame Museum "seeks materials that will tell the stories of Hall of Fame inductees and other significant artists." The museum website provides a list of materials it is interested in collecting. *See Donating Artifacts*, THE ROCK AND ROLL HALL OF FAME, http://rockhall.com/donate/donating-artifacts/.

decedent established a trust, the fiduciary is known as a trustee. There may be instances when both a trustee and an administrator or executor should coordinate with one another if the decedent did not place all of his or her property in a trust. For purposes of this chapter, the representative of the decedent's property is simply referred to as a fiduciary.

A fiduciary is expected to satisfy multiple duties, some of which may seem to conflict with one another. First, a fiduciary has the duty of loyalty to not manage the assets in a manner that is self-dealing.[21] Next, a fiduciary has the duty to administer the estate in the interest of the beneficiaries without the influence of third parties.[22] This particular duty can be complicated when the musician has fans that want to buy or access certain assets, but selling those assets would be against the interest of the beneficiaries. A fiduciary also has a duty of impartiality, which can prove difficult when there are multiple beneficiaries. Despite conflicting responsibilities, the fiduciary has a duty to make assets productive.[23]

Generally speaking, it is wise for a fiduciary to do the following: stay up to date with changing law; be aware of exceptions or nuances in the law; continue accounting to payees;[24] decide whether to litigate wrongful uses of

---

21. Although related to visual art, the dealings of the executors of the Estate of Mark Rothko were scrutinized when they did not satisfy their fiduciary duties. *In re* Estate of Mark Rothko, 362 N.Y.S.2d 673 (N.Y. Sur. 1974).

22. The trustee has the duties of administering the trust in accordance with its terms and applicable law, loyalty, income productivity, and prudent investment, among others. *See* RESTATEMENT (THIRD) OF TRUSTS §§ 76–79 (2007). Similarly, when Bob Marley's widow, Rita Marley, admitted to forging Bob Marley's name to a will, she was removed from control of the estate as one of the administrators. *See* Danielle Mayoras & Andy Mayoras, *Are Bob Marley's Heirs Destroying His Legacy?,* FORBES, Dec, 5, 2011, http://www.forbes.com/sites/trialandheirs/2011/12/05/are-bob-marley-heirs-destroying-his-legacy/.

23. For example, the Estate of Elvis Presley lobbied the Tennessee Legislature to pass legislation protecting the descendability of the right of publicity and has pursued numerous cases of infringement of Elvis's right of publicity. However, the Estate must balance which matters to pursue due to the high costs of litigation. *See* Neil Caulkins, *A Fiduciary's Duties When a Celebrity Persona Is the Asset,* 24 COLUM. J.L. & ARTS 235 (2001).

24. Not all Estates have been diligent about accounting to payees and as a result have been the subject of litigation. For example, the Estate of Merl Saunders sued the Estate of Jerry Garcia over rights and royalties associated with a project released by the Estate of Garcia entitled "Pure Jerry: Jerry Garcia & Merl Saunders Band, Keystone Berkeley September 1, 1974." The Estate of Garcia allegedly failed to account to the Estate of Saunders. *See* Susan Mora, Merl Saunders, Jr., Anthony Saunders Washington v. Jerry Garcia Estate, LLC, No. 08-5772, (N.D. Cal. filed 2008). Additionally, Courtney Love was served with a lawsuit by a management firm, London & Co, over profits from the sale of the rights to songs by Kurt Cobain, *see*

copyrights,[25] trademarks,[26] or the right of publicity;[27] and review the terms of any agreements executed by the decedent.[28]

---

Barnaby Smith, *Courtney Love Settles Lawsuit Over Kurt Cobain Song Rights*, SPINNER (Aug. 18, 2010), http://www.spinner.com/2010/08/18/courtney-love-lawsuit-kurt-cobain-rights/.

25.  Copyright lawsuits cover a range of issues, but notably the James Ambrose Johnson, Jr., 1999 Trust filed suit against UMG Recordings, asserting that royalties due to Rick James for digital downloads should be calculated as licenses, applying the holding in F.B.T. Productions, LLC v. Aftermath Records, 621 F.3d 958 (9th Cir. 2010) as precedent. *See* Rick James, by and through The James Ambrose Johnson, Jr., 1999 Trust v. UMG Recordings, No. 11-1613, (N.D. Cal. filed 2011). On a separate issue, Yoko Ono Lennon brought suit against Premise Media over unauthorized use of "Imagine" in a documentary film. *See* Yoko Ono Lennon, Sean Ono Lennon, Julian Lennon, and EMI Blackwood Music, Inc. v. Premise Media Corp., L.P., 556 F. Supp. 2d 310 (S.D.N.Y. 2008). Additionally, the Estate of Jimi Hendrix was engaged in a forty-year legal battle over rights to sound recordings from two of Hendrix's concerts at Royal Albert Hall in 1969.

26.  The Beastie Boys filed suit against Monster Energy Drink for unauthorized use of the band's trademark. Beastie Boys, Michael Diamond, Adam Horovitz v. Monster Energy, No. 12 CV 6065, (S.D.N.Y. filed Aug. 8, 2012).

27.  Due to his faith as a Rastafarian, Bob Marley died without a will, and his assets passed by intestate succession under Jamaican law. Certain family members allegedly purchased Marley's right of identity for over $11 million and have sought to enforce those rights. *See* Fifty-Six Hope Road Music, Ltd. & Zion Rootswear, LLC v. A.V.E.L.A., Inc., 458 Fed. Appx. 892, (Fed. Cir. 2011). Bob Marley's right of publicity is now co-administered by venture capitalist James Salter, and the family continues to establish new business opportunities for exploitation. *See* Rob Kenner, *The Business of Bob Marley: Billboard Cover Story*, BILLBOARD (February 4, 2011), http://www.billboard.com/#/features/the-business-of-bob-marley-billboard-cover-1005022242.story?page=1.

28.  As technology changes, it is important for the administrators of an estate to be aware of the terms embodying the contracts signed by the decedent. For example, Pink Floyd was victorious over EMI when it invoked language from a 1999 agreement instructing EMI, "Not to couple records delivered hereunder with other master recordings [for example, in compilations] or to sell in any form other than as the current albums." The label was also instructed, "To exploit the albums in exactly the same form as to track listing and timing," and was informed, "There are no rights to sell any or all of the records as single records, other than with [PFM's] permission." This language prevented EMI from selling Pink Floyd's sound recordings on iTunes for individual downloads. Although not an estate issue, this case illustrates the importance of staying informed about signed agreements. *See Pink Floyd Win EMI Court Ruling Over Online Sales*, BBC NEWS (Mar. 11, 2010), http://news.bbc.co.uk/2/hi/8561963.stm; *see also* Rodgers & Hammerstein Organization v. UMG Recordings, Inc., 60 U.S.P.Q.2d 1354 (S.D.N.Y. 2001) ("Mechanical License" covered distribution of certain forms of fixed recordings of musical compositions did not cover streaming over the Internet). Moreover, the Estate should be clear on what it actually owns, and only license those rights, not the rights of others. *See* David Porter, *Jimi Hendrix Estate Sued By Former Bandmate*, BILLBOARD, July 15, 2010, http://www.billboard.com/news/jimi-hendrix-estate-sued-by-former-bandmate-1004104561.story#/news/jimi-hendrix-estate-sued-by-former-bandmate-1004104561.story.

## Copyright

One type of income-producing asset that the fiduciary may exploit is copyrights the musician owned or transferred during his or her life. These copyrights may be in musical compositions, sound recordings, and other works of authorship if the musician was a multidisciplinary artist. As discussed in previous chapters, licensing copyrights can be a substantial source of income.

The copyright for a published or unpublished[29] work of authorship lasts for the duration of the author's life plus seventy years.[30] The existence of a postmortem period of protection means that the successors in interest to the copyright will have substantial rights and responsibilities associated with their inheritance.[31] These rights and responsibilities include the right to terminate a copyright transfer and the responsibility to renew the copyright in certain works.[32] The deadlines associated with these rights and responsibilities should be properly docketed to ensure lasting protection.[33]

---

29. *See* Shloss v. Sweeney, 515 F. Supp. 2d 1083 (N.D. Cal. 2007). Although dealing with the estate of a literary author, *Shloss v. Sweeney* involved the estate of author James Joyce's attempts to restrict Carol Shloss's use of unpublished materials. Works by Joyce that were not published during his lifetime and were not published posthumously at any time before December 31, 2002, entered the public domain in the U.S. on January 1, 2012. For another examination of a literary author's unpublished materials, see also Ofer Aderet, *Kafka's Estate Unveiled: Unpublished Works, Personal Letters*, HAARETZ (Jan. 1, 2012), http://www.haaretz.com/print-edition/news/kafka-s-estate-unveiled-unpublished-works-personal-letters-1.261160. *See also* Estate of Martin Luther King, Jr., Inc. v. CBS, Inc. 194 F.3d 1211 (11th Cir. 1999); Bartok v. Boosey & Hawkes, 523 F.2d 941 (2d Cir. 1975) (the 1976 Act followed the definition used in this case); *and* William Patry, *Posthumous Works and Renewal,* THE PATRY COPYRIGHT BLOG (Sept. 26, 2006), http://williampatry.blogspot.com/2006/09/posthumous-works-and-renewal.html.

30. One very useful resource to track the duration of a particular work's copyright is a chart created by Cornell University and published on its website. *See* Peter B. Hirtle, *Copyright Term and Public Domain in the United States*, CORNELL COPYRIGHT INFORMATION CENTER, 2012, http://copyright.cornell.edu/resources/publicdomain.cfm.

31. *See* Estate of Brown v. Arc Music Group, 830 F. Supp. 2d 501 (N.D. Ill. 2011). The estate of the deceased owner of three record labels failed to state a claim for copyright infringement with regard to seventy-seven works when the complaint did not allege that the musical compositions were registered as copyrighted works or that the estate currently owned the copyrights to those works.

32. The process for renewal is not detailed in this chapter. For more information about renewal see *Renewal of Copyright*, THE U.S. COPYRIGHT OFFICE (2006), http://www.copyright.gov/circs/circ15.pdf.

33. 17 U.S.C. § 302. *But see* Capitol Records v. Naxos of Am., 4 N.Y.3d 540 (2005) (sound recordings made in the United Kingdom in the 1930s that had entered the public

## Termination of Transfer

Since the nuances of the right to terminate a copyright transfer are fairly complicated, they are detailed in this section. The copyright termination right was created to "permit authors, originally in a poor bargaining position, to renegotiate the term of the grant once the value of the work has been tested."[34] That unwaivable[35] right was codified in the Copyright Act, and allows the author of musical compositions or sound recordings to terminate the grant of an exclusive or nonexclusive license or transfer to a third party.[36] However, the termination right does not apply to works made for hire, dispositions by will, or foreign rights.[37]

The termination right is powerful because once the termination is effective, all rights under the original grant revert back to the original author(s) or other person(s) owning termination interests. After recapturing the copyright, the author(s) or person(s) owning the termination rights may choose to transfer the rights again to the original grantee, but under terms more favorable to the rights-holder.[38]

When the author is deceased, the Copyright Act sets forth explicit rules for who can terminate the transfer, as well as when and how. If the rules are not followed, the original grant will persist for the life of the copyright.

---

domain there in the 1980s, 50 years after their creation, were still eligible for copyright protection under the common law of the state of New York, even though they were in the public domain in the U.K).

34. H.R. Rep. No. 2222, 60th Cong., 2d Sess. (1909); *see also* MELVILLE B. NIMMER & DAVID NIMMER, NIMMER ON COPYRIGHT § 9.02 (1989).

35. 17 U.S.C. § 304(c)(5) (2011). Termination of the grant may be effected notwithstanding any agreement to the contrary, including an agreement to make a will or to make any future grant.

36. *See* 17 U.S.C. § 101 (2011). A transfer of copyright ownership is defined as an assignment, mortgage, exclusive license, or any other conveyance, alienation, or hypothecation of a copyright or of any of the exclusive rights comprised in a copyright, whether it is limited in time or place of effect, but not including a nonexclusive license. *See also* 17 U.S.C. § 204 (2011). Transfer is effective by operation of law, or "Instrument of conveyance or note or memorandum of the transfer, is in writing and signed by the owner of the rights conveyed or such owner's duly authorized agent. A certificate of acknowledgment is not required for the validity of the transfer, but is prima facie evidence of the execution of the transfer . . ." based on certain conditions.

37. *See* Siegel v. Warner Bros. Entm't Inc., 542 F. Supp. 2d 1098, 1140 (C.D. Cal. 2008) (terminating party only recaptures the domestic rights of the grant to the copyright in question).

38. 17 U.S.C. § 304(c)(6)(D) (2011); *see* Bourne Co. v. MPL Communications, Inc., 675 F. Supp. 859, 864–65 (S.D.N.Y. 1987), *opinion modified*, 678 F. Supp. 70 (S.D.N.Y. 1988).

Section 304 of the Copyright Act[39] covers works in their first or renewal term that were transferred before January 1, 1978, and Section 203 pertains to transfers that occurred on or after January 1, 1978.[40] The strict requirements to effect the termination under each of these Sections are detailed below.

### Section 304 of the U.S. Copyright Act (pre-1978 grants)

Under Section 304(c)(2) of the Copyright Act, the termination interest of a deceased author is owned and may be exercised in accordance with the following:

(1)  If the author has a surviving widow and surviving children, the widow owns one-half of the author's interest and the children own the other one-half, divided amongst the children per stirpes.

(2)  If the author does not have a surviving spouse, then the entire interest goes to the children and vice versa.

(3)  In the event that the author's widow or widower, children, and grand-children are not living, the author's executor, administrator, personal representative, or trustee shall own the author's entire termination interest.

(4)  In the case of a grant exercised by more than one author of the work, the termination is only effective if executed by the person or persons entitled to exercise a majority of the total termination interest.[41]

After determining who can terminate the grant, the next considerations are: (1) the timing of the termination, (2) notice to the grantee, and (3) recordation in the Copyright Office.

Termination of the grant may be effected during a period of five years beginning at the end of the fifty-six years from the date the copyright was originally secured, or beginning on January 1, 1978, whichever is later.[42] Additionally, there is a fail-safe for a pre-1978 grant of a copyright transfer or license to be terminated within the five-year termination window

---

39.  Roger Miller Music, Inc. v. Sony/ATV Pub., LLC, 672 F.3d 434 (6th Cir. 2012).
40.  17 U.S.C. §§ 203–204 (2011).
41.  17 U.S.C. § 304(c)(1) (2011).
42.  17 U.S.C. § 304(c)(3) (2011).

beginning at the end of seventy-five years from the date the copyright was secured, if the end of the fifty-sixth year expired by October 27, 1998, and termination was not executed at that time.[43]

Notice of the termination shall be served upon the grantee or the grantee's successor in title[44] during a window of time that is not less than two years or more than ten years before the termination date and must be signed by the owners of the termination interest or their duly authorized agents, in writing.[45] The notice must also state the date of the termination. Finally, a copy of the notice shall be recorded in the Copyright Office before the effective date of termination.

Note that a derivative work prepared under authority of a grant of rights may continue to be used under the terms of the original grant even after the termination of that grant. But this privilege does not extend to the preparation of new derivative works based on the copyrighted work after the termination of the grant.[46]

### Section 203 of the U.S. Copyright Act (post-1978 grants)

The primary difference between Section 203 terminations and Section 304 terminations are that Section 203 terminations cover post-1978 grants. Next, terminations under Section 203 must be effected during a five-year window that begins thirty-five years after the date of execution of the grant.[47] If the original grant covers the publication of the work, the five-year period begins at the end of thirty-five years from the date of publication or forty years following the date of execution of the grant, whichever term ends earlier. The remaining aspects of the process are identical to Section 304 terminations.

### Termination of Transfer and Litigation

Although the Copyright Act outlines the procedure for copyright termination, the practical application of termination is still relatively unknown. This is

---

43. 17 U.S.C. § 304(d) (2011).

44. 17 U.S.C. § 304(c)(4) (2011).

45. 17 U.S.C. § 304(c)(4)(A) (2011).

46. 17 U.S.C. § 304(c)(6)(A) (2011); *see also* Mills Music, Inc. v. Snyder, 469 U.S. 153, 156 (1985); Woods v. Bourne ,60 F.3d 978 (2d Cir. 1995).

47. 17 U.S.C. § 203(a)(3) (2011).

likely to change in the coming years because 2013 is the first year that terminations for post-1978 grants become effective. For example, musicians such as Bob Dylan, Tom Petty, Loretta Lynn, and Tom Waits are allegedly already pursuing termination of copyright transfers in sound recordings.[48] These terminations are expected to face tough scrutiny by record labels that want to retain rights. It is anticipated that the record labels will argue that the sound recordings are excluded from termination as works for hire, compilations, or part of collective works.[49]

Presently, at least one notable music copyright termination dispute is making its way through the courts. In January 2011, Victor Willis of the Village People served his notice of termination for thirty-three musical compositions, including "YMCA," on Scorpio Music. On July 14, 2011, Scorpio Music S.A. and its administrator in the United States filed a declaratory judgment action challenging Willis's terminations. Although Scorpio originally attempted to argue the works were made for hire, which are not terminable, it withdrew that argument. Instead, Scorpio relied on the argument that Willis's terminations were not effective because he was a joint author and the notices of termination did not reflect the majority of the termination interests. Willis argued that since he originally transferred his rights in separate agreements from the other joint authors, he had the ability to terminate the transfer unilaterally. The United States District Court for the Southern District of California found in favor of Willis and dismissed Scorpio's complaint. Willis's counterclaim is still pending.[50]

Despite Willis's victory, many other legal questions surrounding copyright termination still exist.[51] For example, the issue of whether a musician can work around the Copyright Act to prevent his statutory successors from owning the musician's termination interest is illustrated in the following case.

48. Larry Richter, *Record Industry Braces for Artists' Battles Over Song Rights*, N.Y. TIMES, Aug. 15, 2011, *available at* http://www.nytimes.com/2011/08/16/arts/music/springsteen-and-others-soon-eligible-to-recover-song-rights.html?_r=0.

49. *See* Mary LaFrance, *Authorship and Termination Rights in Sound Recordings*, 75 S. CAL. L. REV. 375, 389 (2002).

50. Scorpio Music S.A. v. Victor Willis, No. 3:11-CV-01557-BTM-RBB (S.D. Cal., filed July 14, 2011).

51. *See* DC Comics v. Pacific Pictures Corp., No. CV-10-3633 ODW (C.D. Cal. Order, Jan. 10, 2013).

Before his death, Ray Charles created revocable trusts in the amount of $500,000 each for most of his twelve children. The trusts were conditioned on the children's waiver of any future interest in the estate.[52] Despite the existence of the trusts, some of Ray Charles's children accepted the money and later served copyright termination of transfer notices on the publishers of roughly fifty-one musical compositions authored in whole or in part by Ray Charles.

As a result, the Ray Charles Foundation brought suit against Ray Charles's children for a declaration of the Foundation's rights and an injunction to prevent the children or any third parties from representing that they own any rights in and to Ray Charles's compositions, entering into license agreements, or transferring the rights at issue.

On January 28, 2013, the court found in favor of the children, stating:

> The Foundation is not a grantee of the rights to be terminated or its successor. Congress did not even require the statutory heirs provide it with statutory notice of the termination, let alone give it a seat at the table during the termination process.[53]

Although the court made a definitive ruling, it will likely be appealed by the Foundation. Clearly, the landscape of copyright terminations is ever-evolving and should be closely watched by representatives of musician's and their estates.

## Trademark

Trademarks are another income-producing asset that should be on the radar of a musician's representatives.[54] A musician may already own a registered trademark in his or her name or the band's name, or the estate may choose to file an application. Either way, keeping track of a musician's trademark rights is important for the estate, especially in light of the filings required

---

52. Ray Charles Found. v. Raenee Robinson, et al., Defendants, No. 12-02725 (C.D. Cal., filed Mar. 29, 2012).

53. *Id.*

54. Barbara Singer, *Rose By Any Other Name: Trademark Protection of the Names of Popular Music Groups*, 14 HASTINGS COMM. & ENT. L.J. 331 (1992).

to maintain trademark rights (§§ 8 and 15 filings between the fifth and sixth year after the trademark is registered) and renewing the trademark (§§ 8 and 9 filings required between the ninth and tenth year after registration and every ten years thereafter). To satisfy these filing requirements, the estate must submit an affidavit of use. This means that for trademark rights to exist indefinitely, the estate and the assignee of those rights after the estate closes must continue to use the musician's trademark posthumously.

As discussed in other chapters, part of using the trademark is enforcing the rights. To enforce trademark rights, the representatives of a musician's estate should stay apprised of what uses in commerce may infringe on the estate's rights. For example, the estates of Lynrd Skynrd, Elvis Presley, Notorious B.I.G., Jim Morrison, Bradley Nowell, and others have targeted potential infringers through cease and desist letters or full-blown litigation to ensure that the musician's brand is maintained.[55]

## Right of Publicity

Another asset of the estate is the musician's right of publicity. The right of publicity is "the inherent right of every human being to control the commercial use of his or her identity."[56] Like copyrights and trademarks, these rights can be licensed to accumulate income for the estate. Yet, unlike many other freely assignable assets, rights of publicity cannot be involuntarily sold to creditors.[57]

---

55. Grondin v. Rossington, 690 F. Supp. 200 (S.D.N.Y. 1988); Presley's Estate v. Russen, 513 F. Supp. 1339 (D.C.N.J. 1981); Estate of Jim Morrison a/k/a Lou & Pearl Courson v. Rick Sentieri, Communications Serv. Group, D2009-0334 (WIPO 2009) (rights to jim-morrison.com transferred to complainant); Densmore v. Manzarek 2008 WL 2209993 (Cal. Unrep. 2008) (injunction enjoining Raymond Manzarek and Robert Krieger from holding themselves out as the band The Doors); *see also* Sean Ryon, *Estate of Notorious B.I.G. Denies Association with "Ready to Die" Musical*, Hip Hop Dx (July 21, 2012), http://www.hiphopdx.com/index/news/id.20513/title.estate-of-notorious-big-denies-association-with-ready-2-die-musical; Matt Belloni, *Judge Blocks Sublime Bandmembers from Using Name*, Hollywood Reporter, Esq. (Nov. 3, 2009), http://www.hollywoodreporter.com/blogs/thr-esq/judge-blocks-sublime-bandmembers-63444.

56. J. Thomas McCarthy, The Right of Publicity and Privacy § 1:3 (2d ed. 2002).

57. Ron Goldman's father, Fred Goldman, attempted but failed to transfer O.J. Simpson's right of publicity to satisfy a debt. *See* Lawrence Rosenthal, *Celebrity Rights of Publicity: For Sale, But Not Necessarily Available for Creditors*, 19(3) Intell. Prop. & Tech. L.J. 7 (2007). *But see* Carmela Kelly, *Courtney Love Loses Rights to Kurt's Image*, The Fix, May 2, 2012, http://www.thefix.com/content/courtney-love-frances-cobain-publicity-rights91000 (last visited

Although every individual has a right of publicity during life, postmortem rights of publicity vary depending on the state in which the musician dies. In New York, the right of publicity is extinguished upon death of the individual possessing the right.[58] In contrast, other state legislatures have gone to great lengths to establish and extend a postmortem right of publicity. For example, in California, the legislature created a statutory right of publicity pursuant to the California Celebrities Rights Act.[59]

Similarly, after the Sixth Circuit decided in *Memphis Development Foundation v. Factors, Etc., Inc*, that there was no descendible right to Elvis Presley's right of publicity,[60] the legislature changed the law in Tennessee. The new law changed the right of publicity to begin for a period of exclusivity for ten years and to continue for however long the image or likeness is used continuously.[61] Other jurisdictions have also analyzed the question of postmortem publicity rights through case law.[62]

The following chart details the duration of the postmortem right of publicity by state:[63]

| State | Duration of postmortem right |
| --- | --- |
| California | seventy years |
| Florida | forty years |
| Illinois | fifty years |

May 10, 2013) (Courtney Love accepted a loan in exchange for Kurt's publicity rights), *see also* Brittney L. Villalva, *Courtney Love Sued By Lawyers: Sent Love But No Money*, CHRISTIAN POST (June 25, 2012), http://www.christianpost.com/news/courtney-love-sued-by-lawyers-for-500000-sent-love-but-no-money-77210/. However, rights of publicity have been used to satisfy judgments for federal taxation and divorce purposes. *See* Estate of Andrews v. United States, 850 F. Supp. 1279 (E.D. Va. 1994); *Piscopo*, 555 A.2d 1190; Golub v. Golub, 527 N.Y.S.2d 946 (N.Y. Sup. Ct. 1988); Elkus v. Elkus, 572 N.Y.S.2d 901 (N.Y. App. Div. 1991).

58. Milton H. Greene Archives, Inc. v. Marilyn Monroe, LLC, 692 F.3d 983 (9th Cir. 2012); Pirone v. MacMillan, Inc., 894 F.2d 579 (2d Cir. 1990).

59. Celebrities Rights Act, CAL. CIV. CODE § 3344.1.

60. Memphis Dev. Found. v. Factors, Etc., Inc., 616 F.2d 956 (6th Cir 1980).

61. Protection of Personal Rights, TENN. CODE ANN. § 47-25-1101.

62. *See* McFarland v. Miller, 14 F.3d 912 (3d Cir. 1994) (the estate of George McFarland, the actor who played "Spanky" in *The Little Rascals*, maintained a postmortem right of publicity); *see also* Martin Luther King, Jr. Ctr. for Soc. Change v. American Heritage Prods., 694 F.2d 674 (11th Cir.1983) (Georgia recognized a postmortem right of publicity).

63. Alexander Lindey, *The Right of Publicity*, 1 LINDEY ON ENTERTAINMENT, PUBL. & THE ARTS § 3 (3d ed) (2013).

| State | Duration of postmortem right |
|-------|------------------------------|
| Indiana | one hundred years |
| Kentucky | fifty years |
| Nevada | fifty years |
| New York | no descendible right |
| Oklahoma | one hundred years |
| Tennessee | ten years of initial exclusivity, then the right continues for however long a person's name, image, and likeness are used continuously |
| Texas | fifty years |
| Virginia | twenty years |

In addition to ranging durations, different states have varying registration requirements to maintain the right of publicity. For example, in Texas,[64] California,[65] Oklahoma,[66] and Nevada,[67] registration and a fee are required to enforce a decedent's right of publicity during the first year following death. After that first year, the right can be exercised with or without registration.

Just as the administrators of the musician's estate should be aware of potential infringers of a musician's copyright and trademark rights, the administrators should also stay informed of potential breaches of a musician's right of publicity to determine whether litigation is an appropriate avenue to enforce those rights. To illustrate, on October 18, 2012, the Estate of Marlon Brando filed an action for trademark infringement and breach of Marlon Brando's right of publicity against Madonna for her use of Brando's image on tour during her performance of "Vogue."[68] The matter

---

64. Tex. Prop. Code Ann. § 26.010 (1999).
65. Celebrities Rights Act, Cal. Civ. Code § 3344.1 (2000).
66. Okla. Stat. tit. 12 § 1448 (1999).
67. Nev. Rev. Stat. Ann. §§ 597.770–597.810 (2000).
68. CMG Worldwide and the Estate of Marlon Brando settled a dispute over whether a valid agreement existed between the parties for use of Marlon Brando's name and likeness during Madonna's performance of the song "Vogue." See CMG Worldwide, Inc. v. Brando Enters., LP, No. 12-01384 (S.D. Ind., filed Sept. 26, 2012). Note that Madonna need not license the rights from the Estate of Marilyn Monroe in connection with her performance of "Vogue" because Monroe does not have a protectable right of publicity. See Milton H. Greene Archives, Inc. v. Marilyn Monroe, LLC, 692 F.3d 983 (9th Cir. 2012).

settled outside of court, but still illustrates the need of an estate to enforce rights of publicity.

Similarly, various estates raised concerns after Digital Domain Media used technology to project the image of Tupac Shakur, a deceased rapper, on stage at the Coachella Valley Music and Arts Festival in 2012. Although Digital Domain Media had plans to do the same for Marilyn Monroe, Elvis, Jim Morrison, and Jimi Hendrix, it reportedly filed for bankruptcy before completing the projects.[69]

## Digital Assets

The musician's estate is also composed of digital assets,[70] which may be an additional source of income. According to a survey conducted by McAfee, "U.S. consumers value their digital assets, on average at nearly $55,000."[71] These digital assets include all downloaded content, including music, e-books, and other entertainment, and all Internet-based accounts, including e-mail, blogs, Facebook, and Twitter.

For each digital asset that may be a part of the musician's estate, a determination should be made as to who owns the copyright. In certain instances, such as downloaded music, the estate is probably not the copyright owner, unless the musician downloaded his or her own, wholly owned music.[72]

Next, it is useful to have access to the decedent's online accounts, passwords, usernames and answers to security questions.[73] Unfortunately, if this information is not known by the administrators of the estate or family members, certain digital accounts may not be accessible. Due to this hurdle,

69. *Maker of Tupac Shakur Hologram Files for Bankruptcy*, ROLLING STONE (Sept. 12, 2012), http://www.rollingstone.com/music/news/maker-of-tupac-shakur-hologram-files-for-bankruptcy-20120912.

70. Dennis Kennedy, *Of Sound Mind: Make Plans for Your Digital Estate*, ABA J. MAG., Aug. 2012. *See generally*, The Digital Beyond, www.Thedigitalbeyond.com; Digital Estate Resource, www.Digitalestateresource.com; Death and Digital Legacy, www.Deathanddigitallegacy.com.

71. Kelly Greene, *Passing Down Digital Assets*, WALL ST. J., Aug. 31, 2012, *available at* http://online.wsj.com/article/SB10000872396390443713704577601524091363102.html.

72. *See*, 17 U.S.C. § 106A (2011). The Visual Artists Rights Act (VARA) may also be a consideration when determining digital assets.

73. Kennedy, *supra* note 70; Hoops, *supra* note 18.

a musician should create a chart during his or her life that lists passwords, accounts, etc., and save that information in a safe place.

Even if the account information is known, a website's or digital media platform's terms of service control whether a digital asset passes to the decedent's successors. If the decedent accepted terms of service that prohibit assignment, the personal representative is bound by the terms of that agreement.[74] Of course, a fiduciary could bring suit against a particular website to compel access to an account or seek declaration of the estate's right to access the account.[75]

For example, the terms of service for Google, Gmail, Hotmail, Yahoo, LinkedIn, YouTube and Twitter do not allow user accounts to be transferred or assigned. For Facebook, only an authorized representative of the subject matter may administer the page. Even if the digital assets are transferred to a device, such as a Kindle, or iPod, and the device is put in a will, the musician should be aware that companies such as Apple or Amazon may actually have the right to take the digital content away from the estate.[76]

However, case law is not clear-cut on implementation of these terms of service. To facilitate consistency, the Uniform Law Commission is drafting recommendations for legislators to enact concerning rights of a fiduciary to manage and distribute digital assets.[77] Until this information is clearer, digital assets should be analyzed on a case-by-case basis.

## Updating Payors: SAG, AFTRA, ASCAP, BMI, etc.

If a musician is affiliated with a Performing Rights Organization (PRO) during his or her life, then the information provided to the PRO must be updated to reflect the FEIN, bank account information, address, and executor of the estate. Accounts with other organizations, such as SAG, AFTRA,

---

74. *See* Transactions Authorized for Personal Representatives, Uniform Probate Code § 3-715(3).

75. Hoops, *supra* note 18.

76. Jeff John Roberts, *3 Ways to Deal with Digital Media When You Die*, Gigaom (Sept. 5, 2012), http://gigaom.com/2012/09/05/3-ways-to-deal-with-digital-media-when-you-die/. *But see* Imposition and Rate of Tax, I.R.C. § 2001. Digital assets may be subject to estate and gift tax if the asset generates income and can be transferred by the decedent.

77. Becky Yerak, *Online Accounts After Death: Remember Digital Property When Listing Assets*, Chi. Trib., Aug. 26, 2012, http://articles.chicagotribune.com/2012-08-26/business/ct-biz-0826-digital-assets--20120826_1_online-accounts-digital-assets-digital-property.

and SoundExchange should also be updated to ensure that payors of royalties or other income will know where to send payment.

## Tribute Bands

The representatives of a musician's estate should also be aware of the existence of tribute bands. Tribute bands may violate a deceased musician's right of publicity, trademark rights,[78] and even copyrights.[79] These violations may occur because tribute bands publicly perform the songs of a specific musician and attempt to recreate that musician's shows.[80] For example, the tribute band Beatlemania was sued by Apple Corps Ltd. A California court held that the tribute band violated the Beatles's right of publicity and was not protected by fair use or the First Amendment.[81] The court also held that Beatlemania caused unfair competition and consumer confusion.

Another example of enforcement of copyright and trademark rights against tribute bands is illustrated by the representative of Frank Zappa's estate, Gail Zappa. Specifically, the attorneys for the Zappa Family Trust sent numerous cease and desist letters to Zappa tribute bands and venues alleging that public performance blanket licenses do not cover tribute shows and such performances violate dramatic rights.[82] The Trust has also

---

78. *See* Herb Reed Enters., LLC v. Florida Entm't Mgmt., Inc. & Larry Marshak, No. 12-00560 (N.D. Nev., filed Apr. 4, 2012) (Lawsuit for unauthorized use of the trademark THE PLATTERS in connection with entertainment services); *see also MJ Tribute Band— The Battle Over Neverland*, TMZ (Mar. 9, 2010), http://www.tmz.com/2010/03/09/mj-tribute-band-the-battle-over-neverland/ (the Estate of Michael Jackson pursued legal action against a tribute band using the registered trademark NEVERLAND); Jay Allen Sanford, *Which One's Pink? The One Suing Local Tribute Band!*, SAN DIEGO READER (May 23, 2011) *available at* http://www.sandiegoreader.com/weblogs/jam-session/2011/may/23/which-ones-pink-the-one-suing-local-tribute-band/.

79. Steve Lynn, *Rock Stars Sue 8150, Van Halen, Jimmy Page and Others Allege Copyright Violations by Vail Business Owner*, VAIL DAILY, Feb. 22, 2007; *see also* Susan Butler, *Rock Band's Lawsuit Takes Aim at Videogame*, REUTERS (Dec. 8, 2007), *available at* http://www.reuters.com/article/2007/12/09/us-romantics-idUSN0842944420071209.

80. *See* Michael Newman, *Imitation Is the Sincerest Form of Flattery, but Is It Infringement? The Law of Tribute Bands*, 28 TOURO LAW REVIEW 391 (2012).

81. Apple Corps Ltd. v. Leber, 229 U.S.P.Q. 1015 (Cal. App. Super. 1986), *citing* Estate of Presley v. Russen, *supra* note 448 ("entertainment which merely imitates, does not have a creative component of its own and is not protected by the First Amendment").

82. Letter from Owen J. Sloan, Berger Kahn, A Law Corporation, Attorneys for Zappa Family Trust, *available at* http://www.uglyradiorebellion.com/visuals/Ugly%20Radio%20Rebellion%20.PDF.

asserted that advertisements for tribute shows violate Frank Zappa's trademark rights and cause consumer confusion.

## Conclusion

In conclusion, a musician's legacy may prosper after the musician dies. If estate planning experts are consulted, the inventory is created, the relevant filing deadlines are met, and the estate enforces the musician's copyright, trademark and publicity rights, the estate may generate enough income to timely discharge its creditors, pay taxes, and make disbursements to beneficiaries.

# Chapter Eleven
# Music and the General Business Client

Music law issues do not always involve musicians, music producers or distributors. Most general businesses will encounter music-related issues in one form or another at some time, which is the topic of this chapter.

## Advertising and Music Branding

Few radio or television advertisements are prepared without the use of music in some fashion. Music can set a mood or environment, conjure an emotion, or punctuate text or an image. When attention must be grabbed and a message delivered unambiguously in a very short period, music helps get the job done.

Music can also play a role in helping brand a business. The NBC chime is a classic example of a sound trademark that has identified NBC programming to listeners since the late 1920s. Anyone who ever spent time watching television or listening to the radio in Chicago after 1977 will hear familiar music in their head when they read the telephone number 588-2300. Music has tremendous mnemonic power that can be engaged to create brand identity. This is recognized by the fact that sounds may be registered on the Principal Register of the United States Patent & Trademark Office when they are "arbitrary, unique or distinctive and can be used in a manner so as to attach to the mind of the listener and be awakened on later hearing in a way that would indicate for the listener that a particular product or service was coming from a particular, even if anonymous, source."[1]

If a company is seeking to acquire original music to associate with their advertisements as part of their overall branding strategy, they are likely to engage a production company, sometimes referred to as a "jingle house," to compose the music and produce the musical recording that will be used in the advertisement. This is sometimes done directly by the company, or the production company may be engaged through the company's advertising agency. In the end, it will be critical for the company to own all rights in and to the composition and the recording being produced. In order to ensure that occurs, each agreement in the series of agreements—the production company with the advertising agency and the advertising agency with the client company—will need to be in writing and contain language that identifies the deliverables under the agreements as works made for hire (if the material is intended for inclusion in an audiovisual commercial) with appropriate alternative assignment language of all copyright interests in the deliverables as well. Without such language, the rights actually lodged with the company to use the composition and/or recording going forward may be unclear, which could impair the company's adoption of the material for branding purposes. One right the composer might preserve is the right to receive his or her portion of any performance income generated by the public performance of the composition in broadcast commercials that is logged by the composer's performing rights organization.

Use of preexisting music for commercial and promotional purposes requires consent of the owners of the works being used, whether that is a composition being rerecorded by the company producing the commercial or both the composition and the record master if use of an existing recording is being sought. There is no statutory compulsory license for any such uses. The copyright owner has the absolute right to deny any such use, and

---

1. *In re* Vertex Grp. LLC, 89 U.S.P.Q.2d 1694, 1700 (T.T.A.B. 2009).

the terms under which such uses might be made are completely open for negotiation. The fee for use of an iconic song in a national television campaign can exceed $1,000,000,[2] while a local commercial featuring a more modest, regionally successful song will be much less. The variables to be determined include the territory of the advertisement, duration and media of use, lyric changes (if any), scope of exclusivity, and options to extend. Also, as noted in the discussion about trademark rights and individual's rights of publicity, if the client company wants a new recording of a composition to be used in a commercial to sound like a preexisting recording, consent of the performers in the original recordings may need to be obtained. While the Copyright Act permits the production of "soundalike" recordings of musical compositions that are independent fixations of sound,[3] the use of such recordings in commercials may create liability for claims that the identity of the performer in the original recording has been wrongfully used or the trademark rights of such performers have been violated if listeners are likely to believe that the original performer is the performer in the recordings used in the advertisements.

Several services exist to facilitate the connection between owners of sound recordings and those seeking music to use in advertisements and other audiovisual works. These services provide indexing, search, and sampling access to a range of recorded works whose producers and composers they represent and further process the purchase and delivery of material that is selected. These services include Taxi, Musicdealers, Getty Images, You License, Musync, Jingle Punks, and Rumblefish. While such services have not been without some criticism from within the production music community,[4] they are a viable alternative for companies seeking music for use in advertising that do not require "hit" songs or recordings or exclusive, long-term rights. Sound recordings are also available for commercial uses from archives such as Getty Images through SoundCloud and Corbis Greenlight Music.

---

2. Jeffrey Brabec & Todd Brabec, *Music, Money, and Success* 296 (Schimer Trade Books 2011).

3. 17 U.S.C. § 114(b) (2011).

4. *Ron Mendelsohn on Signing with a Non-Exclusive Retitling Library*, Film Music Mag., June 18, 2010, http://www.filmmusicmag.com/?p=5673.

# Sponsorships and Endorsements

Celebrities have allure. They can gather an audience, or enhance the commercial prospects of one's products or services when associated with their resonant values. Whatever the reason, companies frequently call upon celebrities, including musicians, to associate themselves in some way with the companies and their products or services in a range of arrangements.

It is important to distinguish between a sponsorship and an endorsement. Sponsorship simply means that a company has given consideration for the right to associate itself in some manner with a performer. It may be as basic as the purchase of an advertisement in an event's program booklet or as comprehensive as an international tour. Although an endorsement by an artist might be implied by the circumstances of the sponsorship, an actual endorsement of a product or service is a specific action that must be bargained for in any agreement for the artist's services. For example, a sponsor of a performance might receive a "Presented by" credit in the announcements for the performance, but to quote the performer as recommending the sponsor's product or service will require additional, specific authorization. The following are some key issues that are important in such an agreement, in addition to the amount of the artist's fee, expenses, and hospitality requirements.

## What the Artist Will Be Required To Do

The range of activities and deliverables for a sponsorship or endorsement agreement is broad. At its simplest, an artist may be engaged to appear at a particular event meant to mark a company's business development (a store opening or significant sale) or perhaps to attract customers to aid inducement of product sampling. In such cases, a description of what the artist is required to do may include speaking, signing autographs or memorabilia (or perhaps *not* memorabilia[5]), posing for pictures, performing, making a presentation, being interviewed, participating in a broadcast or other

---

5. Some performers refuse to sign memorabilia on the grounds that the purpose of the request is simply to increase the value of an item intended for sale and not for keepsaking.

recording of the event, facilitating a contest, drawing, or other activity, or interacting with others.

The scope and other terms of an expanded sponsorship arrangement with an artist are broad and will be driven principally by the marketing goals of the company engaging the artist. The sponsorship could include a range of activities specific to the company engaging the artist or could be in association with a more general event, such as a performance tour. Some of the deliverables required by an artist under such circumstances could include appearing at so-called meet and greet events, press conferences, performances, creation of special material such as recordings or videos, interviews, voiceovers for advertisements, recorded out-bound telephone greetings, blogs, social media postings, contests, words of endorsement, receptions, autographs, autographed property or memorabilia, the prominent use of a product or service during period of the agreement, links between the artist's and the company's respective websites, or event tickets.

## Artist's Identity and Trademark Rights

Fundamental to a sponsorship or endorsement agreement is the company's ability to use the artist's identity and trademarks in connection with the activities contemplated by the agreement. The identity includes not only the artist's name and likeness but also the artist's biography, voice, and other items that personally identify the artist. The artist's trademarks could include logos, names, or such things as distinctive costuming. The two principal issues to negotiate concerning these uses are (1) approval and (2) how and where the identity and marks may be used. Artists will generally have the ability to approve their biography and how they are depicted and quoted (particularly if an endorsement is to be provided). Once approved, consent is generally not required for how the approved image or quote may be implemented, although approval of overall ad copy, advertisements, and other forms of messaging may be negotiated as well. Use may also be generalized for the company and its products and services or keyed to a specific campaign, such as a new product launch.

## Creation of Special Material

Sponsorship relationships with musical artists frequently involve the development of creative works, such as compositions, recordings, or videos, which are used to help deliver the sponsoring company's commercial message. A sponsor may want to permit streaming or downloading of exclusive recordings from the company's website, or use such recordings in the soundtrack of commercials. A sponsor may also want to record a special performance given by the artist under the auspices of the company and permit streaming or downloading of the recording. This may create issues if the artist is a party to an exclusive recording agreement with a record label that would bar the artist's involvement in the production of sound recordings or videos with a third party. Similarly, an exclusive songwriter agreement could bar the delivery of a musical composition to a third party. In such instances, each record or publishing company will have its own requirements for granting consent. In some cases, the consideration given for the artist's participation in the sponsor's recording activities may be to either permit the record company to use the recordings in certain ways after the sponsor's promotional period has passed, or to assign the recordings to the record company, with a reservation by the sponsor of the right to continue using the recordings in certain ways.

## Scope of Exclusivity

Sponsoring companies will generally want to have the exclusive right to the artist's association during the period of the sponsorship relationship and for a term thereafter. The company does not want to expend resources to exploit the goodwill associated with the artist and find that the association is being diluted with other related products or services. Even worse, the company does not want a competitor to piggyback on the attention created by the company. The scope of this exclusivity implicates product categories, territories, and time periods. From the company's point of view, the product category should be defined as generally and broadly as possible, which may conflict with an artist's existing or anticipated agreements with others.

The territory of exclusivity could reasonably be broader than the actual territory where the sponsorship relationship will be promoted. Media in which a competing sponsoring relationship is promoted might not observe territorial limitations and could be likely to surface in the licensed territory, particularly if the sponsored products or services are directly competitive. Finally, it is reasonable for a sponsor to obtain an extension of the exclusivity provisions of the sponsorship agreement for a period following the actual period of sponsorship activity to protect the residual effect of such association and prevent a competitive sponsorship from causing confusion with an immediate follow-on promotion.

## Morals Clause

It is the nature of celebrity that an individual, once well regarded by the public, can fall into disrepute. When that happens, the goodwill bargained for by a sponsoring company to associate with its products or services disappears. A so-called morals clause in a sponsorship agreement permits a sponsoring company to terminate an agreement with an artist in the event the artist engages in any activity that causes them to be held in lesser regard by the public. Given that misconduct can also be committed by business organizations, which can fall into disrepute by reason of a variety of legal or ethical violations, some artists have begun negotiating so-called reverse morals clauses in sponsorship agreements, which permit them to disassociate themselves from organizations in the event the organization experiences a fall in public regard and the artist believes they would be harmed by seeming to support the organization.

## Non-disparagement

As a counterpart to the express or implied endorsement obtained by a sponsoring company from the artist under the sponsorship agreement, the company will want to obtain a commitment by the artist not to publicly comment upon the artist's experience in participating with the company without the company's consent or in a manner which is "off message" from the promotion. The sponsoring company will of course want to receive as much coverage of its sponsorship as it can, but comments in news stories, articles, publicity, and social media platforms in any form (other than unalloyed praise) can derail the commercial message a company may be seeking to convey. Further, comments that are disparaging of the experience or revealing of the "inside" story of the experience can erase the value bargained for by the sponsor.

## Music at the Work Site

Music has become almost ubiquitous in our lives. Its use and consumption does not stop at the workplace entrance. This has implications in several circumstances.

### Performance of Music in Customer Environment

As mentioned earlier, the public performance of musical compositions is one of the enumerated rights under the Copyright Act. It has long been held that performance of music in such places as hotels[6] and restaurants,[7] on radio and television,[8] by means of the playing of musical recordings,[9] and staging karaoke performances[10] constituted a performance for which the copyright owner was entitled to compensation. On the other hand, playing a radio broadcast to the public in a commercial establishment by means of "a single receiving apparatus of a kind commonly used in private homes" is not a performance of music for which payment is due under an ASCAP, BMI, or SESAC license unless there is a charge to see or hear the transmission or the transmissions is retransmitted.[11]

---

6. Remick Music Corp. v. Interstate Hotel Co., 58 F. Supp. 523 (D. Neb. 1944), aff'd, 157 F.2d 744 (8th Cir. 1946), cert. denied, 329 U.S. 809 (1947).

7. Leo Feist, Inc. v. Lew Tendler Tavern, Inc., 267 F.2d 494 (3d Cir. 1959).

8. Buck v. Jewell-LaSalle Realty Co., 283 U.S. 191 (1931).

9. Associated Music Publishers, Inc. v. Debs Mem'l Radio Fund, Inc., 141 F.2d 852 (2d Cir.), cert. denied, 323 U.S. 766 (1944).

10. Morganactive Songs v. K&M Fox Inc., 77 U.S.P.Q.2d 1064 (S.D. Ind. 2005). However, there is a division of authority about whether karaoke discs are audiovisual works. See Leadsinger, Inc. v. BMG Music Publ'g, 512 F.3d 522 (9th Cir. 2008); ABKCO Music, Inc. v. Stellar Records, Inc., 96 F.3d 60 (2d Cir.1996) (karaoke discs are audiovisual works). But see EMI Entertainment World, Inc. v. Priddis Music, Inc., 505 F. Supp. 2d 1217 (D. Utah 2007) (karaoke discs are not audiovisual works).

11. 17 U.S.C. § 110(5) (2011).

In 1998, Congress passed the Fairness in Music Licensing Act,[12] essentially expanding the exemptions available to restaurants and other establishments from the requirements of obtaining public performance licenses from ASCAP, BMI, and SESAC for the retransmission of regular broadcast, cable system, or satellite carrier signals. No license is required in the case of establishments other than food service or drinking establishments where the establishment either has less than 2,000 square feet of space or, if more space, the performance is communicated by no more than six loudspeakers (no more than four of which are in any one room) and no more than four audiovisual screens having a diagonal screen size no greater than fifty-five inches (no more than one of which is in any one room). The same requirements apply to food service and drinking establishments, but the triggering space size of the establishment is 3,750 square feet.[13]

Businesses that use music within a customer environment, whether in the form of live performances or recorded music, are advised to obtain appropriate agreements with the performing rights organizations if they are not exempt by reason of the space dimensions mentioned above. There are two strong reasons for this advice. First, while the performing rights organizations in the United States only hold nonexclusive rights to the compositions whose rights they enforce and it is possible for a company to obtain permission to perform compositions directly from the owners of the compositions, the effort to do so is inefficient, at best. The performing rights organizations issue blanket licenses of their full catalogs, which guarantee access to all compositions and reduce transaction costs.

Second, the performing rights organizations are diligent in the enforcement of the rights of the publishers and songwriters they represent[14] and enjoy a strong history of success in litigating when faced with recalcitrant unlicensed music users.[15] As an alternative to obtaining direct licenses from performing rights organizations, businesses may elect to subscribe to cer-

---

12. Fairness in Music Licensing Act of October 27, 1998, Pub. L. No. 105-298, 112 Stat. 2827 (1998).

13. 17 U.S.C. § 110(5) (2011).

14. *See, e.g.*, John Bowe, *The Music-Copyright Enforcers*, N.Y. Times, Aug. 6, 2010.

15. Certain state statutes regulate the licensing practices of performing rights organizations. *See, e.g.*, Music Licensing Fees Act, 815 ILCS 637.

tain background music services such as Mood (formerly Muzak), DMX, or DMI, which obtain performance rights in the material that they distribute to their client users so that the music user is only responsible for paying a single fee for the bundle of rights required for their music use.

## Other Workplace Use of Music

Copyright infringement is a tort, and liability for infringement of copyright, as with any other tortuous acts, may extend to persons other than the direct performer or publisher of the infringing work. The infringing acts of a company's employees will create liability for the company.[16] Further, under the concepts of vicarious or contributory liability, where the company is in a position to control the activities of the primary infringer and has a direct financial interest in the activities, liability can be extended to the company. For example, the operator of a flea market where infringing material is sold was found liable for the acts of the client sellers at the market.[17]

As a result, companies should take care to establish and enforce policies with respect to the use of music in the workplace. Companies cannot afford the blinkered view that unauthorized internal uses of music will remain undiscovered.[18] The following are some examples of workplace use of music outside the customer environment.

### Employee Downloading and Music Subscription Services

Use of company computers or systems to either upload or download music files through the use of file-sharing software or sites should be barred. At this point there should be little ambiguity or doubt whether such activity is wrongful, no matter how urgent the arguments in support, but communicating such a policy is nevertheless recommended.

Companies should also remain mindful that music subscription services such as Pandora, Rhapsody, MOD, and others may only be used in a

---

16. Famous Music Corp. v. Bay State Harness Horse Racing & Breeding Ass'n, Inc., 554 F.2d 1213 (1st Cir. 1977).

17. Arista Records Inc. v. Flea World Inc., 78 U.S.P.Q.2d (D.N.J. 2006).

18. Note the effort by the Business Software Association to solicit confidential information concerning software misuse from disgruntled ex-employees. *See* Business Software Association, https://reporting.bsa.org/r/report/add.aspx?src=us&ln=en-us (last visited Feb. 8, 2013).

commercial environment if the company has entered an appropriate agreement with such service. An individual employee who is an authorized user of a service only has the right to use that service for personal purposes, which does not extend to broader deployment and transmission within the workplace.

## Music on Hold

Playing music through the company's telephone system to callers who are placed on hold constitutes a public performance of that music which must be authorized.[19] Companies are advised to avoid retransmission of broadcast, cable, or satellite signals through their telephone systems and to use only recordings of compositions for which they have obtained the right to use in an on-hold feature.

## Office or Warehouse Performance of Music

Under clause (1) of the definition of "publicly" in Section 101 of the Copyright Act, a performance or display is "public" if it takes place "at a place open to the public or at any place where a substantial number of persons outside of a normal circle of a family and its social acquaintances is gathered."[20] The House Report that accompanied the passage of the Copyright Act of 1976 stated that "Routine meetings of businesses and governmental personnel would be excluded because they do not represent the gathering of a 'substantial number of persons.'"[21] However, in one case, a group of twenty-one members of a private club and their respective guests who were in the audience for a performance of music were found to constitute a "substantial number."[22] Moreover, music performed for the benefit of a company's employees is also subject to licensing.[23]

Based on the foregoing, companies are advised that use of music performed in routine meetings within a noncustomer environment would not

---

19. Prophet Music, Inc. v. Shamla Oil Co., Inc., 1993 WL 300204 (D. Minn. 1993).

20. 17 U.S.C. § 101 (2011).

21. H.R. Rep. No. 1476, 94th Cong., 2d Sess. 64, *reprinted in* 1976 U.S.C.C.A.N. 5659, 5677–78.

22. Fermata Int'l Melodies, Inc. v. Champions Golf Club, Inc., 712 F. Supp. 1257 (S.D. Tex. 1989).

23. Merrill v. County Stores, Inc., 669 F. Supp. 1164 (D.N.H. 1987).

create liability if not licensed. However, music regularly performed, for example, throughout a warehouse or within an office environment generally, or at overall company meetings, may create liability if the music is not a retransmission of a regular broadcast, cable system, or satellite carrier signal. If so, the company's sound system and space size exceed the limits of the Fairness in Music Licensing Act described earlier.

## Trade Shows and Conventions

Music is often a feature at trade shows and conventions, either as a form of entertainment for attendees, to attract an audience, or to enliven a presentation. Courts have been divided whether the organizers of professional trade shows are liable for the actions of trade show participants that violate the rights of music rights holders.[24] However, organizers of such shows and the facilities in which they are held are generally licensed themselves for their own activities that involve the performance of music.[25]

Companies are advised to carefully review the terms and conditions of the agreement with the organizer of any trade show at which they intend to use music as a feature of their exhibit, or any facility in which they intend to use music as part of a planned activity (such as a hotel), to understand the extent of their responsibility for obtaining any public performance agreements required by their plans. Companies will save fees if their intended activities fall within the scope of the licenses already in place through the event organizers or facilities. Alternatively, the event organizers or facilities may seek to shift responsibility for obtaining the proper licenses to the exhibitors, who would likely be responsible for indemnifying the event organizer or facility for any failure for having done so.

## Reproductions of Recordings

The ease with which preexisting music may be sourced and incorporated into a sales presentation, an electronic press kit, a company website, or social media site is a powerful tool. However, unless any such use may be

---

24. Compare Artists Music, Inc. v. Reed Pub'l (USA), Inc., 31 U.S.P.Q.2d 1623 (S.D.N.Y. 1994), *and* Polygram Int'l Publ'g, Inc. v. Nevada/TIG, Inc., 855 F. Supp. 1314 (D. Mass. 1994).

25. Jeffrey W. King, *Music Licensing at Trade Shows and Conventions: Who Pays the Band?*, LICENSING J. (Nov./Dec. 2007).

excused as a fair use as explained in Chapter Two, using music in any of these ways will require the consent of the appropriate rights holders. This could involve the owner of the composition, the owner of the recording, and the artist whose performance is featured in the recording. The exact nature of the rights necessary to be licensed may also require expert review. Alternatively, companies are advised to avail themselves of such services as Getty Images or Corbis as a "one-stop shop" to license recordings for their particular requirements, to obtain public domain recordings from such places as MusOpen.org., or to obtain rights through Creative Commons.[26]

## Jukeboxes

The Copyright Act of 1976 eliminated the prior statutory exemption from copyright liability for music played on jukeboxes and established a compulsory license for jukebox operators.[27] Operators pay an annual fee for each machine to the Register of Copyright, and operation of a jukebox without paying this fee is a copyright infringement.[28] The current annual rate for each jukebox may be found at 37 C.F.R. § 254.3. The collected jukebox royalties are distributed to ASCAP, BMI, SESAC and any person unaffiliated with a performing rights society that proves entitlement.

---

26. CREATIVE COMMONS, http://creativecommons.org/about (last visited Feb. 8, 2013).
27. 17 U.S.C. § 116 (2011).
28. Broadcast Music, Inc. v. Fox Amusement Co., 551 F. Supp. 104 (N.D. Ill. 1982).

# Chapter Twelve
# Representing the Musician

The relationship between artists and lawyers has at times been marked by mistrust and misunderstanding. Finding the balance between aesthetic creativity and order has never been easy.

Lawyers have been historically stereotyped by artists as persons "whose avarice is exceeded only by [their] monkey-like cunning,"[1] or akin to the man from Porlock who interrupted Coleridge as he wrote "Kubla Kahn"—we just get in the way and spoil everything. Lawyers on the other hand often disdain the antithetical artistic world for its ambiguity and nonconformity. It was the view of Oliver Wendall Holmes that "the law is not the place for the artist or the poet. The law is the calling of thinkers."[2]

For an attorney, becoming engaged with the creative community is enlightening, fun, and makes a change. It also is not unusual for friendships and long-term client relationships to develop from this arrangement. Creative artists are grateful for the assistance they receive for problems that

---

1. David Apatoff, *The Unhappy Relationship Between the Lawyer and the Artist*, 1 PAIDEIA: A JOURNAL OF LEGAL EXPERIENCE 8 (1975).

2. *See Speeches 22–25* (1913), *reprinted in* THE MIND AND FAITH OF JUSTICE HOLMES: HIS SPEECHES, ESSAYS, LETTERS, AND JUDICIAL OPINIONS, 31 (M. Lerner ed., Transaction Publishing 1988) (Oliver Wendell Holmes delivering the speech "The Profession of the Law" at the conclusion of a lecture to undergraduates of Harvard University on February 17, 1886).

can seem quite overwhelming. In return, they enthusiastically acknowledge those who help them by sharing access to the creative process in sometimes singular experiences.[3]

In one sense, representing musical talent is like representing any other client: you are engaged to provide your legal services to solve a problem, or to provide your best judgment and experience to give advice. And musicians want you to do what they can not or do not want to do. The matters they will entrust to you will be very dear to them. They are not looking for something they can find elsewhere, such as more fans or critics. Like many individual clients, they quite often may feel overwhelmed by the need to deal with the legal system without succumbing to its afflictions. However, musicians do present some unique issues for practitioners that one should be mindful of to enjoy a successful relationship, both personally and professionally.[4]

## Beauty Contest

It often happens that a musician will receive recommendations for, or have otherwise heard of, several attorneys to consider for representation. The artist will then meet with those attorneys to determine whether there is a "fit" professionally and personally before engaging them. There will be a temptation by the attorneys in such beauty contests to prove their expertise and perhaps provide some advice as an example of the kind of insight and value they could bring to the relationship. Attorneys frequently find themselves in such circumstances when trying to win new clients, but there is a special sensitivity that should be brought to the development of a relationship with artists, who may not be experienced consumers of legal services. Even though the attorney may not believe that an attorney-client relationship is

---

3. Of course, matters do not always follow a smooth course. For some interesting examples of where it seems to all go wrong between lawyers and artist clients, see STAN SOOCHER, THEY FOUGHT THE LAW: ROCK MUSIC GOES TO COURT (Schirmer Books 1999).

4. For an excellent discussion of ethics and entertainment law generally, see Kenneth J. Abdo, Esq. & Jack P. Sahl, *Entertainment Law Ethics* (2012), http://www.lommen.com/pdf/SXSW-2012/Entertainment-Law-Ethics.aspx.

being formed during the initial interview process, the artist may not understand that to be the case and may rely upon the advice given during such initial interviews. In a well-known case involving the singer/songwriter Jim Croce, an attorney representing a production company seeking to sign Croce for his recording and composing services was introduced to Croce and his wife as "the attorney," who then proceeded to provide explanations of the proposed relationship to Croce and his wife. When Croce later sought to extricate himself from these agreements, the attorney was successfully sued for breach of his fiduciary duty to Croce for having not advised him to obtain independent counsel to assist him concerning the agreements when the Croces reasonably believed they could rely upon his advice.[5] Counsel should also be mindful under such circumstances of Rule 1.18 of the ABA Model Rules of Professional Conduct concerning prospective client obligations.[6] Rule 1.18 bars the use or revelation of information learned during a consultation with a prospective client and can further bar representing a client with interests materially adverse to those of a prospective client in the same or a substantially related matter if the lawyer received information from the prospective client that could be significantly harmful to that person in the matter.

## Payment of Fees

It is often the case that a musician may present himself or herself as having modest resources for the payment of fees, but that there are others who are supporting the musician, such as parents, managers, or investors, who will pay the fees on the musician's behalf. It also sometimes occurs that the party on the opposite side of a transaction with an artist client, such as a record company, may pay an amount to the attorney for the attorney fees to the artist. Such arrangements are ethically permissible, as long as certain criteria are met. Rule 1.8(f) of the ABA Model Rules of Professional Conduct provides as follows:

---

5. Croce v. Kurnit, 565 F. Supp. 884 (S.D.N.Y. 1982).
6. MODEL RULES OF PROF'L CONDUCT, R. 1.18 (2004).

"(f) A lawyer shall not accept compensation for representing a client from one other than the client unless:

(1)  the client gives informed consent;
(2)  there is no interference with the lawyer's independence of professional judgment or with the client-lawyer relationship; and
(3)  information relating to representation of a client is protected as required by Rule 1.6."[7]

Compliance with Rule 1.8(f) can be reflected in the engagement agreement with the client. Compliance in practice may require some diligence, particularly if the party paying the fees is the artist's manager and most material communications concerning the artist's professional matters take place through the manager.

## Dealing with Representatives

As noted earlier, the entertainment industry is based on intermediaries, such as managers, agents, and business managers. Because of this circumstance, the attorney may find himself or herself dealing principally with a manager or an agent rather than the client artist. This can present problems.

First, the attorney should always understand the full extent of the intermediary's authority to act on behalf of the artist. That authority should not be presumed as to either its scope or its duration. Confirmation may be as simple as reviewing the management agreement. No matter what the understanding of authority may be, the attorney should be sensitive to certain requests that an intermediary might make that should raise suspicion. Requests to change payment directions, for example, or to register trademarks or other intellectual property in the name or co-name of the intermediary rather than the artist, should alert the attorney to confirm such requests with the artist.[8] If the artist is not available to discuss the terms of

---

7. MODEL RULES OF PROF'L CONDUCT R. 1.8(f) (2004).
8. *See, e.g.,* Reznor v. J. Artist Mgmt., Inc., 365 F. Supp. 2d 565 (S.D.N.Y. 2005).

a proposed agreement and seeks to rely upon the attorney and the artist's representative to finalize the agreement, the attorney may need to memorialize any advice concerning the agreement that is addressed to the artist to insure that their own exposure is not compromised. Finally, unless the document requiring the artist's signature is of minor consequence and the intermediary's signature on the artist's behalf is acceptable, the artist should sign such documents themselves to ensure enforceability.

It is not uncommon for an artist's attorney and the artist's representative to develop a close working relationship, particularly if most of the communication concerning the artist is conducted through the manager. It is not unusual under such circumstances for the representative to view the artist's attorney as a source for legal advice that pertains to the representative personally or with respect to matters not directly concerning the artist. Unless the advice is of the most general type, such as factual information about resources that might assist the representative, the artist's attorney should generally resist providing legal advice under such circumstances and should instead refer to the representative to other counsel. While arrangements might be documented in accordance with Rule 1.7 of the ABA Model Rules of Professional Conduct between the attorney and his or her artist client to waive the conflict in the representation of both the artist and the representative, the highly personal relationship between the artist and the representative, particularly personal managers, and the sometimes frequent volatility of such relationships creates additional tensions that disfavor representing both parties even in unrelated matters.[9]

Counsel should also be mindful of maintaining the attorney-client privilege in connection with communications with agents and personal managers. The attorney-client privilege generally extends to those serving as an agent of either the attorney or the client.[10] However, to be protected, the communications must be intended to facilitate the provision of legal services by the attorney to the client. Agents and managers generally will be considered agents of their clients, but the exact nature of the relationship between a

---

9. Given the highly relational makeup of the music industry, some lawyers have promoted their multiple representations of parties in transactions as a desirable and value-adding practice. *See, e.g.*, Joel v. Grubman, No. 261-55-92 (N.Y. Sup. Ct. 1992).

10. Robert V. Straus Prods. v. Pollard, 734 N.Y.S.2d 170 (N.Y. App. Div. 2001).

representative and the talent may not always be clear.[11] Further, the privilege may be lost if communications occur in the presence of third parties that are not characterized as agents.

## Dealing with Groups

Musicians often perform as groups, and it is as a group that the musicians will approach the attorney for representation. The issues that arise under such circumstances are the same as those presented when multiple people elect to start a venture and seek the services of an attorney to organize and represent that venture.

The first question that needs to be answered is, "Who is the client?" If the group is organized as a separate legal entity, or seeks such organization, the client generally would be the entity. If a separate entity is not formed, then the question of how the group is organized should be resolved. Is the group really a sole proprietorship of one of the members with everyone else an employee, or are the group members a general partnership? If the group members are unincorporated joint owners of the group, it is advisable to obtain waivers of conflict of interest from each of the group members in accordance with the requirements of Rule 1.7 of the ABA Model Rules of Professional Conduct.

When representing multiple members of a musical group, communication between one member of the group and the attorney is not treated as confidential between the attorney and the other members of the group. The group members may not understand that—they may believe they can conduct communication with the attorney that is not sharable with other members. Therefore, it is a good practice to advise the group members in either the engagement agreement or the waiver agreement that communications

---

11. Public relations agents have been deemed both subject and not subject to the privilege. *See* Roy Simon, *The Attorney-Client Privilege and Third-Party Consultants: An Update*, THE NEW YORK PROFESSIONAL RESPONSIBILITY REPORT (2010), http://lazar-emanuel.com/The%20Attorney%20Client%20Privilege%20And%20Third-Party%20Consultants%20An%20Update%202.pdf.

between individual group members and the attorney cannot be kept from the others.

The makeup of a musical group can be fluid, with people leaving and joining for a variety of reasons. When representing multiple members of a group, the attorney cannot be drawn into discussions concerning the replacement of band members. The attorney cannot be an advocate for one or several of the group members against another.[12]

While the attorney cannot be the advocate of one group member against another, the attorney should be instructed as to how decisions are made within the group and whose authority the attorney can rely upon to undertake action on behalf of the group.

## Shopping Groups

The music industry is highly competitive, and although the paths to public appeal have expanded in recent years, there are certain traditional opportunities performers seek to achieve for themselves to improve their chances for success. Access to these opportunities, whether recording agreements with major record labels, song publishing agreements with influential music publishing companies, or agreements with powerful managers or agents, is sometimes restricted given the great number of people seeking entry through the same doors. As a result, attorneys are often sought out by artists to open those doors and help present the artists and the results of their talents to decision makers with the hope that the favorable inroad will make the difference. This door-opening is often referred to as "shopping" the artist, and it is often the service beginning performers want the most.

Shopping an artist to important decision makers is often the way an attorney begins developing a practice representing artists. If an attorney is successful in such efforts, it becomes a powerful practice development tool—the attorney is able to demonstrate that he or she is able to advance

---

12. *See, e.g.*, Adler v. Manatt, Phelps, Phillips & Kantor, BC 05307 (L.A. Supr. Ct., filed Apr. 1992) (former member of group Guns N' Roses sued the group's law firm for malpractice in connection with group settlement agreement).

an artist's career in a major way. It is also a way for an attorney to meet others in the industry, which may also lead to productive business development. However, it is also an activity that often has for its fee structure a contingent arrangement based upon the success of the effort. To be effective, and as required by Rule 1.5 of the ABA Model Rules of Professional Conduct, such fee agreements should be in writing, should be reasonable in the manner in which the fee is determined, and should be independently reviewed on behalf of the artist by another attorney to ensure its reasonableness as to the amount of the fee and its other terms.

The reasonableness of a fee for seeking to secure a recording or publishing agreement for an artist will turn on the amount of time involved, the level of success of the effort, and fees customarily charged by others for corresponding services. Given that the customary fees for agents is in the range of 10 percent to 15 percent and the customary contingent compensation arrangement between attorneys and entertainment clients for handling general entertainment business matters is 5 percent, a fee of 10 percent for shopping an artist would seem reasonable.[13] In the event of a termination, the attorney is still entitled to recover the value of his or her services prior to discharge in quantum meruit.[14]

Among the practical risks for an attorney shopping a band are that the group could become unstable or break up for any number of reasons, leaving the attorney without a transaction from which to collect their fee. Also, the act of shopping a band may spark interest in some of the members of the group but not all, which could create a conflicts problem for the attorney if a member is pushed out or otherwise left behind.

## Alternative Fee Arrangements

It is not uncommon for some attorneys representing musicians, particularly successful, high-income performers, to charge the musician on a percentage

---

13. *See, e.g.*, DONALD E. BIEDERMAN ET AL., LAW AND BUSINESS OF THE ENTERTAINMENT INDUSTRIES 22–28 (5th ed. Praeger 2007).
14. Musburger v. Meier, 394 Ill. App. 3d 781 (1st Dist. 2009).

basis rather than hourly. The customary amount is 5 percent, which is usually applied to the musician's income from contracts entered during the course of the attorney's representation.

As with respect to the shopping agreement discussed above and Rule 1.5 of the ABA Model Rules of Professional Conduct, a contingent fee agreement should be in writing, and an attorney is best advised to have their client obtain independent advice concerning entering such an agreement. A key issue that should be addressed in such an agreement is the scope of services to be provided for the contingent fee. Negotiation and drafting of the agreements upon which the fee will be calculated will certainly be included, but what about real estate transactions, tax planning, litigation, or corporate transactions? Another key issue is the length of time the commission will be payable. Unlike management agreements, which generally provide that the management commission will be payable on all income derived from an artist's contract entered during the term of the management agreement (whether the payment occurs during or after the term of the management agreement), payment of contingent attorney fees after the attorney-client relationship has ended may not be enforceable.

In the case of *Hirsch Wallerstein Hayum Matlof & Fishman v. Hirsch Jackoway Tyerman Wertheimer Austin Mandelbaum & Morris*,[15] a law firm sought to enforce contingent fee arrangements, both oral and written, with former clients who followed a partner who left the firm to start another. The law firm took the position that the fee arrangement bound the former clients to pay their former firm in perpetuity for any revenue derived from agreements that had been entered while they were clients of the firm. This position was rejected by the trial court as unconscionable and unenforceable for several reasons, including that such an arrangement would conflict with a client's absolute right to discharge an attorney at any time and select another.[16]

The fact that a perpetual fee arrangement may not be enforceable, however, does not necessarily mean that an attorney is without a remedy for the

---

15. Hirsch Wallerstein Hayum Matlof & Fishman v. Hirsch Jackoway Tyerman Wertheimer Austin Mandelbaum & Morris, BC 320128 (L.A. Super. Ct., filed Aug. 13, 2004).

16. Michael I. Rudell & Neil J. Rosini, *Block to Perpetual Attorney Fees*, Ent. L. & Fin., Sept. 2007.

payment of fees that may have been earned. In the Illinois case of *Musburger v. Meier*,[17] an attorney who represented radio talent on a contingent fee basis was discharged during the course of a negotiation with a radio station. The attorney's fee arrangement with the radio talent had previously been in written form, but that agreement had not been renewed at the time of the negotiation at issue. While the court in *Musburger* noted that an attorney may be discharged at any time by a client, with or without cause, the attorney is still entitled to recover the value of his or her services prior to discharge in quantum meruit. Musburger was able to reconstruct the time he devoted to representing the radio talent in the negotiation and was thus able to recover his fee on that basis. The lesson for attorneys generally from the case may be to maintain time records of their services, even when the matter they are handling is on a contingent fee basis.

## Practical Issues

Relating to a musician client may involve a certain amount of simpatico. Unless you are handling something that will not involve much direct contact with a musician client, it is generally not enough to be a good tactician. As with all creative individuals, artists' talents, and the results of their talents, are very important to them on a highly personal basis. It is not just their livelihood, but a reflection of their identity. Your respect for that talent is key to a successful long-term relationship. I am not suggested a fawning approach or the mustering of an insincere enthusiasm for their work, as musicians are no less capable of detecting such expressions than anyone else. They are usually better since they may encounter it more often than others. The best approach is consistent with the role you are actually being engaged to fulfill, which is the advocate of the musician's interests and the protection of their rights. You do not need to understand the musician's work, or even enjoy it. If you do, that is a bonus. The most important thing is that you respect the work and the talent and effort that the musician is bringing to their career and the process of creating that work. It has been

---

17. *Musburger*, 394 Ill. App. 3d. 781 (1st Dist. 2009).

my experience that this support is the most appreciated—that creative artists most value the trust they have in the attorney's commitment to their interests, much more than they care whether the attorney likes everything they do.

Respect may take many forms. It may mean understanding when the creative process leads to unexpected changes of direction or decisions and being prepared to accommodate those changes within the deal-making process. It may mean giving appropriate weight to intuitive analysis when you might otherwise strictly insist upon reason. It may mean exercising greater patience to bring an understanding of a situation to a musician client without condescension when that musician turns out to be a less sophisticated purchaser of legal services than one customarily works with. It may also mean reminding yourself of the strength you summon when seeking the positive judgment of one or a small group of judges, then multiplying that group by the many hundreds or thousands from which a musician risks rejection whenever they perform—that is a special strength worthy of much respect.

# Appendix A

# Recommended Further Reading

Jeffrey Brabec & Todd Brabec, *Music, Money and Success* (7th ed., Schrimer Trade Books 2011).

David Byrne, *How Music Works* (McSweeney's Books 2012).

Xavier M. Frascongna, Jr., & H. Lee Hetherington, *This Business of Artist Management* (Billboard Books 1997).

Steve Gordon, *The Future of the Music Business* (3d ed., Hal Leonard 2011).

Martin Kamenski, *Minding Your Business: A Guide to Money and Taxes for Creative Professionals* (Hal Leonard 2013).

Al Kohn & Bob Kohn, *Kohn on Music Licensing* (4th ed., Aspen Publishers 2010).

William Krasilovsky & Sydney Shemel, *This Business of Music* (10th ed., Billboard Books 2007).

Schuyler M. Moore, *Taxation of the Entertainment Industry* (10th ed., CCH 2009).

Kevin Parks, *Music & Copyright in America* (ABA 2012).

Donald S. Passman, *All You Need to Know About the Music Business* (8th ed., Free Press 2012).

Mary Hutchings Reed, *IEG Legal Guide to Sponsorship* (International Events Group 1989).

Richard Schulenberg, *Legal Aspects of the Music Industry* (Billboard Books 2005).

Ray D. Waddell, Rich Barnet & Jake Berry, *This Business of Concert Promotion and Touring* (Billboard Books 2007).

Loren Wells, *The Discography: Legal Encyclopedia of Popular Music, available at* http://thediscography.org.

# Appendix B

# List of Dispute Resolution Service Organizations

## Arts Mediation Group
253 Prospect Place
Brooklyn, NY 11238
Jackie Goodrich
www.artsmediation.com
E-mail: Jackie.goodrich@artsmediation.com
Phone: (718) 757–4919

## California Lawyers for the Arts
Arts Arbitration and Mediation Services
Fort Mason Center, C-255
San Francisco, CA 94123
Phone: (415) 775–7200, ext. 101/102
Fax: (415) 775–1143

## JAMS Headquarters
Entertainment and Sports Group
1920 Main Street
Suite 300
Irvine, CA 92614
Phone: (949) 224–1810
Fax: (949) 224–1818
E-mail: tlunceford@jamsadr.com

## JAMS International Headquarters
70 Fleet Street
London EC4Y 1EU, UK
Phone: +44 (207) 583–9808
Fax: +44 (207) 936–3325
E-mail: info@jamsinternational.com

## Lawyers for the Creative Arts
213 West Institute Place
Suite 403
Chicago, IL 60610
Phone: (312) 649–4111
Fax: (312) 944–2195

## National Assn. of Record Industry Professionals (NARIP)
Recommended Mediators
P.O. Box 2446
Toluca Lake, CA 91610–2446
Phone: (818) 769–7007
E-mail: info@narip.com

## World Intellectual Property Organization (WIPO) Arbitration and Mediation Center
Film and Media
34, chemin des Colombettes
CH-1211 Geneva 20, Switzerland
Phone: +41 (22) 338–8247 or 0800 888 549
Fax: +41 (22) 338-8337 or 0800 888 550

# Index

**A**

AAIM. *See* American Association of Independent Music (AAIM)

ABA Model Rules of Professional Conduct
  Rule 1.7, 236
  Rule 1.18, 232

Abandoned property, 183–185

ABKCO Music, Inc. v. Harrisongs Music, Ltd., 722 F.2d 990 (1983), 134

Accountings, 58–60, 103–105

Adaptations, 62

Administration agreements, 69–71

Advances, 95–97, 156–158, 174–175

Advertising, 217–220

AFTRA. *See* American Federation of Television and Radio Artists (AFTRA)

Agents, 126–127

AIFF file format, 4

Aimster, 162

ALAC compression format, 4

Amazon.com, Inc., 214

American Association of Independent Music (AAIM), 167

American Federation of Television and Radio Artists (AFTRA), 214

American Society of Composers, Authors and Publishers (ASCAP), 42–45, 51, 54, 65, 166, 185, 224, 225

Apple Corps Ltd., 215

Apple Inc., 4, 214

Approvals, 55–57, 104–106

ASCAP. *See* American Society of Composers, Authors and Publishers (ASCAP)

Assignments, 13

ATRAC file format, 4

Audio Home Recording Act of 1992, 160

Audits, 58–60, 103–105, 186–188

**B**

Beatlemania, 215

Benefits provisions, 143–144

Berlin v. E.C. Publications, Inc., 329 F.2d 541 (2d Cir. 1964), *cert. denied*, 379 U.S. 822 (1964), 19

Bill Graham Archives LLC v. Dorling Kindersley Ltd., 386 F. Supp. 2d 324 (2005), 17

Billing, 144–145

BMI. *See* Broadcast Music, Inc. (BMI)

Brabec, Jeffrey, 44

Brabec, Todd,, 44

Branding, 217–220

Brando, Marlon, 212

Broadcast Music, Inc. (BMI), 42–45, 51, 54, 65, 166, 224, 225

Broadway Music Corp. v. F-R Pub'g Corp., 31 F. Supp. 817 (1940), 18

Brownmark Films, LLC v. Comedy Partners, 682 F.3d 687 (2012), 19

Budgets, 95–97

Business expenditures, 179–180

Business managers, 137–138

Busking, 139–141

C

Cable music services, 167–168

Campbell v. Acuff-Rose Music, Inc., 510 U.S. 569 (1994), 18

Cancellations, 145–146

Capital gains income
musical compositions, 172–173
ordinary vs., 171–173

C-corporations, 192

Channel of trade adjustments, 100–101

Charles, Ray, 209

Choice of entity, 187–190

Clothing, 181–182

Coachella Valley Music and Arts Festival, 213

Collaboration, 15–16

Compensation
for personal appearances, 142–143
for services rendered, 173–174
unqualified deferred, 174–175

Conflict resolution, 136

Container charges, 99–101

Contractual rights, 35–36

Controlled compositions, 105–107

Conventions, 228–229

Copublishing agreements, 64–66

Copyright
as income-producing asset, 204–205
assignments, 13
basics of, 8
collaboration and, 15–16
fair use and, 16
federal protection for, 9
myths, 19–21
notice, 10–12
parody and, 18–19
registration of claim, 9–11

scope of claim, 13–16
termination right, 205–206
term of, 11–12, 13
work for hire and, 12–13
Copyright Act of 1909, 47–49
Copyright Act of 1976, 47, 89, 90,
      229
Copyright Royalty Board, 160,
      167
Corbis, 228
Corporations, 192
Creative Commons, 228
Credit, 37–39, 59–61, 119
Croce, Jim, 232
Crowd-funding, 176–177,
      184–185
Customer environments, 224–226

D
Data, 32–33
Demo costs, 57
Development agreements,
      121–123
Digital assets, 213–214
Digital distribution
   overview of, 158–159
   revenue, 159–160
Digital Domain Media, 213
Digital Millennium Copyright
      Act of 1998 (DMCA),
      160–162
Digital music, 3–5
Digital Performance Right In
      Sound Recordings Act of
      1995 (DPRA), 160–162

Digital phonorecord deliveries.
      *See* Permanent downloads
Digital rights management (DRM),
      165
Distribution
   advances, 156–158
   digital, 158–159
   DIY, 157–159
   functions, 153–154
   of physical products, 151–153
   process, 156–158
   scope of agreement, 154–156
   warranties and representations,
      156–157
DIY distribution, 157–159
DMCA. *See* Digital Millennium
      Copyright Act of 1998
      (DMCA)
DMI, 225
DMX, 225
Domain names, 27
Downloads, 165–167, 226–227
DPRA. *See* Digital Performance
      Right In Sound Recordings
      Act of 1995 (DPRA)
Dramatic rights, 50–52
Dylan, Bob, 30, 207

E
Eagles, 131
Elsmere Music, Inc. v. National
      Broadcasting Co., 482 F.
      Supp. 741 (1980), *aff'd*,
      623 F.2d 252 (2d Cir.
      1980), 19

Employee downloading, 226–227
eMusic, 164
Endorsements, 220–221
Estate considerations
    elements of musician's estate,
        197–198
Exclusive recordings, 222–223
Exclusive songwriter agreements,
    62–64
Exclusivity, 35, 146–147, 222–223

**F**
Facebook, 23, 28, 213, 214
Fairness in Music Licensing Act,
    225, 227
Fair use
    copyright and, 16
    trademark, 26–28
Fair Use Golden Rule, 17
Fan Freedom Project, 148
Fees, 233–234, 238–240
Fiduciary duties, 201–204
Financing, 81–82
First Amendment, 31
FLAC file format, 4
Flat fees, 142–143
Ford Motor Company,, 29
Foreign tax credits, 185–186
Format adjustments, 100–101
Free goods, 101–102
Frito Lay, 29

**G**
General partnerships, 190–191
Getty Images, 219, 228

GigMasters, 129
Gmail, 214
Google, 214
Grokster, 162
Grooveshark, 163
Group member capitalization,
    81–83
Guitar Hero, 30

**H**
Harrison, George, 134, 195
Harry Fox Agency, 48
Hendrix, Jimi, 213
Hill, Lauryn, 170
Hirsch Wallerstein Hayum Matlof
        & Fishman v. Hirsch
        Jackoway Tyerman
        Wertheimer Austin
        Mandelbaum & Morris,
        BC 320128 (2004), 239
Hobby-loss, 178
Home-office workspace, 180–181
Hospitality provisions, 143–144
Hotmail, 214
House concerts, 140–141

**I**
Identity, 59–61, 221–222
Income
    capital gains, 172–173
    crowd-funded, 176–177
    generated in foreign territory, 61
    ordinary, 173–174
    ordinary vs. capital gains,
        171–173

Indemnifications, 57–58
Independent contractors, 12
Infringement, 24
Instruments, 180–181
Intent-to-use (ITU), 22
Internal Revenue Service (IRS),
     178, 181, 183, 184, 186,
     200
International Organization for
     Standardization (IOS),
     4
International presence, 60–62
*International Royalties Tax
     Reporting Guide*, 185
Interviews, 34–35
Inventory, 198–199
Investors, 84–85
IOS. *See* International
     Organization for
     Standardization (IOS)
IRS. *See* Internal Revenue Service
     (IRS)
Italian Book Corp. v. American
     Broadcasting Cos., 458 F.
     Supp. 65 (1978), 17

**J**
Jackson, Michael, 195
*Jesus Christ Superstar* , 51–52
Jingle Punks, 219
Jukeboxes, 229

**K**
Karll v. Curtis Pub'g Co., 39 F.
     Supp. 836 (1941), 17

Keep Thomson Governor Comm.
     v. Citizens for Gallen
     Comm., 457 F. Supp. 957
     (1978), 17
Key man provision, 37–38
Kickstarter,, 184–185
Klein, Alan, 134

**L**
Lady Gaga, 181
LaGuardia, Fiorello H., 139
Lanham Act, 21, 29
Laws of the Twelve Tables, 139
Lawyers
     alternative fee arrangements,
          238–240
     dealing with groups, 236–237
     dealing with representatives,
          234–236
     fit issues, 232–234
     payment of fees, 233–234
     practical issues, 240–241
     shopping groups, 237–238
Leaving member provisions, 80–81
Lennon, John, 195
Lennon v. Premise Media Corp.
     L.P., 556 F. Supp. 2d 310
     (2008), 17
Levitin, Daniel J., 1
License agreements, 115
Licensing income, 98–99
Lil Wayne, 170
Limewire, 162
Limited liability companies (LLCs),
     193–194

Limited partnerships, 191–192
Lindsay, John V., 139
LinkedIn, 214
LLCs. *See* Limited liability
    companies (LLCs)
Loans, 85–86
Lombardo, Guy, 30
Lynn, Loretta, 207
Lynrd Skynrd, 210

**M**
Management agreements, 132
Marathon v. Blasi, 42 Cal. 4th 974
    (2008), 136
Marley, Bob, 195
Mechanical licenses, 46–49
MediaNet, 164
Megaupload, 163
Merchandising, 107–109, 144–146
Merit advances, 63
Microsoft Corporation, 4
Midler, Bette, 29
Minors, 136
MOD, 226
Monroe, Marilyn, 213
Mood, 225
Moral rights, 40
Morals clause, 223–224
Morrison, Jim, 210, 213
Most favored nations clause,
    38–40
Moving Pictures Experts Group, 4
MP3, 4
MP3.com, 163
MTV Video Music Awards, 181

Music
    advertising and branding,
        217–220
    at work site, 224–225
    digital, 3–5
    elements of, 1–2
    limitations in Western, 2–3
    office or warehouse
        performance of,
        227–228
    on hold, 227–228
    performance in customer
        environment, 224–226
    reproductions of recordings,
        228–229
    sponsorships and endorsements,
        220–221
Musical groups
    financing, 81–82
    leaving member provisions,
        80–81
    organization of, 73–75
    other agreement provisions,
        78–80
    recording agreements, 80–81
    settlements, 86
    treatment of assets, 74–77
Music Choice, 167
Musicdealers, 219
*Music, Money, and Success* (Brabec
    & Brabec), 44
Music Publishers Association, 48
Music publishing
    dramatic rights and, 50–52
    mechanical licenses and, 46–49

overview of, 41–42

performance rights organizations and,, 42–45

publisher agreements, 52–54

synchronization rights, 49–51

Music services, 162–164

Music subscription services, 226–227

Musync, 219

Muve, 164

Myspace, 23

**N**

Napster, 162

National Conference of Personal Managers, 130

Nelson, Willie, 170

Nine Inch Nails, 133

Nondisclosure provisions, 39–40

Non-disparagement, 223–225

Notorious B.I.G., 210

Nowell, Bradley, 210

**O**

Obligation to promote, 56–57, 95–96

Online agencies, 129–131

Online presence, 27–28

Ordinary income

capital gains vs., 171–173

compensation for services rendered vs. royalties, 173–174

Originality, 14

Outkast, 31

Outside financing, 82–84

**P**

Pandora, 226

Parker, Colonel Thomas A., 132

Parks, Rosa, 31

Parody, 18–19

Partnerships,, 190–191

Passive loss deductions, 182–183

Patronage, 83–85

Payment, 54–56

Percentage compensation, 142–143

Performance rights organizations (PROs), 42–45, 54, 214–216

Performing group names, 23–25

Permanent downloads, 165–167

Personal appearances

busking, 139–141

house concerts, 140–141

proceeds of, 147–148

public venues, 141–142

ticketing, 147–149

Personal holding companies, 193–194

Personal managers, 130–132

Personal representatives

agents, 126–127

business managers, 137–138

overview of, 125–126

personal managers, 130–132

Petty, Tom, 207

Piano rolls, 47

Pinterest, 113

Presley, Elvis, 132, 195, 210, 213
Preston v. Ferrer, 552 U.S. 346
　　(2008), 136
Proceeds, 147–148
Producer agreements, 117–120
Production and release
　　commitment, 94–95
Production company agreements,
　　120–121
Production credits, 185–186
Profit sharing deals, 116
PROs. *See* Performance rights
　　organizations (PROs)
Psychoacoustics, 4
Public domain, 11, 14, 20, 38, 49
Publicity. *See* Right of publicity
Public venues, 141–142
Published price to dealers (PPD),
　　97
Publisher agreements
　　administration agreements,
　　　69–71
　　copublishing agreements,
　　　64–66
　　exclusive songwriter
　　　agreements, 62–64
　　single song agreements, 53–54
Publishing income, 174–175

**R**
Ray Charles Foundation, 209
Rdio, 164
Record companies
　　deals, 111–114
　　functions of, 87

Recording agreements
　　accountings and audits,
　　　103–105
　　alternative, 115–117
　　approvals, 104–106
　　controlled compositions,
　　　105–107
　　leaving member provisions in,
　　　80–81
　　merchandising, 107–109
　　nature of relationship, 88–91
　　overview of, 87–88
　　producer agreements,
　　　117–120
　　production and release
　　　commitment, 94–95
　　production company
　　　agreements, 120–121
　　recording budgets and
　　　advances, 95–97
　　royalties, 96–97
　　scope of, 91–94
　　signatory parties, 91–92
　　term of, 92–94
　　videos, 109–110
Recording Industry Association
　　of America (RIAA),
　　160
ReDigi, 163
Representations, 156–157
Representatives,, 234–236
Reproductions, 228–229
Revenue, 159–160
ReverbNation, 129
Reznor, Trent, 133

Reznor v. J. Artist Mgmt., Inc., 365
 F. Supp. 2d 565 (2005),
 133
Rhapsody, 164, 226
Right of first negotiation, 36–37
Right of first refusal, 37
Right of publicity, 28–30
Right of reproduction, 49
Ringbacks, 166–168
Ringtones, 166, 166–168
Rock and Roll Hall of Fame, 201
Roman Republic, 139
Royalties
 accountings and audits,
  103–105
 basis, 97–98
 calculation example, 102–103
 compensation for services
  rendered vs., 173–174
 container charges, 99–101
 digital, 101–103
 format, territory, and channel
  of trade adjustments,
  100–101
 free goods, 101–102
 licensing income, 98–99
 of permanent downloads, 165
 producer, 118
 rates, 97–99
Royalty compensation, 63
Rumblefish, 219

S
SAG. See Screen Actors Guild
 (SAG)

Satellite radio, 167–168
Scorpio Music S.A., 208
S-corporations, 192–193
Screen Actors Guild (SAG), 214
Security, 144
Service provider agreements,
 116
SESAC. See Society of European
 Stage Authors and
 Composers (SESAC)
Settlements, 86
Shakur, Tupac, 213
Shapiro, Bernstein & Co. v. P.F.
 Collier & Son Co., 26
 U.S.P.Q. 40 (1934), 18
Signatory parties, 91–92
Sinatra, Nancy, 30
Single song agreements, 53–54
Sirius XM Radio, 167
Slacker, 164
Society of European Stage Authors
 and Composers (SESAC),
 42–45, 51, 54, 166, 224,
 225
Sole proprietorship, 189–190
Songwriters Capital Gains Tax
 Equity Act of 2007, 172
Sonicbids, 129
SoundExchange, 160–162, 167,
 214
Sound recordings, 89–91
Sponsorships, 220–221
Spotify, 164
StubHub, 148
Synchronization rights, 49–51

**T**

Tape, 117

Tax considerations
  audits, 186–188
  choice of entity, 187–190
  credits, 185–186
  exemptions, 186–187
  gross income, 171–172
  types of taxes, 177–178

Taxi, 219

Technical riders, 146–147

Termination rights, 205–206

Territory adjustments, 100–101

The Beatles, 30, 134, 215

*The Onion*, 23

The Romantics, 30

*This Is Your Brain on Music*
  (Levitin), 1

360 deals, 112–114

Ticketing, 147–149

TicketsNow, 148

Titles, 26–28

Todd W. Musburger, Ltd. v. Meier,
  394 Ill. App. 3d 781
  (2009), 239

Touring income, 173–174

Trademarks
  acquisition of rights, 21–23
  artist's identity, 221–222
  as income-producing asset,
    209–211
  fair use and, 26–28
  online presence and, 27–28
  performing group names, 23–25
  titles and, 26–28

Trade shows, 228–229

Translations, 62

Tribute bands, 215–216

Tumblr, 28, 113

Twitter, 28, 113, 213, 214

2 Live Crew, 18

**U**

Uniform Law Commission, 214

Uniform resource locator (URL),
  27

United States Copyright Act, 17
    U.S.C. 101-1332 (2011)
  101, 89, 227
  106, 8
  107, 16
  114(d)(2), 167
  203, 207–208
  304(c)(2), 206
  1101(a), 9
  Copyright Act of 1909, 47–49
  Copyright Act of 1976, 47, 89,
    90, 229
  digital music services and, 164
  fair use in, 16, 30
  permanent downloads and,
    165
  right of publicity and, 28
  SoundExchange and, 160

United States Copyright Office,
  9–11, 85, 167

United States Patent and
    Trademark Office
    (USPTO), 85, 217

Universal Music Group, 163

URL. *See* Uniform resource locator
    (URL)
Uruguay Round Agreements Act of
    1994, 9
U.S. Customs and Border
    Protection Service, 23
U.S. Department of Labor, 7
USPTO. *See* United States Patent
    and Trademark Office
    (USPTO)

**V**
Valuation, 79–81, 199–201
Videos, 109–110
Village People, 208

**W**
Waits, Tom, 29, 207
Wal-Mart, 131
Warranties, 57–58, 156–157

WAV file format, 4
Webcasting, 160–162
Willis, Victor, 208–209
WMA compression format, 4
Work for hire
    circumstances determining, 89
    copyright and, 12–13

**Y**
Yahoo, 214
You License, 219
YouTube, 214

**Z**
Zacchini v. Scripps-Howard
    Broadcasting Co., 435 U.S.
    562 (1977), 28
Zappa Family Trust, 215
Zappa, Frank, 215
Zappa, Gail, 215